The Coming of the Lord

Gerald N. Lund

The Coming of the Lord

Bookcraft
Salt Lake City, Utah

Library of Congress Catalog Card Number: 79-175135
ISBN 0-88494-229-5

27th Printing, 1996

Lithographed in the United States of America
PUBLISHERS PRESS
Salt Lake City, Utah

To Lynn

My helpmate in this and
other endeavors

There never was a generation of the inhabitants of the earth in any age of the world who had greater events awaiting them than the present. . . . And an age fraught with greater interest to the children of men than the one in which we live never dawned since the creation of the world.

—Wilford Woodruff, *Journal of Discourses,* Volume 18, page 110; September 12, 1875

Contents

Preface

My purpose in preparing this book was twofold. First, for reader convenience I have sought to bring together from many sources, reliable statements on the important subject of the Savior's second coming, while avoiding the sensational, speculative and otherwise questionable material which abounds on this subject. With this and space considerations in mind I have deliberately confined the quotations to passages from scripture and statements by those men sustained by the Church in this dispensation as prophets, seers and revelators.

My second desire was to stimulate a positive, exciting outlook toward the future, thereby helping to overcome the negative, anxious feelings about predicted events which I have frequently observed in my contacts with young people of the Church. True, difficult days are ahead. But the Lord has words of comfort for his saints which should produce an eager desire to prepare for his coming and a joyous anticipation of that great event.

This work is far from an exhaustive treatment of the subject. Space limitations dictated the omission of many significant quotations. Nor is the arrangement meant to imply a definite chronological order of events, sequence being difficult to determine in some instances. My hope is that the book will impel the reader to further study in this absorbing and vital area.

I am grateful for the mental and spiritual gains which came to me while I was preparing this work—especially for the enhanced respect I gained for the counsel of the "living prophets." I am grateful too to my wife Lynn for her unstinted assistance and involvement in this work. The time and effort she put in are impossible to measure. I appreciate also the helpful suggestions of many others.

Most of all I am deeply grateful to the Lord for inspiring his prophets to instruct us so completely on how to prepare for his coming.

Introduction

Shortly after Great Britain declared war against Nazi Germany in 1939, her king broadcast a message of hope and encouragement to the British Empire. In that speech he quoted from a dialogue between a man and the Keeper of the Gate of the Year:

> I said to the man who stood at the gate of the year, "Give me a light that I may tread safely into the unknown," and he replied, *"Go out into the darkness, and put your hand in the hand of God. That shall be to you better than a light, and safer than the known way."*

During the height of World War II when the United States was engaged heavily in combat in Europe and the Pacific, when thousands of young members of the Church were in the fierce areas of battle, Elder Harold B. Lee referred to that quote in an address to the saints during April Conference. He went on to say:

> To the Latter-day Saints in this troublous day, when the perils of the earth are round about us, it is well that we take stock as to how we may approach him and what may be our blessings. The Savior himself spoke of the Comforter, which he said would guide into all truth, would bring all things to our remembrance, should show us things to come; and would teach us all things whatsoever the Lord our God had commanded. . . . So too may we in this day distinguish among the babble of voices that are to be heard on every side, the voice of the true shepherd, that we be not found to be barbarians in the day of our need for direction and guidance. The Apostle Peter declared that way when he said:
> "We also have a more sure word of prophecy; whereunto ye do well that ye take heed, as unto a light that shineth in dark places, until the day dawn, and the day star arise in your hearts. . . . Know-

ing this first, that no prophecy of the scripture is of any private interpretation. For the prophecy came not in old time by the will of man: but holy men of God spake as they were moved by the Holy Ghost." (2 Peter 1:19-21)[1]

Those days in 1943 were grim and ominous days, days in which men cried for some light to guide them through the coming years. To many, the times in which we presently live are times of equal gravity and uncertainty. Crime abounds, anarchy rages, violence is common fare, and immorality has become a way of life to vast numbers of people. Campus unrest, terrorist bombings, wars and threats of war, racial strife, graft, corruption, kidnappings and assassinations fill the pages and screens of the mass media.

So we, too, of this age stand at the gates of the future, pleading for light to guide us safely into the lowering storm clouds. We, too, as Elder Lee has said, desperately need to distinguish from the babble of voices around us, that voice which will alone lead us safely through the dark night. And that voice in this day, as in 1943 and as in countless years before our own century, is the voice of the Master, as given through "holy men of God who spake as they were moved by the Holy Ghost." Through their inspired utterances they declare once again to an anguished world that the Lord's all-seeing eye pierces the shrouded gloom, and that his gentle hand is extended to those venturing into the night. *Prophecy is the hand of God extended in love to a groping, floundering world.*

Members of The Church of Jesus Christ of Latter-day Saints are taught from early youth that God is ever anxious to guide his children through perilous times, and even today has called prophets who are once more warning, predicting, and testifying to the world. These prophets are also concerned by the lowering clouds in world and national events, but their attitude is one of hope rather than despair. As an example of this, Heber J. Grant, seventh president of the Church, said:

> While the world is in a state of commotion and there is perplexity among the nations, *the Latter-day Saints have no fears for*

---

[1]Harold B. Lee, *Conference Report,* April, 1943, pp. 124-125.

the future. The signs of the times indicate the near approach of the coming of the Lord, and the work that we are engaged in is a preparatory one for that great event.[2]

President Jedediah M. Grant, second counselor to President Brigham Young, stated it in this way:

> When we see nation stirred up against nation, and on the other hand see nations exerting a powerful influence to bring about negotiations of peace, shall we say they can bring it about? Do we expect they can stay the onward course of war? *The Prophet of God has spoken it all, and we expect to see the work go on—and see all things fulfilled as the prophets have declared by the spirit of prophecy in them.*
>
> *Why is it that the Latter-day Saints are perfectly calm and serene among all the convulsions of the earth—the turmoils, strife, war, pestilence, famine and distress of nations? It is because the spirit of prophecy has made known to us that such things would actually transpire upon the earth. We understand it, and view it in its true light. We have learned it by the visions of the Almighty. . . .*[3]

Too often, however, this "perfect calmness and serenity" expressed by the prophets is not felt by other members of the Church. Ironically, this is true not because they fail to accept the prophets, but rather because they do. Emotions of fear, anxiety, dread, gloom, and discomfort are prevalent in many people whenever the subject of the future comes up. After a fireside speaker had reviewed some of the prophecies concerning the future of the world, one of the youth present was heard to say with grim sincerity, "I hope I am lucky enough to die before all of these things happen."

Such attitudes are understandable, but tragic nevertheless. These concepts arise from a misunderstanding of the nature of prophecy. These people seem to see God's word, not as the loving message from a concerned Father, but as a curse from a wrathful deity bent on the destruction of all those not willing to toe the mark. To them, it is almost as though God were trying to scare his children into repentance. They are

---

[2]Heber J. Grant, *Conference Report,* October, 1930, p. 5. (Italics added)
[3]Jedediah M. Grant, *The Improvement Era,* Vol. 18, February, 1915, pp. 285, 286. (Italics added)

obviously better prepared for future crises than one who rejects the idea of prophecy completely, but they still have not found the comforting clasp of God's hand. To them, prophecy seems more like a clenched, threatening fist, than an open, loving hand.

It is to this end that this book is written, that all who read it may come to see prophecy for what it really is—proof of the loving hand of a deeply concerned Father extended to all who find fear and anxiety in their hearts as the night and the future close in around them.

A Look at Prophecy

Prophecy—More Than Prediction

Traditionally, people most commonly think of prophecy as being a prediction of future events. The word "prophet" evokes images of men caught up in visions or thundering out promises of destruction upon the wicked. Prediction of future events is an important and essential element of prophecy but is only part of the total concept.

John the Revelator was told by an angel that the spirit of prophecy was "the testimony of Jesus."[1] Peter implied the same thing when he stated that "To him [Jesus] give *all* the prophets witness. . . ."[2] Paul taught that the foundation of the early Church was "apostles and prophets,"[3] and yet it is immediately obvious to one reading the New Testament that these men did much more than simply predict future events. John the Baptist announced that he was preparing the way for one mightier than he. Other than that testimony, we have no record of John the Baptist working miracles or uttering great prophetic promises in the normal sense of the word. And yet Christ says of him: "Among those that are born of women *there is not a greater prophet* than John the Baptist. . . ."[4] As Peter pointed out, prophecy is better defined as the utterances of ". . . holy men of God [spoken] as they were moved by the Holy Ghost."[5]

---

[1]Revelation 19:10.
[2]Acts 10:43. (Italics added)
[3]Ephesians 2:20.
[4]Luke 7:28. (Italics added)
[5]2 Peter 1:21.

This larger meaning is carried in the etymology of the word itself. Our English word "prophet" is derived from two ancient Greek words, viz., *pro* and *phanai*. *Pro* is a Greek preposition meaning both "for" and "before." *Phanai* is the infinitive form of the verb "to speak." Thus, a prophet is one who both speaks *for* God and also speaks *before* an event takes place. The Hebrew word *nabi,* which we translate as "prophet," carries this same wider connotation, meaning simply "one who speaks for God."

Most prophets fulfill three major responsibilities in their callings: first, they testify of the divinity of the Savior; second, they warn the inhabitants of the earth of the things which will result if wrong choices are made; and third, they predict future events that will profoundly affect the destiny of men. This has been the basic message of the prophets since time began. It is this threefold nature of prophecy that has made the voices of the true prophets distinguishable from the babble of voices which arise from the many false prophets and priests of mankind.

It is important to keep this broader concept of prophecy in mind as one discusses the messages of the prophets. The narrower concept of prophecy as prediction may lead one to draw erroneous conclusions, such as that drawn by the seminary student who declared to his teacher that he didn't know if he should sustain President Joseph Fielding Smith as prophet of the Church because he had been unable to find anything that he had "prophesied."

The Purposes of Prophecy

Another error that one may fall into when studying prophecies is that of holding too narrow a concept of the purposes of prophecy. As we mentioned above, there are some in the Church who view prophecy primarily as the Lord's "scare technique." It is unquestionable that some of the prophetic utterances foretell grim and horrible things and that these things are frightening—so frightening that they become a source of strong motivation to repent. Because of this, many people see only the warning nature of prophecy and conclude that God seeks to scare us into doing his will.

While it is clear that warning the inhabitants of the earth is one major purpose of prophecy,[6] the conclusion that the Lord seeks to strike terror into the hearts of his children is unfounded. When a parent describes to his child the pain and suffering that may result from playing with electrical outlets, he may have to use rather ominous predictions and graphically plain terms. But it is plain that this parent is motivated out of love for the child, not out of some desire to see him cowering in fear. So it is with God. At times what he predicts is necessarily terrible to contemplate, but this is so because the choices his children make bring upon themselves terrible consequences.

It should not be forgotten, however, that to warn is only one of the purposes of prophecy. Another important function is to prepare people for the crises in life that will confront them. This is especially true of the signs of the times. The Lord has enumerated them so that when one sees them being fulfilled, he will immediately know that the coming of the Lord is nigh and make the necessary preparations. Jesus told the disciples that these signs were like the leaves appearing on the fig tree. Unlike many other trees, the fig tree of Palestine puts forth its leaves very late in the spring, and thus "When his branch is yet tender, and putteth forth leaves, ye know that summer is nigh: So likewise ye, when ye shall see all these things, know that it is near, even at the doors."[7]

Prophecy is one of the most direct ways that the Lord has for preparing his people. A good example of this is contained in an interesting prophecy concerning the rainbow, given by the Prophet Joseph Smith. It will be remembered that the Lord set the rainbow as a token to Noah of his covenant that the earth would never again be destroyed by flood.[8] Evidently, this same token will serve as a sign to warn us of

---

[6]*Doctrine and Covenants* 1:4.
[7]Matthew 24:32-33.
[8]Genesis 9:11-17.

the nearness of Christ's coming so that we may make necessary preparations. Said the Prophet:

> I have asked of the Lord concerning His coming; and while asking the Lord, He gave a sign and said, "In the days of Noah I set a bow in the heavens as a sign and token that *in any year that the bow should be seen the Lord would not come; but there should be seed time and harvest during that year; but whenever you see the bow withdrawn, it shall be a token that there shall be famine, pestilence, and great distress among the nations, and that the coming of the Messiah is not far distant.*"[9]

It becomes immediately obvious how such a small prophetic bit of information could serve to prepare those aware of it for times which are to come.

In addition to warning and preparation, prophecy serves another vital purpose—that of giving comfort. Even though it seems paradoxical, this may be true of some of the most terrifying of the prophecies. For example, consider a prediction out of the twenty-ninth section of the Doctrine and Covenants. This particular prophecy describes the state of the wicked in the most vivid and gruesome terms.[10]

How could anyone possibly derive any comfort from such a terrible picture? And yet even such scriptures as this may become a source of comfort. A prominent BYU professor told of reading this particular scripture to his young daughter. In her tenderheartedness, it caused her to weep and she begged her father to stop. But, as he explained, he felt it was better that she should weep now while they were still only words on paper than to wait unprepared for such events and then have them happen before her eyes. If this were the case, in her tenderheartedness she might falter; but now, knowing of these things, even though horrified, she may take comfort knowing that God had foretold their occurrence so that she could be better prepared for them.

More clearly evident is the comfort that comes to the soul from knowing that God has foreseen the end and has assured

---

[9]Joseph Smith, *DHC,* Vol. 6, p. 254; March 10, 1844. (Italics added)
[10]*Doctrine and Covenants* 29:17-20.

us that, no matter how dark the intervening days, eventually his work shall emerge triumphant. The prophetic promises of the new Jerusalem, of the millennial reign, of the absence of war, disease, pain, sorrow, and of course, greatest of all, the promise of eternal life—all of these promises light the lamps of our hopes and brighten the gloom that is deepening all around. The prophets point out to us clearly that, even in crises and disaster, the hand of the Lord may be moving to bring about his greater purposes for the children of men.

Let us not forget that one of the great and significant purposes of the Lord in sharing his vision of the future with us is to give us comfort.

The True and the False in Prophecy

In a discussion of prophecy and its effect upon one's destiny, one last important consideration is necessary, viz., how can one tell false prophecy from true prophecy? The future has always held a strong fascination for most men. Throughout history there has always been an abundance of those who sought to make a profit from this innate curiosity. Soothsayers, diviners, astrologers, fortune tellers, spiritualists, witch doctors, and self-styled prophets have long thrived in their occupations.

Unfortunately, too often these fraudulent prophets prove to be more successful, in terms of their following, than do those called by God. Typically the money, praise, and adulation of the masses go to the false prophets, while the true prophets are more often ignored, scorned, abused, and perhaps even martyred. One of the true prophets, who himself escaped assassination only through the intervention of the Lord, explained why this is so:

> But behold, if a man shall come among you and shall say: Do this, and there is no iniquity; do that and ye shall not suffer; yea, he will say: Walk after the pride of your own hearts; yea, walk after the pride of your eyes, and do whatsoever you desireth— and if a man shall come among you, and say this, *ye will receive him, and say that he is a prophet.*
>
> Yea, ye will lift him up, and ye will give unto him of your substance; ye will give unto him of your gold, and of your silver, and

ye will clothe him with costly apparel; and because he speaketh flattering words unto you, and he sayeth that all is well, then *ye will not find fault with him.*[11]

The test for determining what is true and what is false in prophecy was clearly set down for members of The Church of Jesus Christ of Latter-day Saints. In a statement issued in August, 1913, by the First Presidency of the Church (consisting of President Joseph F. Smith, President Anthon H. Lund, and President Charles W. Penrose) one reads:

> When visions, dreams, tongues, prophecy, impressions or any extraordinary gift or inspiration conveys something out of harmony with the accepted revelations of the Church or contrary to the decisions of its constituted authorities, *Latter-day Saints may know that it is not of God, no matter how plausible it may appear.* Also, they should understand that directions for the guidance of the Church will come, by revelation, *through the head.* All faithful members are entitled to the inspiration of the Holy Spirit for themselves, their families, and for those over whom they are appointed and ordained to preside. *But anything at discord with that which comes from God through the head of the Church is not to be received as authoritative or reliable.* In secular as well as spiritual affairs, Saints may receive Divine guidance and revelation affecting themselves, but this does not convey authority to direct others, *and is not to be accepted when contrary to Church covenants, doctrine or discipline, or to known facts, demonstrated truths, or good common sense.* . . . The Lord's Church "is a house of order." It is not governed by individual gifts or manifestations, but by the order and power of the Holy Priesthood as sustained by the voice and vote of the Church in its appointed conferences.[12]

If all members of the Church would remember these guidelines when they are tempted to pass on the newest exciting rumor or "prophecy," much of the spurious and false reports could be eliminated. In the General Priesthood Meeting of the Church during April conference of 1970, President Harold B. Lee warned members of the Church against heeding such items of questionable information.

---

[11]Helaman 13:27-28. (Italics added)
[12]"A Warning Voice," Official letter of declaration by the First Presidency, quoted by Harold B. Lee, *Conference Report,* April, 1970, p. 55. (Italics added)

It never ceases to amaze me how gullible some of our Church members are in broadcasting sensational stories, or dreams, or visions, or purported patriarchal blessings, or quotations, or supposedly from some person's private diary.

For instance, there is one vicious story to the effect that one of our General Authorities is allegedly being urged to present himself to lead the Church contrary to the Lord's revelation and to make people think there is some division among the authorities of the Church. Investigations have indicated that the named writer of these forged letters is fictitious and does not exist—can't be found in the records of the Church or anywhere. Addresses given are spurious, and yet the amazing thing is that we find that these spurious writings and some of these purported revelations, which we found upon investigation are absolutely false, *are finding their way into our Relief Society meetings, into priesthood quorums, firesides, institutes, and seminaries.*

Brethren of the priesthood, you defenders of the faith, we would wish that you would plead with our Saints to *cease promoting the works of the devil.* Spend your time promoting the works of the Lord, and don't allow these things to be found under your charge, *for they are the works of Satan, and we are playing his game whenever we permit such things to be heralded about and repeated and passed about on every side.*

One of our brethren is supposed to have had a patriarchal blessing saying that he would preside over the Church when the Savior came. This is, of course, false. Another one among us has been said to have declared that there are some living today who will see the Savior when he comes. This is again fictitious. Well, the Master said that the time of his coming would be as a thief in the night, that of the time of his coming not even the angels of heaven would know. If we would stop to think of it, nobody with any authority would ever say that such a declaration could be authentic.

So we could go on and on. One of our brethren was reported to have said that the people of California should move up to the tops of the Rocky Mountains, that only there would be safety. Contrary to that, we are constantly saying to our people that safety is where the pure in heart are, and that there is just as much safety wherever you are, if you are living and keeping the commandments of God.

Brethren, I repeat, *don't allow the works of the devil to be paraded in our midst* and become the subject of discourses or lesson materials. Speak of the works of righteousness and the power of the devil will begin to cease among you.[13]

---

[13]Harold B. Lee, *Conference Report,* April, 1970, pp. 55-56. (Italics added)

Men of God in Our Midst

In summary, then, as one begins a study of the prophecies relating to the coming of the Lord, several important considerations must be remembered. First, it is essential that prophecy be seen as more than simply the predicting of future events. True prophets do foretell what lies in the future but they also warn the earth's inhabitants of the results of evil living. Most important, they testify to the world of the divinity of the Savior.

A study of prophecy would not be accurate if one did not understand the purposes for which prophecy is given. Many see prophetic statements as the Lord's way of frightening his children into righteous living; but as was shown, warning is only one of the purposes of prophecy. Prophets help us to prepare ourselves for whatever the future may hold, both in this life and the next, by teaching us the principles by which one may achieve the abundant life.

A third important point to remember is that the potential for good which the prophets of God carry for mankind can be negated by our refusal to heed their words. If one does not discriminate carefully between the voices of the chosen servants of God and the other voices that cry loudly for one's allegiance, it may be that the beneficial effect of the prophecy will be lost. Although living prophets provide a great source of potential power for mankind, we may never come to know this power until we can heed the men of God in our midst.

President Harold B. Lee summed the whole matter up most adequately when he said: "We do not need more prophets to speak, we need more ears to listen."[14]

---

[14]Harold B. Lee, as quoted by A. Theodore Tuttle, *Conference Report,* April, 1970, p. 85.

How Soon the End?

Christ Is Coming

> While they beheld, he was taken up; and a cloud received him out of their sight.

> And while they looked steadfastly toward heaven as he went up, behold, two men stood by them in white apparel;

> Which also said, Ye men of Galilee, why stand ye gazing up into heaven? This same Jesus, which is taken up from you into heaven, shall so come in like manner as ye have seen him go into heaven.[1]

With this angelic promise ringing in their ears, the disciples of the Master returned to Jerusalem with a firm hope that the Savior would return again. It is only natural that since that time nearly every generation of Christians has earnestly hoped that theirs would be the generation in which this promise would be fulfilled. The mind thrills at the thought that one might actually see the realization of the millennial dream come true in his own life. And so from the earliest history of Christianity, there have been those who earnestly believed that Christ's second coming was imminent.

Within twenty years of the death of Christ, the Apostle Paul had to rebuke the saints in Thessalonica for being deceived as to the closeness of the return of the Master. Evidently, some of the saints had even quit their occupations to await the great event, and had become little more than "busy-

---

[1]Acts 1:9-11.

bodies."[2] Therefore, Paul clearly explained that such a day could not come before a great falling away had come first.[3]

Down through the centuries, one reads here and there of groups predicting the day, and sometimes the hour of his coming. For example, in 1818, a farmer by the name of William Miller, in an earnest and sincere search of the Bible became convinced that the return of the Lord would take place in about twenty-five more years. He concluded that the second advent would undoubtedly occur somewhere between March 21, 1843, and March 21, 1844.

Mr. Miller began to tell others of his conclusions with some success. The "Adventist" movement began to sweep the United States and thousands began their preparations for the end. But 1843 came and went with only a comet to temporarily raise their hopes. Miller was deeply disappointed, but one of his disciples recalculated and discovered an "error" in the original figures and announced the new date as October 22, 1844. Again a new wave of hope swept the movement as people quit their jobs, farmers did not plant their winter grain, and the believers gathered to await the end. Again their only reward was bitter disappoinment. [4]

Such movements down through the history of time naturally raise some questions for members of The Church of Jesus Christ of Latter-day Saints. The belief in the nearness of the Millennium is a central part of Mormon theology. One then could logically ask, "What evidence do you have that you shall not also be disappointed in your hope as have so many others before you? Granted that your scriptures point to the reality of that event; but how can you confidently say that it will be soon? Why could it not still be three, or four, or five hundred years away?" The question is a legitimate one and one that requires careful consideration.

---

[2]2 Thessalonians 3:10-12.

[3]*Ibid.*, 2:1-4.

[4]For an interesting treatment of the early history of the Adventist movement see Francis D. Nichol, *The Midnight Cry*, (Review and Herald, 1944).

Not Even the Angels of Heaven

When Christ was telling his disciples of the signs that would signal that his second coming was near, he cautioned them:

> But of that day and hour knoweth no man, no, not the angels of heaven, but my Father only. . . .
>
> Watch therefore: for ye know not what hour your Lord doth come.[5]

Through revelation to the Prophet Joseph Smith, the Lord reaffirmed that this was still the case and will be until the Lord actually comes. "I, the Lord God have spoken it; but the hour and the day no man knoweth, neither the angels in heaven, nor shall they know until he comes."[6] The Latter-day Saints accept the full implication of these scriptures and have been taught to avoid trying to place the date or fix the year of the coming of the Lord.

The Adventist movement was contemporary with the life of Joseph Smith. The predicted date set by William Miller caused some consternation among the early members of the Church, but the Prophet made it clear that this was an error. On March 10, 1844, after referring to the rainbow, he unequivocally stated:

> But I will take the responsibility upon myself to prophesy in the name of the Lord, that Christ will not come this year, as Father Miller has prophesied, for we have seen the bow; and I also prophesy in the name of the Lord that Christ will not come in forty years; and if God ever spoke by my mouth, He will not come in that length of time. Brethren, when you go home, write it down, that it may be remembered.
>
> *Jesus Christ never did reveal to any man the precise time that He would come. Go and read the Scriptures, and you cannot find anything that specifies the exact hour He would come; and all that say so are false teachers.*[7]

---

[5]Matthew 24:36, 42.
[6]*Doctrine and Covenants* 49:7.
[7]Joseph Smith, *DHC,* Vol. 6, p. 254, March 10, 1844. (Italics added)

Seven years later, after the majority of the saints had moved west to the valleys of the Great Salt Lake, the First Presidency (consisting of Brigham Young, Heber C. Kimball, and Willard Richards) issued a general epistle to the membership of the Church. Once again the saints were cautioned against attempting to place the hour or the day of the Lord's advent.

> . . . of the day and the hour of the coming of Christ no man knoweth. It is not yet, neither is it far off; there are prophecies yet to be fulfilled before that event takes place; therefore, *let no man deceive the saints with vain philosophy and false prophecy;* for false prophets will arise, and deceive the wicked, and, if possible, the good; but while the wicked fear and tremble at surrounding judgments, the Saints will watch and pray; and, waiting the final event in patience, will look calmly on the passing scenery of a corrupted world, and view transpiring events as confirmation of their faith in the holy gospel which they profess, and rejoice more and more, as multiplied signs shall confirm the approach of the millennial day.[8]

It Is Nigh, Even at Our Doors

The above fact that no one knows the hour or day of his coming does not answer the question as to why the second coming could not yet be a long way off. Indeed, it only seems to lend more credence to the idea that no one can safely say that the Lord will come soon. However, this is not so. It is important to keep in mind that no date can be set, but there is much evidence that the Lord's coming is near.

In a parable to the disciples, Jesus gave the key for knowing when the great day of his return was near. Said he:

> Now learn a parable of the fig tree; when his branch is yet tender and putteth forth leaves, ye know that summer is nigh:
> So likewise ye, when ye shall see all these things, know that it is near, even at the doors.[9]

So even though no man may know of the day or the hour, the Lord himself indicated the method for determining when

---

[8]"Fifth General Epistle of the Presidency of the Church," issued April 7, 1851, found in *Millennial Star,* Vol. 13, p. 210, July 15, 1851. (Italics added)
[9]Matthew 24:32-33.

his return was near. Many of the prophets have testified that this parable is now being fulfilled. In the conference of April, 1948, President Joseph Fielding Smith stated:

> Surely the signs of the times point to the fact that the great and dreadful day is near, even at our doors. The fig tree, figuratively, is putting forth her leaves. The turmoil, trouble, the war and the bloodshed that we have seen, and which we still see, all point to the fact that this day for the coming of the Son of God is near.[10]

On another occasion he wrote:

> I know that there are many, and even some among the Latter-day Saints, who are saying just as the Lord said they would say, "The Lord delayeth his coming." (D&C 45:26; 2 Peter 3:3-14) One man said: "It is impossible for Jesus Christ to come inside of three or four hundred years." But I say unto you, Watch.
>
> I do not know when he is going to come. No man knows. Even the angels of heaven are in the dark in regard to that great truth. (Matt. 24:36-37) But this I know, *that the signs that have been pointed out are here.* The earth is full of calamity, of trouble. The hearts of men are failing them. We see the signs as we see the fig tree putting forth her leaves: and knowing this time is near, it behooves me and it behooves you, and all men upon the face of the earth, to *pay heed to the words of Christ, to his apostles and watch,* for we know not the day nor the hour. But I tell you this, it shall come as a thief in the night, when *many of us will not be ready for it.*[11]

President Heber J. Grant said:

> The hour and day of the Lord's future advent is withheld from the knowledge of both men and angels; yet the signs, so definitely specified as harbingers of His coming, are multiplying apace. The prevailing unrest among men and nations, the fury of the elements, widespread destruction by land and sea, the frequency and intensity of volcanic and earthquake disturbances—all tell to the well-tuned ear that *the gladsome yet terrible day of the Lord is nigh—aye, even at the doors!*[12]

---

[10]Joseph Fielding Smith, *Conference Report,* April, 1948, p. 132.
[11]Joseph Fielding Smith, *Doctrines of Salvation* (Bruce R. McConkie, comp.), Vol. 3, (Bookcraft: Salt Lake City, 1956) pp. 52-53. (Italics in original)
[12]Heber J. Grant, *Millennial Star,* Vol. 91, p. 34, January, 1929. (Italics added)

In 1839, the Prophet Joseph Smith gave a great discourse on priesthood. In that sermon he spoke briefly of prophecy.

> Men profess to prophesy. I will prophesy that the signs of the coming of the Son of Man *are already commenced.* One pestilence will desolate after another. We shall soon have war and bloodshed. The moon will be turned into blood. I testify of these things and that *the coming of the Son of Man is nigh,* even at your doors.[13]

On New Year's Day, 1871, Wilford Woodruff, who was at that time a member of the Quorum of the Twelve, stated:

> The Savior, when speaking to His disciples of His second coming and the establishment of His kingdom on the earth, said the Jews should be scattered and trodden under foot until the times of the Gentiles were fulfilled. But, said He, when you see light breaking forth among the Gentiles, referring to the preaching of His gospel amongst them; when you see salvation offered to the Gentiles, and the Jews—the seed of Israel—passed by, the last first and the first last; *when you see this you may know that the time of my second coming is at hand* as surely as you know that summer is nigh when the fig tree puts forth its leaves; and when these things commence that generation shall not pass away until all are fulfilled.
>
> *We are living in the dispensation and generation to which Jesus referred*—the time appointed by God for the last six thousand years, through the mouth of all the prophets who have lived and left their sayings on record. . . .[14]

On the one hundred and thirty-sixth anniversary of the organization of the Church, President Joseph Fielding Smith, then president of the Quorum of the Twelve, summarized many of the signs that had already been fulfilled, indicating the closeness of the second coming.

> Many things have taken place during the past one hundred and thirty-six years to impress faithful members of the Church with the fact that the coming of the Lord is near. The gospel has been restored. The Church has been fully organized. The priesthood has been conferred upon man. The various dispensations from the beginning have been revealed and their keys and authorities given to the Church. Israel has been and is being gathered

---

[13]Joseph Smith, *DHC,* Vol. 3, p. 390, July 2, 1839. (Italics added)
[14]Wilford Woodruff, *Journal of Discourses,* Vol. 14, p. 5, January 1, 1871. (Italics added)

to the land of Zion. The Jews are returning to Jerusalem. The gospel is being preached in all the world as a witness to every nation. Temples are being built, and ordinance work for the dead, as well as for the living, is performed in them. The hearts of the children have turned to their fathers, and the children are seeking after their dead. The covenants which the Lord promised to make with Israel in the latter days have been revealed, and thousands of gathered Israel have entered into them. Thus the work of the Lord is advancing, and *all these things are signs of the near approach of our Lord.*[15]

Exactly six years prior to that address by President Smith, Elder George Q. Morris, of the Council of the Twelve, discussed three major signs given by the Lord to warn the world that his second advent was near.

I thought I would like to mention three signs that the Lord gave that we might observe and know when we saw them that he had set his hand again to accomplish final preparatory work for the coming of the millennium.

The first of these was to be the restoration of the gospel of Jesus Christ. That has already occurred, and it occurred 130 years ago. The Church speaks for itself. Its literature, its scriptures, its martyrs, over a million testimonies from lips and lives of members of the Church speak to the world and bear witness that this thing has been accomplished that the Lord has set his hand to do, and it is evident that it is spreading all over the world today. . . .

Another sign of great importance was the rise of an evil power. Brother [Ezra Taft] Benson had already very impressively referred to it—communism. . . .

It is that point that I think is very significant. The Savior recognized the domination of Satan over the world generally, and called him the prince of the world, but in a special way—in the way that Brother Benson has referred to—he has entered into the politics of the world among the nations of the world, and already subjugated about one billion people of the world, and by a dire, sanguinary, and deadly philosophy has brought death to millions and has brought slavery to almost a billion people. . . .

A third item is God's promise that he would gather Jews to Jerusalem, and I think perhaps we may well now not continue the

---

[15]Joseph Fielding Smith, "The Signs of the Lord's Coming," *The Improvement Era,* June, 1966, p. 499. (The entire sermon is excellent on the signs of the times and their fulfillment.)

saying the Jews are going to gather in Jerusalem. I think now we may well say they have gathered.[16]

It is significant that all three signs are fulfilled or in the process of fulfillment.

Many other statements by the prophets could be quoted to further support the concept that the fig tree is indeed "putting forth its leaves" and that the coming of the Lord is nigh, "even at the doors." But there are other evidences to consider which bear equal testimony to this fact.

The Savior Comes Tomorrow

Once, when he was asked if he knew when the Lord's coming would be, President Joseph Fielding Smith gave a startling answer. Said he:

> I answered, Yes; and I answer, Yes, now. I know when he will come. *He will come tomorrow.* We have his word for it. Let me read it:
>
> "Behold, now it is called today until the coming of the Son of Man, and verily it is a day of sacrifice, and a day for the tithing of my people; for he that is tithed shall not be burned at his coming. (Now there is a discourse sufficient on tithing.) For after today cometh the burning—this is speaking after the manner of the Lord —for verily I say, tomorrow all the proud and they that do wickedly shall be as stubble; and I will burn them up, for I am the Lord of Hosts; and I will not spare any that remain in Babylon." (D&C 64:23-24)
>
> So the Lord is coming, I say, tomorrow. Then let us be prepared. Elder Orson F. Whitney used to write about the Saturday Evening of Time. This is the sixth day now drawing to its close. When the Lord says it is today until his coming, that, I think is what he has in mind, for he shall come in the morning of the Sabbath, or seventh day of the earth's temporal existence, to inaugurate the millennial reign. . . .[17]

That this is the last day of the earth's normal existence is clearly explained in scripture. In 1832, while working on

[16]George Q. Morris, *Conference Report,* April, 1960, pp. 100-101. (Italics added)

[17]Joseph Fielding Smith, *Conference Report,* April, 1935, p. 98. (Italics added)

the revision of the Bible, Joseph Smith recorded some questions and answers dealing with the Book of Revelation.

> Q. What are we to understand by the book which John saw, which was sealed on the back with seven seals?
>
> A. We are to understand that it contains the revealed will, mysteries, and works of God; the hidden things of his economy concerning this *earth during the seven thousand years of its continuance, or its temporal existence. . . .*
>
> Q. What are we to understand by the sounding of the trumpets, mentioned in the 8th chapter of Revelation?
>
> A. We are to understand that as God made the world in six days, and on the seventh day he finished his work, and sanctified it, and also formed man out of the dust of the earth, even so, *in the beginning of the seventh thousand years will the Lord God sanctify the earth,* and complete the salvation of man, and judge all things, and shall redeem all things, except that which he hath not put into his power, when he shall have sealed all things, unto the end of all things; and the sounding of the trumpets of the seven angels are the preparing and finishing of his work, in the beginning of the seventh thousand years—the preparing of the way before the time of his coming.[18]

It is commonly accepted by most scholars that there were approximately 4,000 years from Adam to Christ, and of course, just under 2,000 years have passed since. The scholars disagree on *exactly* how many years the earth has undergone since the Fall of Adam, however, so it cannot be said that the Millennium will occur in the year 2,000 A.D. (as some enthusiastic interpreters of the scriptures would like to conclude). But the scriptures and the prophets make it clear that this is the "last day" before the Millennium, using Peter's definition that a day with the Lord is as a thousand of our years.[19] Not only is it the last day but we are now in the final stages of that day, according to the Lord. "For the field is white already to harvest; and *it is the eleventh hour,* and the *last time* that I shall call laborers into my vineyard."[20] The Lord indicates in several different places in the Doctrine and Covenants that this

---

[18]*Doctrine and Covenants* 77:6, 12. (Italics added)
[19]2 Peter 3:8.
[20]*Doctrine and Covenants* 33:3. (Italics added)

is the last time he will call missionaries to the work.[21] This is why Orson F. Whitney called it "the Saturday Evening of Time." Brigham Young said:

> Do you know that it is the eleventh hour of the reign of Satan on the earth? Jesus is coming to reign, and all you who fear and tremble because of your enemies, cease to fear them and learn to fear to offend God. . . .[22]

President Wilford Woodruff said:

> We are living at the commencement of the Millennium, and near the close of the 6,000th year of the world's history. Tremendous events await this generation. You can read an account of them in the revelations of St. John; the opening of the seals; the blowing of the trumpets; the pouring out of the plagues; the judgments of God which will overtake the wicked when Great Babylon comes in remembrance before God, and when the sword that is bathed in heaven shall fall on Idumea, or the world, who shall be able to abide these things? *Here we are living in the midst of these tremendous events.*[23]

Elder Charles W. Penrose wrote:

> In answer to questions put by his Apostles, Jesus spoke of certain events which were to be taken as signs of his advent. These things are *now taking place:* therefore we are living in the day of his coming.[24]

This Generation Shall Not All Pass Away

There is another set of evidence which indicates that the return of the Savior as King of kings and Lord of lords is very close. Wilford Woodruff, as already quoted above, noted that although we do not know the hour or the day, the Lord has pointed out the *generation* in which his coming should take

---

[21]*Doctrine and Covenants* 6:3-4; 11:3; 21:9; 31:4-5; 39:17; 43:28; 95:4.

[22]Brigham Young, *Journal of Discourses,* Vol. 10, p. 250, October 6, 1863.

[23]Wilford Woodruff, *Journal of Discourses,* Vol. 25, p. 10, January 6, 1884. (Italics added)

[24]Charles W. Penrose, "The Second Advent," *Millennial Star,* Vol. 21, p. 583, September 10, 1859. (Italics in original)

place. Elder Woodruff then stated plainly: "We are living in the *dispensation and generation* to which Jesus referred. . . ."[25]

This concept is plainly taught both in the scriptures and by the words of the prophets. In the Doctrine and Covenants, under date of September 22nd and 23rd, 1832, the word of the Lord stated that the temple in the city of Zion, or New Jerusalem, would be reared *in this generation.*

> Verily this is the word of the Lord, that the city New Jerusalem shall be built by the gathering of the saints, beginning at this place, even the place of the temple, which temple shall be reared in this generation.
>
> For verily this generation shall not all pass away until an house shall be built unto the Lord, and a cloud shall rest upon it, which cloud shall be even the glory of the Lord, which shall fill the house.[26]

In the *History of the Church* under date of October 15, 1843, Willard Richards recorded a sermon given by the Prophet Joseph Smith in Nauvoo. In that sermon Joseph said:

> I prophesy, in the name of the Lord God of Israel, anguish and wrath and tribulation and the withdrawing of the Spirit of God from the earth await *this generation,* until they are visited with utter desolation.[27]

Wilford Woodruff testified on other occasions that our generation was the one in which Christ would come. In the *Millennial Star* under date of April 21, 1879, he wrote:

> My testimony is unto all men and nations, *that you live in the day and the hour of the judgments of God Almighty. You live in the day and generation when the God of Israel has set his hand to perform his work, his strange work in the latter days. You live in the age in which God will bring to pass the fulfillment of that word of prophecy and prediction which has been spoken by all the prophets since the world began,* which stands recorded in the sacred

---

[25]Wilford Woodruff, *Journal of Discourses,* Vol. 14, p. 5. (Italics added) (For the entire quote, see footnote No. 14 above.)
[26]*Doctrine and Covenants* 84:4-5.
[27]Joseph Smith, *DHC,* Vol. 6, p. 58. October 15, 1843. (Italics added)

books of divine truth, and the fulfillment of these revelations will involve the destiny of the whole world, Jew and Gentile, rich and poor, high and low, saint and sinner, Babylon and Zion.[28]

Just how many years are required to make up a generation is not known. It cannot even be safely said that it is a definite number of years. Elder Orson Pratt spoke of this difficulty in 1877. (In passing it should be noted that Elder Pratt was given the specific charge by the Lord to prophesy. "Therefore prophesy, and it shall be given by the power of the Holy Ghost."[29]) Referring to Doctrine and Covenants 84:5-6, Elder Pratt said:

> As regards the number of years by which a generation shall be measured, we have no specific definite period given to us by revelation; the Lord speaks in terms that are general in relation to generations. Among the Nephites, immediately after Christ's appearance to them a generation was a hundred years, and in the fourth generation they were destroyed, as a nation; except some few who went over to the Lamanites. We find generations numbering from father to son, and from son to grandson, etc., and when we come to average generations, according to the statistics of nations, we find them to be about thirty years to a generation; but when the Lord speaks in general terms, and says, This generation shall not pass away, until a House shall be built to his name, as is given in this "Book of Covenants," and a cloud should rest upon it; in that case I do not think he is limited to any definite period, but suffice it to say that the people living in 1832, when the revelation was given, will not all pass away; there will be some living when the house spoken of will be reared, on which the glory of God will rest. Already forty-five years have passed away since that revelation was given, concerning the building of that House.[30]

Before discussing the implications of his statement, however, another important point needs to be substantiated.

The Dispensation of the Fulness of Times

President Woodruff said that Christ had indicated the *generation* and *dispensation* in which he was to come. Here,

---

[28]Wilford Woodruff, *Millennial Star,* Vol. 41, p. 241, April 21, 1879. (Italics added)

[29]*Doctrine and Covenants* 34:10.

[30]Orson Pratt, *Journal of Discourses,* Vol. 19, p. 215, December 9, 1877.

too, the evidence is persuasive that this dispensation is the *last* one and the one which is to usher in the millennial reign of the Savior. This dispensation is called the dispensation of the fulness of times, for in this dispensation a fulness of the gospel and the blessings held down through time will be gathered together in one great whole.[31] It is the dispensation which will therefore have the power to complete the preparations necessary for the coming of the Lord.

President Joseph Fielding Smith explained it this way:

> The Lord has declared by his own voice and by revelation to his servants, the prophets, that we are living in the *last days.* When we speak of the last days, we do not mean that this is the end of the earth, that it shall cease presently to exist. We mean that we are living in *that period of time known as the dispensation of the fulness of times,* in which the Father has promised to gather all things together in Christ, both which are in heaven and which are on earth. (Ephesians 1:9-10; Doctrine and Covenants 27:12-13) We mean that we are living in the day when unrighteousness shall cease, when wickedness shall no longer be found on the face of the earth, when this earth shall be turned over, according to the promise the Lord made to Daniel the Prophet, to the saints of the Most High, who shall possess it forever and ever.[32]

In October general conference of 1911, President Charles W. Penrose of the First Presidency, discussed the dispensation of the fulness of times.

> We are living in the dispensation of the fulness of times, and in this dispensation—the grandest and greatest of all, will be gathered in one all things that are in Christ, not only His people gathered from the various nations to Zion to build it up, to prepare the place for His feet, but the hosts that have passed away, whom He will bring with Him. Not only are the people to be gathered together, but the glorious truths which have been made manifest in the ages that are past will all be brought forth in the dispensation in which we are living, and things kept hid from the foundations of the world will be made manifest; for the Lord has promised it, and His promises never fail of fulfillment.[33]

---

[31]*Doctrine and Covenants* 128:18.
[32]Joseph Fielding Smith, *Doctrines of Salvation* (Bruce R. McConkie, comp.), Vol. 3, (Bookcraft: Salt Lake City, 1956), p. 14. (Italics added)
[33]Charles W. Penrose, *Conference Report,* October, 1911, pp. 48-49.

Whose Eyes Shall Not Be Closed in Death

Now to return to the remarkable statement by Orson Pratt made in 1877, wherein he gave his opinion that there were those then living upon the earth who would still be alive when the temple was reared in Jackson County, Missouri. It has been nearly 100 years since that statement was made and yet the Church still looks forward to the fulfillment of that prophecy. Since there is not an abundance of people left who were alive when Orson Pratt made that statement, some have concluded that it was simply his opinion and obviously in error. If this were an isolated statement, that explanation would carry more weight, but it is not. Statements by the prophets similar to the statement by Orson Pratt are another of the great evidences we have that the second coming is near at hand. For example, in the 1967 October Priesthood Conference of the Church, Elder Hugh B. Brown of the First Presidency, said:

> It seems to me that of all the signs of the times (and they are ominous and on every side) this is one of the significant signs of the times—that the Church of Jesus Christ, the kingdom of God, is massing its forces, getting ready for that which is to follow. . . .
>
> I hope that every young man under the sound of my voice will resolve tonight, "I am going to keep myself clean. I am going to serve the Lord. I am going to prepare every way I can for future service, because I want to be prepared *when the final battle shall come.*"
>
> *And some of you young men are going to engage in that battle. Some of you are going to engage in the final testing time, which is coming and which is closer to us than we know.*[34]

In a great discourse to the saints assembled in general conference in 1898, President Wilford Woodruff spent some time recalling some experiences he had been privileged to enjoy with the Prophet Joseph Smith. He told of meeting with the Prophet in a log cabin in preparation for the organization of Zion's Camp. Some of the brethren spoke and bore their testimonies. When they finished, Joseph told them they were limited in their vision of what was to come. He told of

---

[34]Hugh B. Brown, *Conference Report,* October, 1967, p. 115. (Italics added)

the time when the saints would go to the Rocky Mountains and do a great work there. Then he said, according to President Woodruff:

> This people will go into the Rocky Mountains; they will there build temples to the Most High. They will raise up a posterity there, *and the Latter-day Saints who dwell in these mountains will stand in the flesh until the coming of the Son of Man.* The Son of Man will come to them while in the Rocky Mountains.

Then President Woodruff went on to say:

> ... I never expected to see the Rocky Mountains when I listened to that man's voice, but I have, and do today. I will say here that I shall not live to see it, [President Woodruff died five months later, before the next General Conference of the Church] you may not live to see it; *but these thousands of Latter-day Saint children that belong to the Sabbath schools, I believe many of them will stand in the flesh when the Lord Jesus Christ visits the Zion of God here in the mountains of Israel.*[35]

Ten years earlier, President Woodruff had echoed this same feeling at a stake conference held in Grantsville, Utah.

> *Many of these young men and maidens that are here today will, in my opinion, if they are faithful, stand in the flesh when Christ comes in the clouds of heaven.* These young people from the Sabbath schools and from the Mutual Improvement Associations, *will stand in the flesh while the judgments of the Almighty sweep the nations of the earth as with a besom of destruction, in fulfillment of the revelations of God, and they will be the very people whom God will bless and sustain.* Therefore, I say, our young men cannot begin too quickly to qualify themselves by treasuring up wisdom and calling upon God and getting the Holy Priesthood; for they have got to stand in holy places while these judgments are poured out upon the earth.[36]

President Joseph Fielding Smith, then a member of the Council of the Twelve, expressed his opinion of the same truth in April conference, 1936.

---

[35]Wilford Woodruff, *Conference Report,* April, 1898, p. 57. (Italics added)
[36]Wilford Woodruff, given at Tooele Stake Conference (at Grantsville, Utah) July 29, 1889. Reported in *Millennial Star,* Vol. 51, p. 595. (Italics added)

The day of the coming of the Lord is near. I do not know when. I am not looking, however, upon the coming of the Son of Man . . . as something that may come in some far distant time—because I sincerely believe *it will come in the very day when some of us who are here today will be living upon the face of the earth.* That day is close at hand.[37]

The Times of the Gentiles

In the forty-fifth section of the Doctrine and Covenants, we are told that when the "times of the Gentiles" are fulfilled, ". . . there shall be men standing in that generation, that shall not pass until they shall see an overflowing scourge; for a desolating sickness shall cover the land."[38] Many other judgments were then listed as happening also. Thus, the fulfilling of the times of the Gentiles is a key in determining how close the coming of the Lord is. In the same section the Lord gives us the key for knowing when the times of the Gentiles shall be completed:

> And this I have told you concerning Jerusalem; and when that day shall come, shall a remnant be scattered among all nations;
> But they shall be gathered again; *but they shall remain until the times of the Gentiles be fulfilled.*[39]

The Savior taught the same thing to his apostles when he said, ". . . And Jerusalem shall be trodden down of the Gentiles, until the times of the Gentiles be fulfilled."[40] It is only in recent years that this prophecy has come to see its fulfillment. As recently as 1967, the city of Jerusalem was taken completely into Jewish power and dominion, for the first time in nearly two thousand years. President Joseph Fielding Smith clearly states that the times of the Gentiles are nearly fulfilled. In an editorial in the Church News in 1931, he said:

> We all know that from the time of the destruction of Jerusalem in the year 70 A.D. until near the close of World War I, Jerusalem

---

[37]Joseph Fielding Smith, *Conference Report,* April, 1936, pp. 75-76. (Italics added)
[38]*Doctrine and Covenants* 45:30-31.
[39]*Ibid.,* 45:24-25. (Italics added)
[40]Luke 21:24.

was trodden down of the Gentiles, and during all of that time the Jews were scattered and almost without privileges in the Holy Land. The Lord said they should remain scattered among the nations *until* the times of the Gentiles were fulfilled. Moroni said the times of the Gentiles were about to be fulfilled. Today we are living in the *transition* period; *the day of the Gentiles has come in, and the day of Judah and the remnant of downtrodden Israel is now at hand.* The sign for the fulfillment of the prophecy has been given.[41]

Then in general conference some thirty-five years later, when the world had come to see Israel established as an independent and courageous nation, President Joseph Fielding Smith said:

Jesus said the Jews would be scattered among all nations and Jerusalem would be trodden down by the Gentiles until the times of the Gentiles were fulfilled. (Luke 21:24) The prophecy in Section 45, verses 24-29, of the Doctrine and Covenants regarding the Jews was literally fulfilled. Jerusalem, which was trodden down by the Gentiles, is no longer trodden down but is made the home for the Jews. They are returning to Palestine, and *by this we may know that the times of the Gentiles are near their close.*[42]

The Angels of Destruction

One last important indication has been given that answers the question, "How can you be so sure that the second coming of the Lord is still not three or four hundred years in the future?" We are indebted to President Wilford Woodruff for this evidence, for it was through his mouth that it was declared. In the summer of 1894, President Woodruff accompanied a group of temple workers on a special outing, and addressed them in the evening. He spoke of the judgments that were going to come upon the nation and its people.

They will come down like the judgments of Sodom and Gomorrah. And none but the priesthood will be safe from their fury. God has held the angels of destruction for many years, lest they should reap down the wheat with the tares. But I want to tell you now, *that those angels have left the portals of heaven, and they stand over this people and this nation now, and are hovering over*

---

[41]Joseph Fielding Smith, *Doctrines of Salvation* (Bruce R. McConkie, comp.), Vol. 3, (Bookcraft: Salt Lake City, 1956), pp. 258-259. (Italics added)
[42]Joseph Fielding Smith, "The Signs of the Lord's Coming," *The Improvement Era,* June, 1966, p. 499. (Italics added)

*the earth waiting to pour out the judgments. And from this very
day they shall be poured out.* Calamities and troubles are increasing in the earth, and there is a meaning to these things. Remember
this, and reflect upon these matters. If you do your duty, and I do
my duty, we'll have protection, and shall pass through the afflictions
in peace and safety.[43]

The angels to which he referred were those mentioned in the
Doctrine and Covenants.

Behold, verily I say unto you, the angels are crying unto the
Lord day and night, who are ready and waiting to be sent forth
to reap down the fields."[44]

Three months after his first mention of these angels, Wilford
Woodruff again spoke of them.

What is the matter with the world today? What has created
this change that we see coming over the world? Why these terrible
earthquakes, tornados, and judgments? What is the meaning of all
these mighty events that are taking place? *The meaning is, these
angels that have been held for many years in the temple of our
God have got their liberty to go out and commence their mission
and their work in the earth, and they are here today in the earth.*[45]

Two years later, in general conference, President Woodruff
said:

*I want to bear testimony to this congregation, and to the heav-
ens and the earth, that the day is come when those angels are
privileged to go forth and commence their work. They are laboring in the United States of America; they are laboring among the
nations of the earth; and they will continue. We need not marvel
or wonder at anything that is transpiring in the earth. The world
does not comprehend the revelations of God.* They did not in the
days of the Jews; yet all that the prophets had spoken concerning
them came to pass. So in our day these things will come to pass.
I heard the Prophet Joseph bear his testimony to these events that
would transpire in the earth. . . . We cannot draw a veil over the

[43]Wilford Woodruff, "The Temple Workers' Excursion," reported by Susan
Young Gates, *The Young Woman's Journal*, Vol. 5, pp. 512-513. (Italics added)
    [44]*Doctrine and Covenants* 86:5.
    [45]Wilford Woodruff, *Millennial Star*, Vol. 56, p. 643, October 8, 1894. (Italics
added)

events that await this generation. No man that is inspired by the Spirit and power of God can close his ears, his eyes or his lips to these things.[46]

During World War II, President Joseph Fielding Smith was asked to deliver a series of lectures to the ladies of the Lion House Social Center on the "Signs of the Times." In one of the discussions, he spent some time explaining the parable of the wheat and the tares which makes reference to the angels reaping down the fields. He quoted President Woodruff's statements on the loosing of these angels and then went on to say:

> One day while I was sitting in the presence of my father back about 1908 or 9, somewhere in there, I called attention to these statements of President Woodruff, and I said I would like to go over the records from the time of the dedication of the Temple up until now and see what we can find in regard to calamities, destructions, plagues; and he encouraged me to do it, and so I did. So I went over the newspapers and over the magazines and jotted down year by year the destructions, the commotions among men, everything in the nature of a calamity, and to my great astonishment each year they increased, and they have been increasing ever since I quit making that record. I was greatly astonished by it. . . .

President Smith referred to a study of wars done by two sociologists, and then continued:

> Out of this study these scientists declare that they have discovered that war has tended to increase over all Europe in the late centuries. They say they have learned that in these countries, war grew from 2.678 in the twelfth century to 13,735.98 in the first twenty-five years of the twentieth century. Their tables show the growth by centuries. Up to the seventeenth century the wars were comparatively insignificant. Beginning with that century war increased during the eighteenth, with a lull in the nineteenth, yet in that century they were more than 100 times greater than in medieval times.
>
> These men conclude that "all commendable hopes that war will disappear in the near future are based on nothing more substantial than hope of a belief in miracles."

---

[46]Wilford Woodruff, *Millennial Star,* Vol. 58, p. 739, November 19, 1896. (Italics added)

And then I made this prediction:

"If prophecy is to be fulfilled, there awaits the world a conflict more dreadful than any the world has yet seen." (Progress of Man, pp. 402-404).

Now I want to make some comments in regard to the statement by President Woodruff and this parable.

The Lord said that the sending forth of these angels was to be at the end of the harvest, and the harvest is the end of the world. Now, that ought to cause us some very serious reflections. And the angels have been pleading, as I have read it to you, before the Lord to be sent on their mission. Until 1893 the Lord said to them no, and then He set them loose. According to the revelation of President Woodruff, the Lord sent them out on that mission.

What do we gather out of that? That *we are at the time of the end.* This is the time of the harvest.[47]

The End Is Near

In summary, then, when the question is asked, "How soon the end?" it must immediately be said that no one knows. But the evidence of scripture and the statements of the prophets make it clear that the time is close at hand. People may try to rationalize or explain away the signs which are being fulfilled all around them, but the evidence is still clear. There are many things predicted which have yet to come to pass, but the signs of the times manifest themselves with increasing rapidity.

Orson Pratt said he believed that some people living in 1877 would live to see the temple erected in the city of New Jerusalem. Some would dismiss that since it has been nearly 100 years and there is still no temple in Zion. But it should be remembered that, as recorded in the Book of Mormon, Samuel the Lamanite prophesied that the signs of Christ's birth would come in five years. When the five years were nearly up, many began to scoff and even threatened the believers with death if they did not deny their belief. *The sign was given on the last night before the five years were finished.*[48]

---

[47]Joseph Fielding Smith, *Signs of the Times,* (Deseret Book Co.: Salt Lake City, 1952), pp. 116, 120-121. (Italics added)
[48]3 Nephi 1:1-20.

It is true that there are not many people alive today [1971] who were alive when Orson Pratt made his prophecy. But it doesn't take many. It is interesting to note that at the writing of this book, the president of the Church of Jesus Christ, President Joseph Fielding Smith, was alive at the time Orson Pratt spoke this prophecy.

One must be cautious about rejecting the words of the Lord's servants because the full meaning and implications are hidden. President Charles W. Penrose stated the proper attitude most adequately:

> Of course, we understand that certain things predicted through the Prophet Joseph Smith are to take place *before this generation shall pass away,* and the Lord will see to it that the generation in which those things were predicted will not all pass away until all shall be fulfilled, but there is no fixed period for a generation, no set time in the revelations of God, no year or date given when these things shall take place, and it is folly for anybody to put a date to it. *Leave that in the hands of the Lord and he will take care that his word is fulfilled. . . .*[49]

---

[49]Charles W. Penrose, *Conference Report,* April, 1918, pp. 20-21. (Italics added)

A Cry of War

Shortly before the close of 1832, the Prophet Joseph Smith described the conditions that were existent in the world at that time. Cholera was prevalent in many of the large cities, India was experiencing an epidemic of the plague, and the United States had just passed through a serious crisis with the state of South Carolina. Whether it was this close brush with civil war or some other cause that caused the Lord to respond is not known. Joseph Smith says simply, "On Christmas day, I received the following revelation and prophecy on war."[1] Then follows one of the most remarkable prophecies ever recorded.

> Verily, thus saith the Lord concerning *the wars* that will shortly come to pass, *beginning* at the rebellion of South Carolina, which will eventually terminate in the death and misery of many souls;
>
> *And the time will come that war will be poured out upon all nations, beginning at this place.*
>
> For behold, the Southern States shall be divided against the Northern States, and the Southern States will call on other nations, even the nation of Great Britain, as it is called, and they shall also call upon other nations, in order to defend themselves against other nations; and *then war shall be poured out upon all nations.* . . .
>
> And thus, with the sword and by bloodshed the inhabitants of the earth shall mourn; and with famine, and plague, and earthquake, and the thunder of heaven, and the fierce and vivid lightning also, shall the inhabitants of the earth be made to feel the

---

[1]Joseph Smith, *DHC,* Vol. 1, p. 301, December 25, 1832.

wrath, and indignation, and chastening hand of an Almighty God, until the consumption decreed *hath made a full end of all nations.*[2]

For a time it looked as though Joseph Smith had prophesied prematurely of a crisis that did not occur. President Jackson's firm stand caused South Carolina to back down and the confrontation was avoided. But the prophecy stood, and was fulfilled most remarkably nearly thirty years later when South Carolina again rebelled and fired against Fort Sumter. The great and costly Civil War was the final result and the words of the Lord were once more vindicated before the full view of the world.

Wars and Rumors of Wars

This prophecy has come to be known as "The Civil War Prophecy." However the revelation is even more remarkable for its other prophetic promises. The Lord promised that wars (note the plural) would be shortly coming to pass, and that "beginning" at the rebellion of South Carolina, war would be poured out "upon all nations."

President Joseph Fielding Smith explained that the Civil War was the Lord's sign that the beginning of the end had come.

> Based upon what the Lord says in this Section 87 of the Doctrine and Covenants—the Section on war which I read—*I place the time of the beginning of the end at the rebellion of South Carolina.* I say I place it there. I beg your pardon. *The Lord places it there* because it says beginning at this place these things would take place.[3]

When the Savior was outlining the events that would transpire before his return, he intimated that war would become a natural phenomenon of the last days. "And they shall hear of wars, and rumors of wars. Behold I speak for mine elect's sake; for nation shall rise against nation, and kingdom against kingdom; there shall be famines, and pestilences, and earthquakes, in divers places."[4] *War is one of the*

---

[2]*Doctrine and Covenants* 87:1-3, 6. (Italics added)
[3]Joseph Fielding Smith, *Signs of the Times,* (Deseret Book Co.: Salt Lake City, 1952), p. 149. (Italics added)
[4]Joseph Smith 1:28-29.

signs of the times. It has become so much a part of modern-day life that it is almost taken for granted. One has only to list such names as The Congo, Biafra, Pakistan, Peru, Korea, Argentina, Viet Nam, Brazil, Hungary, Berlin, Greece, Egypt, India, Red China, Israel, Cambodia, Cuba, and a hundred others. Each evokes a mental picture of war, overthrown governments, civil chaos, or invasion. This century has seen cold and hot wars; civil, religious, racial and revolutionary wars; aerial, naval, trench and guerrilla warfare; chemical, biological, and atomic warfare. Little wonder that Joseph Smith said: "Some may have cried peace, but the Saints and the world will have little peace from henceforth."[5]

War upon All Nations

In the prophecy on war previously cited, the Lord stated that war would be poured out upon all nations "until the consumption decreed hath made a full end of all nations."[6] The prophets of this dispensation have abundantly testified that the nations of the world will be broken up in preparation for the coming of the King of kings when there shall be only one government in the world, the Kingdom of Christ. War is the means by which this end will be brought about. The following is just a sampling of what the prophets of today have told us concerning the fulfillment of the Lord's words concerning war.

In an article written in the *Millennial Star,* Elder Charles W. Penrose stated:

> Through the rejection of this Gospel, which "Shall be preached to all the world as a witness" of the coming of Christ, the world will increase in confusion, doubt, and horrible strife. As the upright in heart, the meek of the earth, withdraw from their midst, so will the spirit of God also be withdrawn from them. The darkness upon their minds in relation to eternal things will become blacker, nations will engage in frightful and bloody warfare, the crimes which are now becoming so frequent will be of continual occurrence, the ties that bind together families and kindred will be disregarded and violated, the passions of human nature will be put

---

[5]Joseph Smith, *DHC,* Vol. 3, p. 390, July 2, 1839.
[6]*Doctrine and Covenants* 87:6.

to the vilest uses, the very elements around will seem to be affected by the national and social convulsions that will agitate the world, and storms, earthquakes, and appalling disasters by sea and land will cause terror and dismay among the people; new diseases will silently eat their ghastly way through the ranks of the wicked; the earth, soaked with gore and defiled with the filthiness of her inhabitants, will begin to withhold her fruits in their season; the waves of the sea will heave themselves beyond their bounds, and all things will be in commotion; and in the midst of all these calamities, the masterminds among nations will be taken away, and fear will take hold of the hearts of all men.[7]

Lorenzo Snow stated that these wars would help bring people to the Church for protection:

By and by the nations will be broken up on account of their wickedness, the Latter-day Saints are not going to move upon them with their little army, they will destroy themselves with their wickedness and immorality. They will contend and quarrel with one another, state after state and nation after nation, until they are broken up, and thousands, tens of thousands and hundreds of thousands will undoubtedly come and seek protection at the hands of the servants of God.[8]

The wars of destruction and change were a constantly recurring theme in Elder Orson Pratt's discourses. For example, in 1879 he stated:

. . . When that day shall come there shall be wars, not such wars as have come in centuries and years that are past and gone, but a desolating war. When I say desolating, I mean that it will lay these European nations in waste. Cities will be left vacated, without inhabitants. The people will be destroyed by the sword of their own hands. Not only this but many other cities will be burned; for when contending armies are wrought up with terrible anger, without the Spirit of God upon them, when they have not that spirit of humanity that now characterizes many of the wars amongst the nations, when they are left to themselves, *there will be no quarter given, no prisoners taken, but a war of destruction, of desolation, of the burning of the cities and villages, until the land is laid desolate.* That is another thing that will come before the coming of the Son of Man.[9]

---

[7]Charles W. Penrose, *Millennial Star,* Vol. 21, p. 582, September 19, 1859.
[8]Lorenzo Snow, *Journal of Discourses,* Vol. 14, p. 309, January 14, 1872.
[9]Orson Pratt, *Journal of Discourses,* Vol. 20, pp. 150-151, March 9, 1879.
(Italics added)

In a letter written to the nation of Great Britain in 1857, Elder Orson F. Whitney said:

> But if you will not, as a nation, repent, and unite yourselves with God's kingdom, then the days are near at hand, woe unto you when that day shall come! For it shall be a day of vengeance upon the British nation; and your armies shall perish; your maritime forces shall cease; your cities shall be ravaged, burned, and made desolate, and your strongholds shall be thrown down; the poor shall rise against the rich, and their storehouses and their fine mansions shall be pillaged, their merchandise, and their gold, and their silver, and their rich treasures, shall be plundered; then shall the Lords, the Nobles, and the merchants of the land, and all in high places, be brought down, and shall sit in the dust, and howl for the miseries that shall be upon them; and they that trade by sea shall lament and mourn; for their traffic shall cease. And thus shall the Lord Almighty visit you, because of your great wickedness in rejecting His servants and His kingdom. . . .[10]

Orson Hyde, the apostle who dedicated the land of Palestine for the return of the Jews, made a startling prediction which has been literally fulfilled in this century. He prophesied:

> You have scarcely yet read the preface of your national troubles. Many nations will be drawn into the American maelstrom that now whirls through the land; and after many days, when the demon of war shall have exhausted his strength and madness upon American soil, by the destruction of all that can court or provoke opposition, excite cupidity, inspire revenge, or feed ambition, *he will remove his headquarters to the banks of the Rhine.*[11]

The Rhine, of course, refers to the Rhine River, one of the most prominent rivers of Germany. In both of this century's great wars, Germany has been a prime protagonist.

A year after the conclusion of World War II, President George Albert Smith prophesied that even greater catastrophes would come than that great global war if people did not repent.

> I fear that the time is coming . . . unless we can call the people of this world to repent of their ways, the great war that has just

---

[10]Orson F. Whitney, *Millennial Star,* Vol. 19, pp. 680-681, October 24, 1857.
[11]Orson Hyde, *Millennial Star,* Vol. 24, p. 274, May 3, 1862. (Italics added)

passed will be *an insignificant thing,* as far as calamity is concerned, compared to that which is before us. And we can avoid it if we will; if we will each do our part, it can be prevented.[12]

A statement made by President David O. McKay may have bearing on this struggle, for he prophesied that Communism must be overthrown so that the gospel could be preached to the peoples in those countries.

A new religious freedom must come. God will overrule it [Communism], for that people must hear the truth and truth in simplicity. Truly there is much for the Church to do in the coming century.[13]

Peace Is Taken from the Earth

All of these prophetic promises only support what the Lord said in his preface to the Doctrine and Covenants. "For I am no respecter of persons, and will that all men shall know that the day speedily cometh; the hour is not yet, but is nigh at hand, *when peace shall be taken from the earth, and the devil shall have power over his own dominion.*"[14] President Joseph Fielding Smith has testified that that hour has now come.

One year after the organization of the Church, peace could not have been taken from the earth, in justice, but the Lord said the time would speedily come. *That time has come. Peace has departed from the world.* The devil has power today over his own dominion. This is made manifest in the actions of men, in the distress among the nations, in the troubles that we see in all lands, including this land which was dedicated to liberty.[15]

More Than War

As if the wars were not terrible enough in and of themselves, they will be accompanied with other calamities so great that men's hearts shall fail them. The Lord has warned his

---

[12]George Albert Smith, *The Improvement Era,* November, 1946, p. 763. (Italics added)

[13]David O. McKay, *Church News,* May 28, 1960.

[14]*Doctrine and Covenants* 1:35. (Italics added)

[15]Joseph Fielding Smith, *Conference Report,* April, 1937, p. 59. (Italics added)

people to remain clean until his coming so that these things could be avoided. In the revelation known as the "Olive Leaf," the Lord said:

> For not many days hence and the earth shall tremble and reel to and fro as a drunken man; and the sun shall hide his face, and shall refuse to give light; and the moon shall be bathed in blood; and the stars shall become exceedingly angry and shall cast themselves down as a fig that falleth from off a fig-tree.
>
> And after your testimony cometh wrath and indignation upon the people.
>
> For after your testimony cometh the testimony of earthquakes, that shall cause groanings in the midst of her, and men shall fall upon the ground and shall not be able to stand.
>
> And also cometh the testimony of the voice of thunderings, and the voice of lightnings, and the voice of tempests, and the voice of the waves of the sea heaving themselves beyond their bounds.
>
> *And all things shall be in commotion;* and surely men's hearts shall fail them; for fear shall come upon all people.[16]

A year and a half earlier, the Lord had explained how both war and calamities would be found together.

> And there shall be earthquakes also in divers places, *and many desolations; yet men will harden their hearts against me, and they will take up the sword, one against another, and they will kill one another.*[17]

In places other than scriptures, the prophets have testified of the other distresses besides war which will precede the second coming of the Lord. John Taylor wrote in one of the Church's newspapers about a year after the Prophet's death:

> So, knowing that there are other judgments in store for the whole earth, we will venture a prediction, and *that there shall be storm and hail enough to cause a famine,* and show the whole of the earth that Jesus Christ, and not the Mormons, vexes the nation. Enough of the present generation shall see, hear, and feel it, to be witnesses that the servants of God tell the truth.[18]

---

[16]*Doctrine and Covenants* 88:87-91. (Italics added)
[17]*Ibid.,* 45:33. (Italics added)
[18]John Taylor, *Nauvoo Neighbor,* August 6, 1845. (Italics added)

President Wilford Woodruff also said:

> *The Lord is not going to disappoint either Babylon or Zion, with regard to famine, pestilence, earthquake or storms, he is not going to disappoint anybody with regard to any of these things, they are at the doors.* . . . Lay up your wheat and other provisions against a day of need, for the day will come when they will be wanted, and no mistake about it. We shall want bread, and the Gentiles will want bread, and if we are wise we shall have something to feed them and ourselves when famine comes.[19]

A New Kind of Sermon

The plagues, the famines, the thunderings and lightnings, the hail and the earthquakes are all necessary, for the children of men will not otherwise heed the warning voice of the Lord. In these times of chaos and catastrophes which are coming, the missionaries of the Church will be called home, and the Lord will preach his own sermons to the people.

Both Heber C. Kimball and Brigham Young taught that the calling home of the missionaries was a literal event and one of the signs of the times.

> The judgments of God will be poured out upon the wicked to the extent that *our elders from far and near will be called home.* Or, in other words, the gospel will be taken from the Gentiles and later on will be carried to the Jews.[20]
>
> Do you think there is calamity abroad now among the people? Not much. All we have yet heard and all we have experienced is scarcely a preface to the sermon that is going to be preached. When the testimony of the Elders ceases to be given, and the Lord says to them, "Come home; I will now preach my own sermons to the nations of the earth," *all you now know can scarcely be called a preface to the sermon that will be preached with fire and sword, tempests, earthquakes, hail, rain, thunders and lightnings, and fearful destruction.* What matters the destruction of a few railway cars? You will hear of magnificent cities, now idolized by the people, sinking in the earth, entombing the inhabitants. The sea will heave itself beyond its bounds, engulfing mighty cities. Famine

---

[19]Wilford Woodruff, *Journal of Discourses,* Vol. 18, p. 121, September 12, 1875. (Italics added)
[20]Heber C. Kimball, *Deseret News, Church Department,* May 23, 1931, p. 3. (Italics added)

will spread over the nations, and nation will rise up against nation, kingdom against kingdom, and states against states, in our own country and in foreign lands.[21]

Orson Pratt also taught the same doctrine.

> When God has called out the righteous, when the warning voice has been sufficiently proclaimed among the Gentile nations, and *the Lord says, "It is enough," he will also say to his servants— "O, ye, my servants, come home, come out from the midst of these Gentile nations, where you have labored and borne testimony for so long a period;* come out from among them, for they are not worthy; they do not receive the message that I have sent forth, they do not repent of their sins, come out from their midst, their times are fulfilled. Seal up the testimony among them and bind up the law."[22]

And yet, according to Melvin J. Ballard, even these testimonies of the elements themselves will go largely unheeded by men.

> The Lord said they would not heed that warning voice *no more than they had heeded the warning voice of his servants.* But I want to call the attention of the Latter-day Saints, and indeed if I had the power, the attention of all the world to the fact that *God is speaking through the elements.* The earthquakes, the sea heaving itself beyond its bounds, bringing such dire destruction as we have seen are *the voice of God crying repentance to this generation,* a generation that only in part has heeded the warning voice of the servants of the Lord.[23]

In Zion and Her Stakes

"But is there to be no hope in such dark times?" one cries out. "How can anyone escape such destruction and warfare?" The words of the prophets once again offer hope in the midst of approaching darkness; once more we are shown

---

[21]Brigham Young, *Journal of Discourses,* Vol. 8, p. 123, July 15, 1860. (Italics added)

[22]Orson Pratt, *Journal of Discourses,* Vol. 18, p. 64, July 25, 1875. (Italics added) See also *Doctrine and Covenants* 43:21-22.

[23]Melvin J. Ballard, *Conference Report,* October, 1923, p. 31. (Italics added)

the hand of God that will lead us through the deepening gloom.

In July, 1839, the Prophet Joseph Smith met with the Twelve who were departing on missions for Great Britain and addressed them. He spoke of the coming wars and pestilences that would come upon the world. His words were grim and foreboding, but they also explained how the righteous could escape from these disastrous events.

> There will be here and there a Stake [of Zion] for the gathering of the Saints. *Some may have cried peace, but the Saints and the world will have little peace from henceforth.* Let this not hinder us from going to the Stakes; for God told us to flee, not dallying, or we shall be scattered, one here, and another there. There your children shall be blessed, and you in the midst of friends where you may be blessed. . . .
>
> I prophesy that that man who tarries after he has an opportunity of going, will be afflicted by the devil. Wars are at hand; we must not delay; but are not required to sacrifice. We ought to have the building up of Zion as our greatest object. When wars come, we shall flee to Zion. . . . *The time is soon coming, when no man will have any peace but in Zion and her stakes.*[24]

Orson Pratt also testified:

> . . . By and by the Spirit of God will entirely withdraw from these Gentile nations, and leave them to themselves. Then they will find something else to do besides warring against the Saints in their midst—besides raising their sword and fighting against the Lamb of God; *for then war will commence in earnest, and such a war as probably never entered into the hearts of men in our age to conceive of. No nation of the Gentiles upon the face of the whole earth but what will be engaged in deadly war, except the Latter-day Kingdom.*[25]

The Lord specifically told the Prophet Joseph in a revelation that the city of New Jerusalem would be a place of refuge and safety and a land of peace for the Saints of the Lord. So great will be its glory that it will strike terror into

---

[24]Joseph Smith, *DHC*, Vol. 3, pp. 390-391. (Italics added)
[25]Orson Pratt, *Journal of Discourses*, Vol. 7, p. 188, July 10, 1859. (Italics added)

the hearts of the wicked so that they dare not come up to battle against it. And those who will not take up the sword against their neighbor will flee to Zion for safety.[26] So to those who trust in the hand of the Lord for guidance during the dark hours, there will be a place of hope and comfort.

The Chastening Hand of the Lord

But even with this hope, it is not a pleasant task to contemplate the terrible events predicted by the Lord's servants. They are so appalling in their destruction that the mind pales at the implications. At first glance they seem to indicate a harshness on the part of the Lord, an eagerness to punish his children when they have erred. Many people find it hard to reconcile such full-scale war and widespread catastrophes with the tender mercies of a loving Father. But the scriptures and the words of the servants of the Lord are abundantly clear. He must take vengeance upon the wicked because they will not repent.[27] However, this vengeance comes only after he pleads over and over for them to forsake their evil ways and come unto him.

> O, ye nations of the earth, how often would I have gathered you together as a hen gathereth her chickens under her wings, but ye would not!
>
> How oft have I called upon you by the mouth of my servants, and by the ministering of angels, and by mine own voice, and by the voice of thunderings, and by the voice of lightnings, and by the voice of tempests, and by the voice of earthquakes, and great hailstorms, and by the voice of famines, and pestilences of every kind, and by the great sound of a trump, and by the voice of judgment, and by the voice of mercy all the day long, and by the voice of glory and honor and the riches of eternal life, and would have saved you with an everlasting salvation, *but ye would not!*
>
> Behold, the day has come, when the cup of the wrath of mine indignation is full.[28]

---

[26]*Doctrine and Covenants* 45:68.
[27]*Ibid.*, 29:17.
[28]*Ibid.*, 43:24-26. (Italics added)

The wrath of his indignation is full because we are so easily turned to evil, and it seems as though it is only through the chastenings of trouble and tribulation that we turn to him.

> *And thus we see that except the Lord doth chasten his people with many afflictions, yea, except he doth visit them with death and with terror, and with famine and with all manner of pestilence they will not remember him.*[29]

And yet, even in spite of our eagerness to turn from him, he still patiently and lovingly seeks to warn us of future destruction so that we can repent and turn his judgments aside.

> I stand here without any fear and say without any danger of anybody successfully being able to prove the contrary, that if the warning voice of the Prophet Joseph Smith and the elders of this Church had been heeded by the nations of the earth, we would not have seen the dreadful calamity of war through which we have passed, that these problems could have been solved and averted.
>
> *The means was provided, and the means was rejected, and then when our Father has done this, though he be God, is yet limited to law, by obedience to which he became God, and he must honor the same, he cannot step beyond those limitations and set aside the law. The law must take its course, and when men refuse the offer and tender the Lord has given by which they may be saved, they cannot blame the Lord if calamities, judgments and destructions come upon them. The Lord cannot avert it, it must take its course, and yet our Father in his kindness and mercy has offered the way and the means of escape.*[30]

The choice is given to us freely and it is ours to make. However, if we make the unwise decision, God has no choice but to let fall the judgments which our acts produce.

---

[29]Helaman 12:3. (Italics added)
[30]Melvin J. Ballard, *Conference Report,* October, 1923, p. 31. (Italics added)

The United States in Prophecy

As one reviews the destiny of the nations of the earth and the prophecies concerning the great struggles and universal warfare which is foretold by the prophets, the question naturally comes to mind: "And what of the United States of America? What of this nation, one of the most wealthy and powerful civilizations ever in the unrolling scene of world history? Have the prophets also spoken concerning this land?"

A Land Choice Above All Others

As early as several thousand years before the birth of the Savior, the land which is now called America was designated as a land to be preferred above all others. Both to the Jaredites, who were led out of central Asia at the time of the confusion of tongues, and to the family of Lehi who left Jerusalem about six hundred years before Christ's birth, the Lord testified that the land to which they were going was the promised land, a land so abundant in wealth that all who lived there in righteousness would prosper. Indeed, it was a land which was "choice above all other lands."[1] The millions who have come to this country in this age have found it to be just as the Lord promised.

But such a land was not to be had without some conditions. A land choice above all other lands requires a people choice above all other peoples. The Lord made it very clear that this land was reserved only for a people willing to serve him and keep his commandments. If the people refused to

---

[1]Ether 2:7; 1 Nephi 2:20.

meet those conditions they necessarily would have to lose the privilege of dwelling in the promised land.

> And he had sworn in his wrath unto the brother of Jared, that whoso should possess this land of promise, *from that time henceforth and forever,* should serve him, the true and only God, *or they should be swept off when the fulness of his wrath shall come upon them.*
>
> And now, we can behold the decrees of God concerning this land, that it is a land of promise; and whatsoever nation shall possess it shall serve God, *or they shall be swept off.* . . .
>
> *For it is the everlasting decree of God. And it is not until the fulness of iniquity among the children of the land, that they are swept off.*[2]

That is the everlasting decree of God for all who possess this land. And the Book of Mormon records the literal fulfillment of this promise to two great and mighty nations. One has only to read the final destruction of both the Jaredite and Nephite nations to know that God's decree is not one to be set aside.

The Wickedness of This Generation

In his preface to the Doctrine and Covenants, the Lord warned the people living in our time that the level of wickedness was rising, and would soon bring the divine promise into play once again if they did not repent.[3]

If the generation which now inhabits the promised land does not serve the only true and living God they too shall be swept off when their iniquity is full. The outlook is not very optimistic, for the prophets have been testifying that the wickedness in this age is rampant. As early as 1833, the Prophet Joseph Smith said:

> The nations of the Gentiles are like the waves of the sea, casting up mire and dirt, or all in commotion, and they are hastily preparing to act the part allotted them, when the Lord rebukes the nations, when He shall rule them with a rod of iron, and break

---

[2]Ether 2:8-10. (Italics added)
[3]*Doctrine and Covenants* 1:11-16.

them in pieces like a potter's vessel. The Lord declared to His servants, some eighteen months since, *that He was then withdrawing His Spirit from the earth;* and we can see that such is the fact, for not only the churches are dwindling away, but there are no conversions, or but a very few: and this is not all, the governments of the earth are thrown into confusion and division; and *Destruction,* to the eye of the spiritual beholder, seems to be written by the finger of an invisible hand, in large capitals, upon almost everything we behold.[4]

Then in a sermon preached to the saints in Nauvoo a few months before his death, the Prophet explicitly declared the state of this generation.

I prophesy, in the name of the Lord God of Israel, anguish and wrath and tribulation and the withdrawing of the Spirit of God from the earth await this generation, *until they are visited with utter desolation. This generation is as corrupt as the generation of the Jews that crucified Christ;* and if He were here today, and should preach the same doctrine He did then, they would put Him to death.[5]

Presidents John Taylor and Wilford Woodruff both testified that the wickedness that prevails in the earth is one of the factors leading to its destruction.

A terrible day of reckoning is approaching the nations of the earth; the Lord is coming out of his hiding place to vex the inhabitants thereof; and the destroyer of the gentiles, as prophesied of, is already on his way. . . . Already combinations are being entered into which are very ominous for the future prosperity, welfare, and happiness of this great republic. *The volcanic fires of disordered and anarchical elements are beginning to manifest themselves and exhibit the internal forces that are at work among the turbulent and unthinking masses of the people.*[6]

The angels of God are waiting to fulfill the great commandment given forty-five years ago, to go forth and reap down the earth because of the wickedness of men. How do you think eternity feels today? Why, *there is more wickedness, a thousand times over,*

[4]Joseph Smith, *DHC,* Vol. 1, p. 314, January 4, 1833. (Italics added)
[5]*Ibid.,* Vol. 6, p. 58, October 15, 1843. (Italics added)
[6]John Taylor, *Journal of Discourses,* Vol. 23, p. 62, April 9, 1882. (Italics added) In light of today's society, President Taylor's remarks seem especially prophetic.

in the United States now, than when that revelation was given. The whole earth is ripe in iniquity; and these inspired men, these Elders of Israel, have been commanded of the Almighty to go forth and warn the world, that their garments may be clean of the blood of all men.[7]

The wickedness committed today in the Christian world in twenty-four hours is greater than would have been committed in a hundred years at the ratio of fifty years ago. And the spirit of wickedness is increasing, so that I no longer wonder that God almighty will turn rivers into blood; I do not wonder that He will open the seals and pour out the plagues and sink great Babylon, as the angel saw, like a millstone cast into the sea, to rise no more forever. I can see that it requires just such plagues and judgments to cleanse the earth, that it may cease to groan under the wickedness and abomination in which the Christian world welters today.[8]

This state of wickedness among the children of men who live upon the promised land must of necessity bring God's judgments upon them, and they will be swept off unless they repent. This was borne out on another occasion, when President Woodruff was shown a vision of what would result from this nation's unwillingness to serve God. He had been visiting the Saints in Northern Utah and had camped in a tent some distance from Brigham City. His biographer, Matthias Cowley, quotes from his journal:

"I went to bed filled with prayer and meditation. I fell asleep and remained in slumber until about midnight, when I awoke. *The Lord then poured out His spirit upon me and opened the vision of my mind so that I could comprehend in a great measure the mind and will of God concerning the nation and concerning the inhabitants of Zion. I saw the wickedness of the nation, its abominations and corruptions and the judgments of God and the destruction that awaited it. . . ."* The revelation was submitted to the Quorum of the Twelve Apostles just prior to the April conference of that year. It was accepted by that body as the word of the Lord, according to Elder Woodruff's journal, under date of April 4th, 1880.[9]

[7]Wilford Woodruff, *Journal of Discourses,* Vol. 18, p. 128, October 8, 1875. (Italics added)

[8]*Ibid.,* Vol. 14, p. 3, January 1, 1871.

[9]Matthias F. Cowley, *Wilford Woodruff, History of His Life and Labors* (Bookcraft: Salt Lake City, 1964), pp. 530-531.

To Vex This Nation

This general state of wickedness violates the decree of God that all who would possess the land must do so in righteousness, and will bring upon all the nations of the promised land swift destruction if they do not repent. But the United States of America, as a government, added a specific crime to their general state of wickedness which will especially add to the fulfillment of the divine promise.

Early in the history of the Church, many of the members of the Church were eager to ascertain the location of the land of Zion. When Joseph Smith indicated through revelation that its center place was in Jackson County, Missouri, thousands of the saints moved there. But it soon became evident that to live in Zion was not to live without problems. The Missourians who lived around Independence were soon expressing open hostility toward the new settlers. Harassment and insults escalated into open mob violence until the saints were finally driven from their homes in the winter of 1833-34. Across the Missouri River and into the northern counties of Missouri, the exiled saints sought new homes where they could live in peace.

It is hard now to imagine the feelings of those saints thus driven from the land of Zion. It had been designated by the Lord as the site of the New Jerusalem, yet now they had been driven off. Many troubled prayers were sent heavenward asking for guidance in such dark hours. In addition to the comfort and explanations, coming in response to those prayers, the Lord gave the Church some instructions on their responsibilities in seeking redress from the United States government.

> Let them importune at the feet of the judge;
> And if he heed them not, let them importune at the feet of the governor;
> And if the governor heed them not, let them importune at the feet of the president;
> *And if the president heed them not, then will the Lord arise and come forth out of his hiding place, and in his fury vex the nation.*[10]

---

[10]*Doctrine and Covenants* 101:86-89. (Italics added)

In response to the commandment, the Prophet Joseph Smith had a list compiled of all the crimes committed against the saints, and petitions were drawn up and sent to Congress. However, before the lists were completed, new problems had arisen. The move to Northern Missouri seemed to solve the conflict between Mormon and non-Mormon for a time, but soon the old problems began to creep in again. After the great apostasy of the Church in Kirtland in 1837, the remaining faithful moved to Missouri. By the summer of 1838 there were nearly fifteen thousand Mormons living in Northern Missouri. To the Missourians it looked as though they would soon be inundated by the hated Mormons. Once again open warfare became the order of the day, and into Church history came such phrases as "The Haun's Mill Massacre," "The Battle of Crooked River," "Governor Lilburn W. Boggs and his Infamous Extermination Order," "The Betrayal at Far West," and "Liberty Jail." With the help of the government of the state of Missouri, the mob drove fifteen thousand saints from their homes in the winter of 1838-39, and Zion was left temporarily in the hands of the enemies of righteousness.

With these new crimes against the Church, the Prophet determined to carry his petitions to the government in person. It was in the lack of response to these petitions that the government of the United States sealed her destiny upon the land of promise.

Journeying to Washington, D.C., late in October, 1839, the Prophet presented the petition of the saints to both the Congress and the President of the United States. In his journal, he reports the disappointing results of his efforts.

> During my stay I had an interview with Martin Van Buren, the President, who treated me very insolently, and it was with great reluctance he listened to our message, which, when he had heard, he said: *"Gentlemen, your cause is just, but I can do nothing for you;"* and *"If I take up for you I shall lose the vote of Missouri."* His whole course went to show that he was an office-seeker, that self-aggrandizement was his ruling passion, and that justice and righteousness were no part of his composition. I also had an interview with Mr. John C. Calhoun, whose conduct towards me very

ill became his station. [Calhoun was a member of the Senate.]
I became satisfied there was little use for me to tarry, to press the
just claims of the Saints on the consideration of the President or
Congress, and stayed but a few days. . . .[11]

Although Elias Higbee was left to continue to plead the
cause of the saints, no action to redress the saints was ever
taken. The Senate Judiciary Committee stated in their final
report of the matter: ". . . the case presented for their investigation is not such a one as will justify or authorize any inter-
position by this government."[12] The Church had fulfilled the
command of the Lord, and the word of the Lord now stood:
"And if the president heed them not, then will the Lord
arise and come forth out of his hiding place, and in his fury,
vex the nation."[13]

Joseph Smith made it clear that this decision on the part
of the government would result in its eventual destruction.
When he arrived home in March of 1840, the Prophet wrote
in his journal:

I arrived safely at Nauvoo, after a wearisome journey, through
alternate snow and mud, having witnessed many vexatious movements in government officers, whose sole object should be the peace
and prosperity and happiness of the whole people; but instead of
this, I discovered that popular clamor and personal aggrandizement
were the ruling principles of those in authority; and *my heart faints
within me when I see, by the visions of the Almighty, the end of
this action, if she continues to disregard the cries and petitions of
her virtuous citizens,* as she has done, and is now doing.[14]

Two years later, in his now famous conversation with Judge
Stephen A. Douglas, the Prophet said:

*I prophesy in the name of the Lord God of Israel, unless the
United States redress the wrongs committed upon the Saints in the
state of Missouri and punish the crimes committed by her officers*

---

[11]Joseph Smith, *DHC*, Vol. 4, p. 80, February 6, 1840. (Italics in original)
[12]*Ibid.*, p. 91, March 4, 1840.
[13]*Doctrine and Covenants* 101:89.
[14]Joseph Smith, *DHC*, Vol. 4, p. 89, March 4, 1840. (Italics added)

> *that in a few years the government will be utterly overthrown and wasted, and there will not be so much as a potsherd left. . . .*[15]

Then once again, late in 1843, another petition was sent to Congress asking for redress. The Prophet commented on that petition.

> While discussing the petition to Congress, I prophesied by virtue of the holy Priesthood vested in me, and in the name of the Lord Jesus Christ, that if Congress will not hear our petition and grant us protection, *they shall be broken up as a government.*[16]

To this day no action has ever been taken by the government of the United States, and thus these clear and prophetic promises stand awaiting their fulfillment.

The Future Destiny of the United States

Joseph Smith was not the only one to testify of the coming destruction of this nation. Many of the apostles and prophets have also borne witness to this fulfillment of God's promises. Brigham Young told of hearing the Prophet speak of the coming destruction of the United States.

> The whole government is gone; it is as weak as water. I heard Joseph Smith say nearly thirty years ago, "They shall have mobbings to their hearts' content, if they do not redress the wrongs of the Latter-day Saints." Mobs will not decrease but will increase until the whole government becomes a mob, and eventually it will be State against State, city against city, neighborhood against neighborhood, Methodists against Methodists, and so on.[17]

In 1881, sixteen years after the close of the Civil War, President John Taylor said:

> Do I not know that a nation like that in which we live, a nation which is blessed with the freest, the most enlightened and magnificent government in the world today, with privileges which would exalt people to heaven if they lived up to them—do I not know that if they do not live up to them, but violate them and

[15]*Ibid.,* Vol. 5, p. 394, May 18, 1843. (Italics added)
[16]*Ibid.,* Vol. 6, p. 116, December 16, 1843. (Italics added)
[17]Brigham Young, *Deseret News,* Vol. 9, p. 2, May 1, 1861.

trample them under their feet, and discard the sacred principles of liberty by which we ought to be governed—do I not know that their punishment will be commensurate with the enlightenment which they possess? I do. And I know—I cannot help but know—that *there are a great many more afflictions yet awaiting this nation.*[18]

President Wilford Woodruff was another who often spoke of the destruction that is to come upon the United States. In his history of the Church he wrote:

> I warn future historians to give credence to my history; for my testimony is true, and the truth of its record will be manifest in the world to come. All the words of the Lord will be fulfilled upon the nations, which are written in this book. *The American nation will be broken in pieces like a potter's vessel, and will be cast down to hell if it does not repent—and this, because of murders, whoredoms, wickedness and all manner of abominations, for the Lord has spoken it.*[19]

In 1880, in an address to the saints, he said:

> *I ask myself the question, "Can the American nation escape?" The answer comes, "No." Its destruction, as well as the destruction of the world is sure; just as sure as the Lord cut off and destroyed the two great and prosperous nations that once ir' ↗bited this continent of North and South America, because of thei. wickedness, so will He them destroy, and sooner or later they will reap the fruits of their own wicked acts, and be numbered among the past. . . .*
>
> There are changes awaiting us, they are even nigh at our very doors, and *I know it by the visions of heaven; I know it by the administrations of angels, and I know it by the inspiration of heaven, that is given to all men who seek the Lord; and the hand of God will not stay these things. We have no time to lose.*[20]

Elder Orson Pratt foretold the destruction and chaos yet coming upon the United States.

---

[18]John Taylor, *Journal of Discourses,* Vol. 22, p. 141, July 3, 1881. (Italics added)

[19]Cowley, *op. cit.,* p. 500. (Italics added)

[20]Wilford Woodruff, *Journal of Discourses,* Vol. 21, p. 301, August 1, 1880. (Italics added)

If it be asked, why is America thus to suffer? The answer is, because they have rejected the kingdom of God, and one of the greatest divine messages ever sent to man; because they have sanctioned the killing of the Saints, and the martyrdom of the Lord's Prophets, and have suffered his people to be driven from their midst, and have robbed them of their houses, and homes, and land, and millions of property, and have refused to redress their wrongs. For these great evils, they must suffer; the decrees of Jehovah have gone forth against them; the sword of the Lord has been -un sheathed, and will fall with pain upon their devoted heads. Their great and magnificent cities are to be cut off. *New York, Boston, Albany, and numerous other cities will be left desolate. Party will be arrayed in deadly strife against party; State against State; and the whole nation will be broken up; the sanguinary weapons of the dreadful revolution will devour the land. Then shall there be a fleeing from one city to another, from one State to another, from one part of the continent to another, seeking refuge, from the devastations of bandits and armies;* then shall their dead be left unburied, and the fowls of heaven shall summer upon them, and the beasts of the earth shall winter upon them. Moreover, the Lord will visit them with the deadly pestilence which shall sweep away many millions by its ravages; for their eyes shall fall from their sockets, and their flesh from their bones, and their tongues shall be stayed in their mouths, that they shall not be able to blaspheme against their Maker. And it will come to pass, that the heavens will withhold their rains and their fruitful fields be turned into barrenness, and the waters of their rivers will be dried up, and left in standing pools, and the fish therein will die; and the Lord will send forth a grievous plague to destroy the horses and cattle from the land. Thus by the sword and by pestilence, and by famine, and by the strong arm of the Almighty, shall the inhabitants of that wicked nation be destroyed.[21]

The Constitution by a Thread

One of the things that has made the United States of America unique in the annals of government is its Constitution. The Church of Jesus Christ of Latter-day Saints teaches that such a document is too unique to have come solely from the minds of men. The Lord has stated clearly in his revelations that he established the Constitution by raising up wise men for that very purpose.[22] These principles of government

---

[21]Orson Pratt, *Millennial Star,* Vol. 28, pp. 633-634, October 6, 1866. (Italics added)

[22]*Doctrine and Covenants* 101:77, 80.

by the people for the preservation of freedom are divinely inspired, and the wars and destruction that are coming will not make them any less so. But the prophets have indicated that these principles established in the Constitution will be forsaken by the country in general and that this will be an important factor in bringing about the destruction of the United States.

Many of the prophets have referred to the time when the constitutional principles would be in danger, and it has been clearly prophesied that these principles would be saved or found only in the Church. Brigham Young reported that Joseph Smith was the first to teach this doctrine. In an Independence Day celebration speech Brigham Young said:

> Will the Constitution be destroyed? No: it will be held inviolate by this people; and, as Joseph Smith said, "The time will come when the destiny of the nation will hang upon a single thread. *At that critical juncture, this people will step forth and save it from the threatened destruction.*" It will be so.[23]

Early in the spring of the following year, Brigham Young intimated that the holders of the priesthood would be the ones to save the Constitution.

> When the Constitution of the United States hangs, as it were, upon a single thread, they will have to call for the "Mormon" elders to save it from utter destruction; and they will step forth and do it.[24]

Some people have argued that such a critical threat was posed to the Constitution during the Civil War and this is what the Prophet Joseph meant. However, this would not account for the "elders of the Church" saving it, for the Civil War passed over the Church with relatively minor effect. In addition, three years after the Civil War was over, Brigham Young again referred to this prophecy as yet being in the future.

---

[23]Brigham Young, *Journal of Discourses,* Vol. 7, p. 15, July 4, 1854. (Italics added)
[24]Brigham Young, *Ibid.,* Vol. 2, p. 182, February 18, 1855.

How long will it be before the words of the Prophet Joseph Smith will be fulfilled? He said if the Constitution of the United States were saved at all it must be done by this people. It will not be many years before these words come to pass."[25]

Elder Orson Hyde of the Council of the Twelve was also present when Joseph Smith made that prophecy, but he made a slight variation in his report.

It is said that brother Joseph in his lifetime declared that the Elders of this Church should step forth at a particular time when the Constitution would be in danger, and rescue it, and save it. This may be so; but I do not recollect that he said exactly so. I believe he said something like this—that the time would come when the Constitution and the country would be in danger of an overthrow; and said he, *"If the Constitution be saved at all, it will be by the elders of this Church."* I believe this is about the language, as nearly as I can recollect it.

The question is whether it will be saved at all, or not. I do not know that it matters to us whether it is or not; the Lord will provide for and take care of his people, if we do every duty, and fear and honour him, and keep his commandments; and he will not leave us without a Constitution.[26]

President John Taylor spoke of it as a saving of the constitutional principles rather than the actual government itself.

When the people have torn to shreds the Constitution of the United States the Elders of Israel will be found holding it up to the nations of the earth and proclaiming liberty and equal rights to all men, and extending the hand of fellowship to the oppressed of all nations. This is part of the program, and as long as we do what is right and fear God, he will help us and stand by us under all circumstances.[27]

Orson Pratt felt that although the United States would lose the power to govern in the chaos that will be present, the spirit of the Constitution would be preserved in the government set up by the members of the Church.

---

[25] *Ibid.,* Vol. 12, p. 204, April 8, 1868.
[26] Orson Hyde, *Journal of Discourses,* Vol. 6, p. 152, January 3, 1858. (Italics added)
[27] John Taylor, *Journal of Discourses,* Vol. 21, p. 8, August 31, 1879. (Italics added)

> . . . *He will speedily fulfill the prophecy in relation to the over-throw of this nation, and their destruction. We shall be obliged to have a government to preserve ourselves in unity and peace; for they, through being wasted away, will not have power to govern;* for state will be divided against state, city against city, town against town, and the whole country will be in terror and confusion; mob-ocracy will prevail and there will be no security, through this great Republic, for the lives or property of the people. When that time shall arrive, we shall necessarily want to carry out the principles of our great constitution and, as the people of God, we shall want to see those principles magnified, according to the order of union and oneness which prevails among the people of God.[28]

President J. Reuben Clark, Jr., issued a solemn warning about the costs of sacrificing the principles of the Constitution.

> Brethren, let us think about that, because I say unto you with all the soberness I can, that we stand in danger of losing our liberties, and that once lost, *only blood will bring them back; and once lost, we of this church will, in order to keep the church going forward, have more sacrifices to make and more persecutions to endure than we have yet known,* heavy as our sacrifices and grievous as our persecutions of the past have been.[29]

President David O. McKay said on more than one occasion that the maintenance of constitutional principles was one of the most important tasks that members of the Church had before them. In an editorial in *The Instructor* in 1956, he said: "Next to being one in worshipping God there is nothing in this world upon which this Church should be more united than in upholding and defending the Constitution of the United States."[30]

So it seems evident from what the prophets have said that the Constitution of the United States of America will be severely threatened in the crises that are to come, but its principles will be preserved by the members of the Church. In view of such developments as the flag burnings, "peace"

---

[28]Orson Pratt, *Deseret Evening News*, Vol. 8, no. 265, October 2, 1875. (Italics added)
[29]J. Reuben Clark, Jr., *The Improvement Era*, May, 1944, p. 337. (Italics added)
[30]David O. McKay, *The Instructor*, February, 1956, p. 34.

marches and slogan chanting of the seventies, President John Taylor's remarks of ninety years ago are particularly appropriate.

> It is our duty [to defend human rights] that our families demand of us; it is a duty that the honest in this nation demand of us, and that God demands of us; and we will try to carry it out, God being our helper. And if other people can afford to trample under foot the sacred institutions of this country, we cannot. And if other people trample upon the Constitution and pull it to pieces, we will gather together the pieces and rally around the old flag, or what is left of it, and proclaim liberty to the world, as Joseph Smith said we would.[31]

In this day of anarchy, bombings, violence and assassinations, it is not too difficult to see the conditions fermenting which could topple the stable government of this nation.

George Q. Cannon also spoke of the day when such factions would rend the government, and there would be no stability outside of the members of the Church.

> . . . The day will come—and this is another prediction of Joseph Smith's—I want to remind you of it, my brethren and sisters, *when good government, constitutional government—liberty—will be found among the Latter-day Saints, and it will be sought for in vain elsewhere;* when the Constitution of this land and republican government and institutions will be upheld by this people who are now so oppressed and whose destruction is now sought so diligently. The day will come when the Constitution, and free government under it, will be sustained and preserved by this people.[32]

The Seeds of Destruction

It is hard to believe that a nation as large and as prosperous and as powerful as the United States is today could lose the power to govern. Even though there are serious problems in this country today, it still has a great governing power and is a world leader in its influence. What conditions could bring such a nation to the brink of destruction? What kinds of

---

[31]John Taylor, *Journal of Discourses,* Vol. 23, p. 239, August 20, 1882.
[32]George Q. Cannon, *Journal of Discourses,* Vol. 23, p. 104, November 20, 1881. (Italics added)

crises could strike with such power as to destroy the United States? Although there is much that is not known concerning the specific events that will bring the Lord's prophecies to fulfillment, he has given several indications of what is to come.

In a scripture quoted in the previous chapter, the Lord said that when the times of the Gentiles were fulfilled, there would be men standing in that generation which would not pass away until they saw an "overflowing scourge cover the land."[33] The Lord often spoke of this scourge coming upon the people, and the devastating results of what would follow. In March of 1829, even before the Church was organized, he said:

> For a desolating scourge shall go forth among the inhabitants of the earth, and shall continue to be poured out from time to time, if they repent not, until the earth is empty, and the inhabitants thereof are consumed away and utterly destroyed by the brightness of my coming.[34]

Webster defines a scourge as "an instrument of punishment or criticism; a cause of widespread or great affliction."[35] This scourge seems to involve many forms of terrible calamities, including great hailstorms,[36] tempests,[37] plagues, pestilence, and war.[38] Such terrible disasters will be such that they will lay to waste those who fight against God and will actually leave mighty cities desolate of their populations. The Lord warned some specific cities, particularly Boston, New York and Albany, of the desolation awaiting them if they did not repent.[39]

Other Nations to Come Against Us

It is not clear from the scriptures whether these various calamities which all go to make up the desolating scourge

---

[33]*Doctrine and Covenants* 45:30-31.
[34]*Ibid.,* 5:19.
[35]*Webster's Seventh New Collegiate Dictionary,* (G.&C. Merriam Co., Springfield, Mass., 1965) p. 773.
[36]*Doctrine and Covenants* 29:16.
[37]*Ibid.,* 88:90.
[38]*Ibid.,* 97:26.
[39]*Ibid.,* 84:96-97.

will come together or at various times. Perhaps, as so often in the past, war will bring with it its attendant evils of disease, famine, starvation, pestilence and the like. This is a distinct possibility, for the Prophet Lehi told his son that if a nation upon the promised land did not serve the Lord, it would result in other nations coming against it.

> . . . If the day shall come that they will reject the Holy One of Israel, the true Messiah, their Redeemer and their God, behold, the judgments of him that is just shall rest upon them.
>
> *Yea, he will bring other nations unto them, and he will give unto them power,* and he will take away from them the lands of their possessions, and he will cause them to be scattered and smitten.
>
> Yea, as one generation passeth to another there shall be bloodsheds, and great visitations among them. . . .[40]

President John Taylor, on several different occasions stated very clearly that the United States would have other nations come against her in war, and that she would see warfare in her own land.

> Were we surprised when the last terrible war took place here in the United States? No. Good Latter-day Saints were not, for they had been told about it. Joseph Smith had told them where it would start in South Carolina. But I tell you today the end is not yet. *You will see worse things than that, for God will lay his hand upon this nation, and they will feel it more terribly than even they have done before. There will be more bloodshed, more ruin, more devastation than ever they have seen before. Write it down! You will see it come to pass; it is only just starting in.* And would you feel to rejoice? No; I would feel sorry. I knew very well myself when this last war was commencing and could have wept and did weep, over this nation; but there is yet to come a sound of war, trouble and distress, in which brother will be arrayed against brother, father against son, son against father, a scene of desolation and destruction that will permeate our land until it will be a vexation to hear the report thereof.[41]

In 1876, speaking of the nations that would come against Jerusalem and the tribulations the Jews would experience,

---

[40] 2 Nephi 1:10-12. (Italics added)
[41] John Taylor, *Journal of Discourses,* Vol. 20, p. 318, October 6, 1879. (Italics added)

President Taylor said: "They [the Jews] will in due time be gathered together to their own lands as we are gathered here; and nations will go up against them, *and then too will certain nations come against us.*"[42] Then in 1883 he stated:

> The world, as I have said, is full of confusion, and there will be worse confusion by and by. We had a great war upon this continent some years ago; *but there will yet be wars pass through these United States,* and through other nations, until it will be mournful to hear the report of the bloodshed, the sorrow and the trouble that will be caused thereby. . . .[43]

City Against City

Nor are these wars to involve simply our struggle against other nations. Many of the prophets have clearly predicted conditions of war that would finally bring the United States to destruction. The war, pestilence, famines, hailstorms, etc., etc., mentioned by so many of the prophets shall evidently cause such chaos in America that ordered government shall cease and the nation shall be wracked by mob violence more terrible than normal warfare. President Taylor, as just cited above, spoke of the time when family members would be fighting against each other and a scene of desolation would permeate the land.

The Prophet Joseph Smith was the first of the modern prophets to speak of this coming terror. In 1833 he said:

> And now I am prepared to say by the authority of Jesus Christ, that not many years shall pass away before the United States shall present such a scene of bloodshed as has not a parallel in the history of our nation; pestilence, hail, famine, and earthquake will sweep the wicked of this generation from off the face of the land, to open and prepare the way for the return of the lost tribes of Israel from the north country.[44]

Six years later, after the saints had been driven from the state of Missouri, the Prophet returned to the same theme in a discourse to the Twelve.

---

[42]*Ibid.,* Vol. 18, p. 281, November 5, 1876. (Italics added)
[43]*Ibid.,* Vol. 24, p. 200, June 18, 1883. (Italics added)
[44]Joseph Smith, *DHC,* Vol. 1, p. 315-316, January 4, 1833.

I saw men hunting the lives of their own sons, and brother murdering brother, women killing their own daughters, and daughters seeking the lives of their mothers. *I saw armies arrayed against armies. I saw blood, desolation, fires.* The Son of Man has said that the mother shall be against the daughter, and the daughter against the mother. *These things are at our doors. They will follow the Saints of God from city to city.* Satan will rage, and the spirit of the devil is now enraged. I know not how soon these things will take place; but with a view of them, shall I cry peace? No; I will lift up my voice and testify of them. How long you will have good crops, and the famine be kept off, I do not know; when the fig tree leaves, know then that summer is nigh at hand.[45]

Elder Jedediah M. Grant, who was very close to the Prophet Joseph during his lifetime, told of Joseph's vision of warfare that would come upon the United States.

The Prophet stood in his own house when he told several of us the night the *visions of Heaven were opened to him, in which he saw the American continent drenched in blood, and he saw nation rising up against nation. He also saw the father shed the blood of the son and the son the blood of the father; the mother put to the death the daughter, and the daughter the mother; and natural affection forsook the hearts of the wicked;* for he saw that the Spirit of God should be withdrawn from the inhabitants of the earth, in consequence of which there should be blood upon the face of the whole earth except among the people of the Most High. The prophet gazed upon the scene his vision presented, *until his heart sickened, and he besought the Lord to close it up again.*[46]

Unquestionably, that prophecy was partially fulfilled during the great and terrible Civil War, but others of the prophets have indicated that much of it is yet to be fulfilled.

Elder Orson Pratt very explicitly described the conditions of anarchy and mobocracy that would sweep the nation to its destruction.

What then will be the condition of that people, when this great and terrible war shall come? It will be very different from the war between the North and the South. Do you wish me to

---

[45]*Ibid.*, Vol. 3, p. 391, July 2, 1839. (Italics added)
[46]Jedediah M. Grant, *The Improvement Era*, February, 1915, pp. 286-287. (Italics added)

describe it? I will do so. *It will be a war of neighborhood against neighborhood, city against city, county against county, state against state, and they will go forth destroying and being destroyed, and manufacturing will, in a great measure, cease, for a time, among the American nation. Why? Because in these terrible wars, they will not be privileged to manufacture; there will be too much bloodshed—too much mobocracy—too much going forth in bands and destroying and pillaging the land to suffer people to pursue any local vocation with any degree of safety.* What will become of millions of the farmers upon that land? They will leave their farms and they will flee before the ravaging armies from place to place; and thus will they go forth burning and pillaging the whole country; and that great and powerful nation, now consisting of some forty millions of people, will be wasted away, unless they repent.[47]

Elder Pratt also spoke of the city of New York and its future in such chaos.

> For instance the great and populous city of New York, that may be considered one of the greatest cities of the world, will in a few years become a mass of ruins. The people will wonder while gazing on the ruins that cost hundreds of millions to build, what has become of its inhabitants. Their houses will be there, but they will be left desolate. So saith the Lord God. That will be only a sample of numerous other towns and cities on the face of this continent.[48]

So terrible will such conditions be that he speaks of people being grateful simply for the privilege of fleeing from city to city.

> . . . The time will come when there will be no safety in carrying on the peaceable pursuits of farming or agriculture. But these will be neglected, and *the people will think themselves well off if they can flee from city to city, from town to town and escape with their lives.* Thus will the Lord visit the people, if they will not repent. Thus will He pour out His wrath and indignation upon them. . . .[49]

As already noted, Brigham Young also spoke of the time when the United States would have mobbings to their hearts' content. He said:

---

[47]Orson Pratt, *Journal of Discourses,* Vol. 20, p. 151, March 9, 1879. (Italics added)
[48]*Ibid.,* Vol. 12, p. 344, December 27, 1868.
[49]*Ibid.* (Italics added)

> *Mobs will not decrease but will increase until the whole gov-*
> *ernment becomes a mob,* and eventually it will be State against
> State, city against city, neighborhood against neighborhood, Meth-
> odists against Methodists, and so on. . . . It will be the same with
> other denominations of professing Christians, and it will be Christ-
> ian against Christian, and man against man, and those who will not
> take up the sword against their neighbors, must flee to Zion.[50]

On another occasion, President Young compared the future
of the United States to the collapse and destruction of the
Jaredite nation.

> Famine will spread over the nations, and nation will rise up
> against nations, kingdom against kingdom, and state against states,
> *in our own country* and in foreign lands; and *they will destroy each*
> *other, caring not for the blood and lives of their neighbors, or their*
> *families, or for their own lives. They will be like the Jaredites who*
> *preceded the Nephites upon this continent, and will destroy each*
> *other to the last man, through the anger that the devil will place*
> *in their hearts,* because they rejected the words of life and are given
> over to Satan to do whatever he listeth to do with them. You may
> think that the little you hear of now is grievous; yet the faithful
> of God's people will see days that will cause them to close their
> eyes because of the sorrow that will come upon the wicked nations.
> The hearts of the faithful will be filled with pain and anguish for
> them.[51]

That is a particularly foreboding prediction, for it will
be remembered that the final destruction of the Jaredites is a
most vivid description of what happens to a people when the
Spirit of the Lord ceases to strive with them.

The Prophet Ether records that the struggle of his people
had been so great and devastating that the whole face of the
land was covered with the bodies of the dead and the "scent
thereof went forth upon the face of the land."[52] With the
smell of death strong in their nostrils one would expect that
people would then turn from the evil ways that were destroying them, but such was not the case with the Jaredites. In-

---

[50]Brigham Young, *Deseret News,* Vol. 9, p. 2, May 1, 1861. (Italics added)
[51]Brigham Young, *Journal of Discourses,* Vol. 8, p. 123, July 15, 1860. (Italics added)
[52]Ether 14:21-23.

stead, the people spent some four years gathering their armies together for a last great struggle. So filled were their hearts with hatred and the desire for revenge, that even women and children were armed and prepared for the battle.[53]

Thus it was that millions of men, women, and children gathered at the Hill Ramah, later called by the Nephites, Cumorah, to begin the final act of destruction. It is hard for the mind to comprehend the awfulness of that final scene; great armies struggling bitterly all day and retiring to their tents at night to rend the air with wailing cries for their dead. But as the Prophet records, even such scenes were not enough to bring them to repentance, for says he: ". . . The Spirit of the Lord had ceased striving with them, and Satan had full power over the hearts of the people . . .wherefore they went again to battle." They were so drunken with anger they would exhaust themselves by day but sleep on their swords by night so that they could continue the battle the next day.[54] The battle continued until only the two commanders remained alive—both wounded and faint from loss of blood—and finally the one gained enough strength to decapitate the other, and then he, too, fainted.[55]

A civilization of millions fighting down to the last man is more than today's world can comprehend, and yet Brigham Young said that such scenes would be repeated in our own age. It is a chilling possibility and sobering to the mind.

To Repent or to Be Swept Off

War, calamities, pestilence, famine, destruction of our own and other nations—all of these things are startling and stagger the mind. It is little wonder that the coming days strike fear and anxiety into the hearts of men. These times predicted so often by the prophets of the Lord will be grim ones indeed. But it is precisely for this reason that the Lord has given us warning of their coming. When they come upon the world, those saints who have been looking forth to the

---

[53]*Ibid.,* 15:15.
[54]*Ibid.,* 15:19-22.
[55]*Ibid.,* 15:23-32.

signs of the times and making preparations, in terms of their own personal righteousness, will then have strength to endure.

In our own day, the fulfillment of these predictions can be seen coming to pass. War is a common world-wide occurrence; violence, anarchy, and crime abound. Joseph Smith, for example, predicted that the time was coming when "natural affection" would forsake the hearts of the wicked.[56] And today one reads in the paper such items as:

> More children under 5 years old are killed by their own parents each year than die of disease, a University of California medical educator reported today. Severe beatings and tortures account for several hundred deaths and thousands of serious injuries to youngsters and the national toll of child abuse is conservatively estimated at 60,000 annually, Dr. James S. Apthorp told in an address to faculty and students of USC's Delinquency Control Institute.[57]

These signs and the other signs of wickedness that are so prevalent in today's world are indications that mankind is losing the guidance of the Spirit of the Lord. In fact, a little over a year after the Church was organized, the Lord said that he was holding back his Spirit from the world because of the wickedness of its inhabitants.[58] This is so not because the Lord wishes to leave his children without light and guidance, but rather because they will not have his Spirit in their lives. Christ does not withdraw from men; men withdraw from him, and it is in consequence of this that the inhabitants of this country and the other nations of the world are racing into the maelstrom of destruction.

This land is still a land choice above all others, and it will be a land of liberty and peace for as long as its peoples serve the God of the land, Jesus Christ. However, as they forsake him and turn to their own gods of material wealth and human learning, the divine decree will once again be invoked, and they, too, "shall be swept off."

---

[56]Joseph Smith, as quoted by Jedediah M. Grant, see footnote 46 in this chapter.

[57]*San Gabriel Valley* [California] *Tribune,* March 12, 1970, p. C8.

[58]*Doctrine and Covenants* 63:32.

Upon My House Shall It Begin

Upon the Wicked

Over and over in the discussion thus far, the phrase "upon the wicked" has been used. The plagues and pestilences shall come "upon the wicked"; wars will sweep "the wicked" off the land; destruction shall come "upon the wicked" if they do not repent; and so on. It is such a common part of any treatment of prophecy that it becomes natural to use it without thinking. However, one must stop and examine that phrase to determine if it is valid to use it so freely, and if so, what implications it has.

Just what is meant by those designated as "the wicked"? How evil must a person be to fall into this "doomed class"? What correlation is there between members of the Church and those who are "righteous"? If one is a member of the Church, or at least an "active" member, will he avoid the great calamities which are to befall "the wicked"? If this is so, just what, or more specifically, *who* is meant by "the Church"? These and many other questions come to mind in any serious study of prophecies concerning the last days. And they are pertinent questions, for the very nature of the terrible judgments discussed in the previous two chapters are such as to motivate a person to do all that he can to avoid their consequences. It is only natural that one becomes concerned about his personal rating on the scale of righteous and evil behavior, if that behavior is to become the criteria for determining who shall escape these judgments.

Judgments on the House of God

To a member of the Church who is anxiously seeking to prepare himself for the coming of the Lord, one of the most disturbing of all revelations is one given to Thomas B. Marsh in 1837, at the time when he was president of the Quorum of the Twelve. The Lord spoke of the condition of darkness which was covering the earth and the resulting day of vengeance which it would bring upon the world.

Then comes the prophetic promise which is so disturbing to members of the Church.

> *And upon my house shall it begin, and from my house shall it go forth, saith the Lord;*
>
> First among you, saith the Lord, who have professed to know my name and have not known me, and have blasphemed against me in the midst of my house, saith the Lord.[1]

It seems to be a natural human tendency to avoid painful and unpleasant images about one's own self. No one likes to think that they are actually part of that group defined by the Lord as "the wicked." But the Lord makes it clear that some of those so defined are found in The Church of Jesus Christ of Latter-day Saints.

When the saints first moved into Jackson County, Missouri, and the other lands of the area, they were warned that they must live up to their covenants if they were to possess the land of Zion.

It was less than a year later that the mob spirit in Missouri boiled over and the saints were driven from Jackson County. Shortly thereafter, the Lord revealed that this suffering had come upon them because of their transgression.

> Behold, I say unto you there were jarrings, and contentions, and envyings, and strifes, and lustful and covetous desires among them; *therefore, by these things they polluted their inheritances.*
>
> *They were slow to hearken unto the voice of the Lord their God; therefore, the Lord their God is slow to hearken unto their prayers, to answer them in the day of their trouble.*[2]

---

[1]*Doctrine and Covenants* 112:25-26. (Italics added)
[2]*Ibid.*, 101:6-7. (Italics added)

A few months before that revelation was given, the Lord had defined Zion as the pure in heart[3] and then he went on to explain what Zion (or the pure in heart) must do if they are to escape the wrath and vengeance of God that is coming upon the wicked.

> Nevertheless, Zion shall escape if she observe to do all things whatsoever I have commanded her.
>
> *But if she observe not to do whatsoever I have commanded her, I will visit her according to all her works, with sore affliction, with pestilence, with plague, with sword, with vengeance, with devouring fire.*[4]

So it is evident that the members of the Church who are not observing the commandments of the Lord in this day will likewise experience the wrath of God. This chastening will serve a valuable purpose in helping the Church prepare the world for the coming of the Lord. Many great tasks await the Lord's people if the world is to be ready for the return of the Savior. These chastening judgments will tend to weed out the wicked and unfaithful membership of the Church so that the Lord will have a people who will carry out his will in all things.

Many of the prophets have testified that the judgments of God would come upon the Church because some of its members do not keep their covenants. Joseph F. Smith, who later became sixth president of The Church of Jesus Christ of Latter-day Saints, bore witness to this fact in a general conference address in 1880.

> . . . I further testify, that *unless the Latter-day Saints will live their religion, keep their covenants with God and their brethren, honor the Priesthood which they bear, and try faithfully to bring themselves into subjection to the laws of God, they will be the first to fall beneath the judgments of the Almighty, for his judgment will begin at his own house.*[5]

In an editorial in *The Improvement Era,* after becoming the prophet of the Church, President Smith discussed the great

[3]*Ibid.,* 97:21.
[4]*Ibid.,* 97:25-26. (Italics added)
[5]Joseph F. Smith, *Conference Report,* April, 1880, p. 6. (Italics added)

earthquake which had recently struck in San Francisco. He explained the Latter-day Saint view of the judgments, both for themselves and for the world.

> We believe that his judgments are poured out to bring mankind to a sense of his power and his purposes, that they may repent of their sins, and prepare themselves for the second coming of Christ to reign in righteousness upon the earth. . . .
>
> We firmly believe that Zion—which is the pure in heart—shall escape, if she observes to do all things whatsoever God has commanded; but in the opposite event, *even Zion shall be visited "with sore affliction, with pestilence, with plague, with sword, with vengeance, and with devastating fire."* (D&C 97:26) *All this that her people may be taught to walk in the light of truth,* and in the way of the God of their salvation.[6]

In 1879 President John Taylor spoke of the judgments coming upon the house of God.

> *But the judgments will begin at the house of God. We have to pass through some of these things, but it will only be a very little compared with the terrible destruction, the misery, and suffering that will overtake the world who are doomed to suffer the wrath of God.* It behooves us, as the saints of God, to stand firm and faithful in the observance of his laws, that we may be worthy of his preserving care and blessing.[7]

President Daniel H. Wells, second counselor to Brigham Young, explained that the saints had been gathered out from the midst of the wicked so they could better keep the commandments of God.

> Now, we are here in obedience to a great command, a command given by the Almighty to his Saints to gather out from Babylon, lest they be partakers of her sins and receive of her plagues. *But if we are going to partake of her sins in Zion, and to nourish and cherish the wicked and ungodly, what better shall we be for gathering? Shall we escape her plagues by so doing? No, there is no promise to that effect,* but if we practice the sins and

---

[6]Joseph F. Smith, *The Improvement Era,* Vol. 9, p. 653, June, 1906. (Italics added)

[7]John Taylor, *Journal of Discourses,* Vol. 21, p. 100, April 13, 1879. (Italics added)

iniquities of Babylon here in Zion, we may expect to receive of her plagues and to be destroyed.[8]

Elder Orson Pratt, of the Quorum of the Twelve, often spoke of the judgments upon the house of God and explained that the Latter-day Saints will escape them only if they keep the commandments.

> If we will not keep the commandments of God, and if our rising generations will not give heed to the law of God and to the great light which has shone from Heaven in these latter days, but turn their hearts from the Lord their God and from the counsels of His priesthood, *then we shall be visited like the wicked, then we shall have the hand of the Lord upon us in judgment;* then that saying that the Lord has delivered in the Book of Doctrines and Covenants will be fulfilled upon us, "that I will visit Zion, if she does not do right, with sore afflictions, with pestilence, with sword, with famine and with the flame of devouring fire."[9]

The Saints to Be Tried

President Joseph Fielding Smith wrote in one of his works of how these judgments will be withheld from the Church if its members would faithfully keep their commandments.

> *All of these things will be withheld while the nations are being punished, if the members of the Church will keep faithfully their commandments. If they will not, then we have received the warning that we, like the rest of the world, shall suffer His wrath in justice.*[10]

President Heber C. Kimball, who knew the Prophet Joseph Smith well, and who was first counselor to President Brigham Young for many years, spoke of when Salt Lake City would become one of the wicked cities of the world as the saints turned their hearts to worldly wealth. He prophesied of the trials that would come upon them.

---

[8]Daniel H. Wells, *Journal of Discourses,* Vol. 18, p. 98, October 7, 1875. (Italics added)

[9]Orson Pratt, *Journal of Discourses,* Vol. 12, p. 345, December 27, 1868. (Italics added)

[10]Joseph Fielding Smith, *The Progress of Man,* (Genealogical Society of Utah: Salt Lake City, 1936), p. 467. (Italics added)

Our sons and daughters must live pure lives so as to be prepared for what is coming.

After a while the gentiles will gather by the thousands to this place, and *Salt Lake City will be classed among the wicked cities of the world. A spirit of speculation and extravagance will take possession of the Saints, and the results will be financial bondage.*

Persecution comes next and all true Latter-day Saints will be tested to the limit. Many will apostatize and others will be still not knowing what to do. . . .

Before that day comes, however, the Saints will be put to tests *that will try the integrity of the best of them. The pressure will become so great that the more righteous among them will cry unto the Lord day and night until deliverance comes.*[11]

Brigham Young spoke of the problems that would come upon the saints if they did not remain faithful.

If the Latter-day Saints do not desist from running after the things of this world, and begin to reform and do the work the Father has given them to do, they will be found wanting, and they, too, will be swept away and counted as unprofitable servants.[12]

Some years earlier, while touring Davis, Weber, Box Elder and Cache Counties in Utah, President Young had spoken of the majority of people being righteous in the Church and the effect it would have.

There is one principle I would like to have the Latter-day Saints perfectly understand—that is, of blessings and cursings. *For instance, we read that war, pestilence, plagues, famine, etc., will be visited upon the inhabitants of the earth; but if distress through the judgments of God comes upon this people, it will be because the majority have turned away from the Lord. Let the majority of the people turn away from the Holy Commandments which the Lord has delivered to us, and cease to hold the balance of power in the Church, and we may expect the judgments of God to come upon us;* but while six-tenths or three-fourths of this people will keep the commandments of God, the curse and judgments of the Almighty will never come upon them, though we will have trials

---

[11]Heber C. Kimball, *Deseret News, Church Department,* p. 3, May 23, 1931. (Italics added)

[12]Brigham Young, *Journal of Discourses,* Vol. 18, p. 262, October 8, 1876. (Italics added)

of various kinds, and the elements to contend with—natural and spiritual elements. . . .[13]

Perhaps one last citation from another president will serve to conclude the array of evidence about the judgments of God coming upon his own house. President Wilford Woodruff summed it up very briefly and yet very succinctly, when he said:

> Zion is not going to be moved out of her place. The Lord will plead with her strong ones, and *if she sins he will chastise her until she is purified before the Lord.* I do not pretend to tell how much sorrow you or I are going to meet with before the coming of the Son of Man. *That will depend upon our conduct.*[14]

Power and Protection to the Righteous

There seems to be little doubt that the judgments of God shall fall upon those defined as "the wicked" as the world is prepared for the second coming of the Lord. It is likewise clear that if the members of the Church do not walk in obedience to the commandments, they, too, shall feel the chastening hand of God. Therefore, it is important that a determination be made of what is necessary to escape these judgments. What is it that makes either the Church or an individual worthy enough so that these terribly destructive calamities will pass over them?

Here, too, the prophets of the Lord have spoken clearly and abundantly to indicate the way of escape. In a most straightforward manner, Joseph Smith outlined the steps necessary to avoid the judgments of God in a letter written to a newspaper editor dated January 4, 1833.

> I will proceed to tell you what the Lord requires of all people, high and low, rich and poor, male and female, ministers and people, professors of religion and non-professors, in order that they may enjoy the Holy Spirit of God to a fulness *and escape the judgments of God, which are almost ready to burst upon the nations of the earth.* Repent of all your sins, and be baptized in water for the remission of them, in the name of the Father, and of the Son,

---

[13]*Ibid.,* Vol. 10, p. 335, June 22 to 29, 1864. (Italics added)
[14]Wilford Woodruff, *Millennial Star,* Vol. 51, p. 547, 1889. (Italics added)

and of the Holy Ghost, and receive the ordinance of the laying on of the hands of him who is ordained and sealed unto this power, that ye may receive the Holy Spirit of God. . . .[15]

Nearly ten years later, writing in his journal, Joseph referred to an editorial in the *Times and Seasons,* the Church newspaper published in Nauvoo. He does not say who wrote it, but it was evidently important enough that he included it in his journal. Part of that editorial reads:

> We have been chastened by the hand of God heretofore for not obeying His commands, although we never violated any human law, or transgressed any human precept; yet we have treated lightly His commandments, and departed from His ordinances, and the Lord has chastened us sore, and we have felt His arm and kissed the rod; let us be wise in time to come and ever remember that "to obey is better than sacrifice, and to hearken than the fat of rams."[16]

After the expulsion of the saints from Jackson County, Missouri, the Lord himself gave the key as to how the saints could triumph over their enemies from that very hour.[17] Evidently that key was not heeded, for a few years later they were once again driven from their homes.

Both Brigham Young and Wilford Woodruff spoke of learning to yield to the direction of the Holy Spirit and the counsel of the servants of God.

> There is not another people on the earth whose faith and works are directed for the accomplishment of good like the Latter-day Saints. But we do not obey counsel as we should. Yet when we look at them and at others on the face of the earth, we have reason to say we are proud of the Latter-day Saints. *But are we all we should be? No. We must learn to listen to the whispering of the Holy Spirit, and the counsels of the servants of God, until we come to the unity of the faith.*[18]

> There are certain events awaiting the nations of the earth as well as Zion; and when these events overtake us *we will be pre-*

---

[15]Joseph Smith, *DHC,* Vol. 1, p. 314, January 4, 1833. (Italics added)
[16]*Ibid.,* Vol. 5, p. 65, July 15, 1842.
[17]*Doctrine and Covenants* 103:1-10.
[18]Brigham Young, *Journal of Discourses,* Vol. 12, p. 241, July 25, 1868. (Italics added)

served if we take the counsel that is given us and unite our time, labor and means, and produce what we need for our own use; but without this we shall not be prepared to sustain ourselves and we shall suffer loss and inconvenience thereby.[19]

Not All Suffering Comes from Wickedness

Thus far in this discussion, the prophets have testified in many different ways that the people who do not keep the commandments of God, whether in or out of the Church, shall be made to suffer the wrath of the Almighty God. And an important point it is. But one must be cautious lest he think that *all* suffering is reserved for the individual who violates the commandments. Joseph Smith made it very clear that this is not so.

> I explained concerning the coming of the Son of Man; also that *it is a false idea that the Saints will escape all the judgments, whilst the wicked suffer;* for all flesh is subject to suffer, and "the righteous shall hardly escape;" still many of the Saints will escape, for the just shall live by faith; *yet many of the righteous shall fall a prey to disease, to pestilence, etc., by reason of the weakness of the flesh, and yet be saved in the kingdom of God.* So that it is an unhallowed principle to say that such and such have transgressed because they have been preyed upon by disease or death, for all flesh is subject to death; and the Savior has said, "Judge not, lest ye be judged."[20]

Obviously, man is subject to natural law. If a man steps off a cliff, he will fall to his death, whether he is righteous or not, whether he did it deliberately or unknowingly. If an innocent child drinks insecticide, it will kill him, even though he thought it was something harmless. When war sweeps a nation, some righteous will be caught up in that phenomenon and suffer because of it. (This does not imply that divine intervention cannot be made in each of these cases through the power of faith and priesthood. At such times, higher laws that we do not understand are brought into play and "miracles" are wrought.) God does not shield the righteous from

---

[19]Wilford Woodruff, *Journal of Discourses,* Vol. 17, p. 70, May 8, 1874. (Italics added)
[20]Joseph Smith, *DHC,* Vol. 4, p. 11, September 29, 1839. (Italics added)

all pain and sorrow, for this is the very purpose of our exist-ence.[21] Hothouse plants are beautiful to behold but they have no durability to weather the heat and cold of everyday life.

In addition to natural law, the Savior taught that the very fact that one makes a commitment to the gospel may bring suffering and persecution upon him.

> Remember the word that I said unto you, The servant is not greater than his lord. If they have persecuted me, they will also persecute you. . . .[22]

He then went on to warn his disciples that the time would come when men would kill them and think they were doing God a service.[23] Down through history, the true follower of Christ has often brought suffering upon himself.

President Joseph Fielding Smith suggested another factor that may bring suffering upon the righteous, namely, the wick-edness of those mingled with the righteous.

> Because of our disobedience and our failure to keep the com-mandments of the Lord, *the righteous, as in times past, may be called upon to suffer with the unrighteous among them.*[24]

President Smith's father, Joseph F. Smith, in the editorial previously mentioned dealing with the San Francisco earth-quake, explained that the judgments sometime fall upon both the righteous and the wicked but both may be benefited there-from.

> . . . Judgment is not an end in itself. Calamities are only permitted by a merciful Father, in order to bring about redemp-tion. Behind the fearful storms of judgment, which often strike the just and the unjust alike, overwhelming the wicked and the righteous, there arises bright and clear the dawn of the day of sal-vation. . . . What he permitted to occur seems clearly to have been for the purpose of calling attention, by the finger of his power, to the wickedness and sins of men—not alone to the sins of the people

---

[21] 2 Nephi 2:11.
[22] John 15:20.
[23] *Ibid.,* 16:2.
[24] Joseph Fielding Smith, *Conference Report,* April, 1937, p. 60. (Italics added)

of the stricken city, for there are many elsewhere who are just as evil minded, but to the transgressions of all mankind, that all may take warning and repent. *Men who stand in the way of God's wise purposes, whether they be good or evil, must suffer in the turmoil. Thus it is that often the righteous suffer for the unrighteous; and it is not satisfactory to the thinking mind to say that therefore God is unjust. The perfect Christ suffered, the just for the unjust. . . .*[25]

Even though the suffering may come upon a person as a result of someone else's wickedness, it still serves to bring him to greater depths of faith and humility. As the Lord suggested to the Missouri saints: ". . . and all things wherewith you have been afflicted shall work together for your good, and to my name's glory, saith the Lord."[26]

Brigham Young prophesied that the very kingdom of God would continue to come under attack from the world as it has so often in the past.

If we live, *we shall see the nations of the earth arrayed against this people; for that time must come in fulfillment of prophecy.* Tell about war commencing! Bitter and relentless war was waged against Joseph Smith before he had received the plates of the Book of Mormon; and from that time till now the wicked have only fallen back at times to gain strength and learn how to attack the Kingdom of God.[27]

In conclusion, then, one must not assume that suffering is necessarily a mark of wickedness, although there seems little question that often it is a result of unrighteous living.

"But," says one, "what good then is the righteous life if it is not guarantee of protection in the dark days ahead?" The first obvious answer to such a question is that there is a joy and satisfaction in obedience to gospel principles which would, in and of itself, justify the Christ-like life. Second, as Joseph Smith suggested, even if the righteous should fall prey to the weaknesses of the flesh, they will be saved in the kingdom of God. In the span of eternity, this life is but for a moment and the eternal reward is of much deeper significance than a brief flash of comfort and painlessness in mortality.

---

[25]Joseph F. Smith, *The Improvement Era,* June, 1906, p. 650. (Italics added)
[26]*Doctrine and Covenants* 98:3.
[27]Brigham Young, *Journal of Discourses,* Vol. 5, p. 339, October 18, 1857. (Italics added)

The third answer to such a question is simply this: Although the righteous have no *guarantee* of escape, the wicked have *no hope*. It is true that *some* of the righteous will suffer, but *all* of the wicked will, and without the assurance of an eternal reward which the righteous have.

Elder Orson Pratt spoke of the promise of the Lord that the judgments of God would come upon the wicked and then said:

> Let the righteous among this people abide in their righteousness, and let them cleave unto the Lord their God; and if there are those among them who will not keep his commandments, they will be cleansed out by the judgments of which I have spoken. *But if the majority of this people will be faithful, the Lord will preserve them from their enemies, from sword, pestilence and plague, and from every weapon that is lifted against them.*[28]

Brigham Young expressed his belief that the righteous never suffer as much as the wicked, even though they sometimes bring suffering upon themselves.

> "But," says one, "I thought that we were to suffer persecution for righteousness' sake." *I would to God that all our persecutions were for righteousness' sake,* instead of for our evil doings. Still, as I have often remarked, *I never believed that the righteous have ever suffered as much as the wicked.* Jesus Christ said to his disciples, "These things I have spoken unto you, that in me ye might have peace. In the world ye shall have tribulation, but be of good cheer: I have overcome the world." I admit that the Saints anciently "were stoned, they were sawn asunder, were tempted, were slain with the sword; they wandered about in sheep skins, and goat skins; being destitute, afflicted, tormented; they wandered in deserts, and in the mountains, and in dens, and caves of the earth. . . ." Yet in all this suffering and persecution, they were blessed and comforted and rejoiced though in tribulation.[29]

To sum it up in terms of the coming judgments of God, the person who seeks diligently to live the obedient life *has nothing to lose, and everything to gain.* And this is how it

---

[28]Orson Pratt, *Journal of Discourses,* Vol. 15, p. 362, March 9, 1873. (Italics added)

[29]Brigham Young, *Journal of Discourses,* Vol. 11, p. 274, December 23, 1866. (Italics added)

always will be in our relationship with the Lord. The Christ-like life is not a burden but a blessing.

The Chastening Hand of God

One other important point needs to be made to complete a discussion of the great judgments which are coming upon the world and the Church. It is very hard for some people to overcome the idea that God's judgments are the expressions of an angry, revengeful deity. They still cannot grasp the principle discussed above by President Joseph F. Smith that behind God's judgment lies his deep desire to bring about the redemption of man. In that same editorial, President Smith concluded:

> But we believe that these severe, natural calamities are visited upon men by the Lord *for the good of His children,* to quicken their devotion to others, and to bring out their better natures, that they may love and serve him. *We believe, further, that they are the heralds and tokens of his final judgment, and the schoolmasters to teach the people to prepare themselves, by righteous living, for the coming of the Savior* to reign upon the earth, when every knee shall bow and every tongue confess that Jesus is the Christ.[30]

On several occasions, the Lord, himself, explained the purpose for the chastening of his people, pointing out that it is part of the preparation for those who wish to be sanctified.[31]

Wilford Woodruff had caught the fuller vision of the positive benefits of the Lord's chastisement when he said:

> *It matters not what the minds and feelings of men are, the Lord is determined to raise up a people that will worship Him; and if He has to whip, and scourge, and drive us through a whole generation, He will chastise us until we are willing to submit to righteousness and truth, or until we are like clay in the hands of the potter. The chastisements we have had from time to time have been for our good, and are essential to learn wisdom, and carry us through a school of experience we never could have passed through without. I hope, then, that we may learn from the experience we*

---

[30]Joseph F. Smith, *op. cit.,* p. 654. (Italics added)
[31]*Doctrine and Covenants* 95:1; 101:4-5; 105:6.

have had to be faithful, and humble, and be passive in the hands of God, and do His commandments. . . .[32]

Strange as it may seem at first glance, these judgments are the work of a *loving* Father, deeply concerned about the eternal and temporal welfare of his children. If the children are wise, they shall heed the warning signs and diligently apply themselves to the task of ordering their lives in accordance with the plan laid down by the Father and his Divine Son. Only in this way will any person be sure that when the judgments start upon the house of God, he will not be in that part of the house that needs to be swept clean.

---

[32]Wilford Woodruff, *Journal of Discourses,* Vol. 2, p. 198, February 25, 1855. (Italics added)

Refuge in the Midst of Terror

A Saturday Night Bath

From the discussion of the last several chapters, it should be quite evident that the United States and the rest of the world will see great disasters and severe chaos before the millennial reign of the Savior begins. War, pestilence, mobocracy, famine, storms, earthquakes and other judgments of the Lord will sweep the wicked of this generation from the face of the earth. These judgments of the Almighty are necessary to cleanse the earth in preparation for the coming of the Lord. Elder Sterling W. Sill, an Assistant to the Quorum of the Twelve, compared the coming judgments to a ritual common in the earlier history of the United States, viz., "the Saturday night bath."

> But the next one-thousand year period will be *the earth's sabbath.* This will be the period when the earth will rest and enjoy its sanctified state. For this period the earth will be renewed and regain its former status as a terrestrial sphere, with all of its paradisiacal beauty, glory, and righteousness fully restored. *But first the earth must be cleansed. During its long history of sin and trouble our earth has become soiled and dirty. And it must have its "Saturday night bath," and be dressed in fresh clean clothing in which it can appropriately live its best 1,000 years.*[1]

It should also be apparent that the righteous will generally be preserved and protected from these judgments, even though some suffering will naturally come upon them. But

---

[1]Sterling W. Sill, "The Earth's Sabbath," *The Improvement Era,* June, 1967, p. 35. (Italics added)

how is this to be done when chaos and mobocracy become so rampant that the United States government will be brought to collapse? How will the Lord preserve his people in such widespread disorder? The Lord has told us that conditions will be so terrible that "fear shall come upon every man."[2] What means will be provided for the escape of the Saints? It is to these questions that we shall now turn our attention.

Gathering for Deliverance

In the scripture just cited, the Lord went on to indicate the key by which he would deliver his saints from the wrath which is to come. That key was the gathering to Zion before the judgments were poured out in full measure.[3]

The Lord clearly testified that he will protect and watch over his people in these coming calamitous times, and they will prevail. Wilford Woodruff, who was at that time president of the Quorum of the Twelve, also bore witness to this fact. Said he: "The Lord is going to make a short work in the earth, and he will defend his anointed, his prophets, his Zion and his people. This is the decree of Almighty God."[4] And the means by which he will do it seems to be the gathering of his people. In April, 1838, the Lord spoke through the Prophet Joseph and said:

> Verily I say unto you all: Arise and shine forth, that thy light may be a standard for the nations:
>
> And that the gathering together upon the land of Zion, and upon her stakes, *may be for a defense, and for a refuge from the storm, and from wrath* when it shall be poured out without mixture upon the whole earth.[5]

Joseph Smith taught the importance of gathering on other occasions. For example, in 1834 he said:

> . . . Without Zion, and a place of deliverance, we must fall; because the time is near when the sun will be darkened, and the

---

[2]*Doctrine and Covenants* 63:33.
[3]*Ibid.,* 63:32-37.
[4]Wilford Woodruff, *Journal of Discourses,* Vol. 18, p. 116, September 12, 1875.
[5]*Doctrine and Covenants* 115:5-6. (Italics added)

moon turn to blood, and the stars fall from heaven, and the earth reel to and fro. Then, if this is the case, and *if we are not sanctified and gathered to the places God has appointed, with all our former professions and our great love for the Bible, we must fall; we cannot stand; we cannot be saved; for God will gather out his Saints from the Gentiles, and then comes desolation and destruction, and none can escape except the pure in heart who are gathered.*[6]

John Taylor, in a work entitled, *The Government of God,* explained that the gathering of the righteous to Zion would be one way the Lord would use to help establish his government.

> Before the Lord destroyed the old world, he directed Noah to prepare an ark; before the cities of Sodom and Gomorrah were destroyed, he told Lot to "flee to the mountains"; before Jerusalem was destroyed, Jesus gave his disciples warning, and told them to "flee out of it;" and before the destruction of the world a message is sent; after this, the nations will be judged, for God is now preparing his own kingdom for his own reign, and will not be thwarted by any conflicting influence, or opposing power. *The testimony of God is first to be made known, the standard is to be raised, the Gospel of the kingdom is to be preached to all nations, the world is to be warned, and then come the troubles.* The whole world is in confusion, morally, politically, and religiously; but a voice was to be heard, "Come out of her, my people, that you partake not of her sins, and that ye receive not of her plagues."[7]

In 1877, Joseph F. Smith, son of the patriarch Hyrum Smith, and later president of the Church, preached that the gathering is as necessary to the people of this dispensation as are the first principles of the gospel.

> In this dispensation there is a principle or commandment peculiar to it. What is that? *It is the gathering of the people to one place. The gathering of this people is as necessary to be observed by believers, as faith, repentance, baptism, or any other ordinance.* It is an essential part of the Gospel of this dispensation, as much so as the necessity of building an ark by Noah for his deliverance, was a part of the Gospel in his dispensation. Then the world was destroyed by a flood, now it is to be destroyed by war,

---

[6]Joseph Smith, *DHC,* Vol. 2, p. 52, April 21, 1834. (Italics added)
[7]John Taylor, *The Government of God,* (S.W. Richards: Liverpool, England, 1852), p. 101. (Italics added)

pestilence, famine, earthquakes, storms, and tempests, the sea rolling beyond its bounds, malarious vapors, vermin, disease, and by fire and the lightnings of God's wrath poured out for destruction upon Babylon.[8]

Faithfulness and Unity Required of Those Who Gather

It is not meant to imply, of course, that one simply has to gather to Zion to be saved. It will be remembered from a scripture quoted in the previous chapter that the Lord defined Zion as the pure in heart.[9] If those who gather are not pure in heart, they obviously have not come to Zion.

In the section of the Doctrine and Covenants quoted above in which the Lord spoke of saving his people by gathering them, it should be noted that the Lord said it was his will that the people assemble upon the land of Zion *and* that "every man should take righteousness in his hands and faithfulness in his loins."[10]

Brigham Young explained that the gathering of the saints is for the purpose of building God's kingdom. Any other motivation is not acceptable.

> . . . We are gathered together expressly to become of one heart and of one mind in all our operations and endeavors to establish Christ's spiritual and temporal kingdom upon the earth, to prepare for the coming of the Son of Man in power and great glory.[11]

No Peace but in Zion and Her Stakes

This gathering of the righteous will take place so that they may escape the wars and desolation that are coming upon the earth. The Lord has told his people that the conditions will be so bad that there will not be peace anywhere on the face of the whole earth except among his people. The City of Zion, also known as the New Jerusalem, will become a city wherein the righteous can find refuge from the wrath and judgments of God. Early in March of 1831, the Lord told

---

[8]Joseph F. Smith, *Journal of Discourses,* Vol. 19, p. 192, September 30, 1877. (Italics added)
[9]*Doctrine and Covenants* 97:21.
[10]*Ibid.,* 63:36-37.
[11]Brigham Young, *Journal of Discourses,* Vol. 12, p. 153, January 12, 1868.

the saints to begin gathering there, so they could escape the wrath to come.

> And it shall be called the New Jerusalem, a land of peace, a city of refuge, a place of safety for the saints of the Most High God;
>
> And the glory of the Lord shall be there, and the terror of the Lord also shall be there, insomuch that the wicked will not come unto it, and it shall be called Zion.[12]

Two years later Joseph also spoke of that city as a place of refuge.

> The city of Zion spoken of by David, in the one hundred and second Psalm, will be built upon the land of America. "And the ransomed of the Lord shall return, and come to Zion with songs and everlasting joy upon their heads" [Isaiah 35:10] ; and then they will be delivered from the overflowing scourge that shall pass through the land. . . .[13]

Thousands of the early members of the Church flocked to the location of the city of Zion in Jackson County, Missouri, only to be driven out a few years later due to their unwillingness to keep the commandments of God. When they were driven completely out of the state of Missouri in the winter of 1838-39, it looked as though there was no more hope for the redemption of Zion. But the Lord explained in a later revelation to the Prophet that Zion would not be moved out of her place notwithstanding the scattering of the saints, and that no other place would be appointed in its stead.[14]

Evidently, however, the Lord has set up other places of refuge and protection for the saints until the redemption of Zion is complete and the city is constructed. It was only a few months after the expulsion from Missouri that the Prophet Joseph again spoke of escaping the judgments of God by fleeing to Zion and her stakes.

> There will be here and there a Stake (of Zion) for the gathering of the Saints. Some may have cried peace, *but the Saints*

---

[12]*Doctrine and Covenants* 45:66-67.
[13]Joseph Smith, *DHC,* Vol. 1, p. 315, January 4, 1833.
[14]*Doctrine and Covenants* 101:17-20.

and the world will have little peace from henceforth. Let this not hinder us from going to the Stakes; for God has told us to flee, not dallying, or we shall be scattered, one here, and another there. There your children shall be blessed, and you in the midst of friends where you may be blessed. The Gospel net gathers of every kind.

I prophesy, that the man who tarries after he has an opportunity of going, will be afflicted by the devil. Wars are at hand: we must not delay; but are not required to sacrifice. We ought to have the building up of Zion as our greatest object. *When wars come, we shall have to flee to Zion.* The cry is to make haste. The last revelation says, Ye shall not have time to have gone over the earth, until these things come. It will come as did the cholera, war, fires, and earthquakes; one pestilence after another, until the Ancient of Days comes, then judgment will be given to the Saints.[15]

The stakes shall be places of refuge and are, as can be seen, an important part of the gathering to Zion.

In 1941, George Albert Smith said essentially the same thing.

He has told us in great plainness that the world will be in distress, that there will be warfare from one end of the world to the other, that the wicked shall slay the wicked and that peace shall be taken from the earth. And he has said, too, that the only place where there will be safety will be in Zion. Will we make this Zion? Will we keep it to be Zion because Zion means the pure in heart? . . .[16]

The Rocky Mountains

When the saints were forced to flee Nauvoo after the martyrdom of the Prophet and his brother and eventually found a home in the valleys of the Rocky Mountains, many people saw this as a fulfillment of the Lord's promise to provide a place of shelter and protection. Two years before his death, the Prophet Joseph had predicted the removal of the main body of the Church to the Rocky Mountains. On August 6, 1842, while the saints were still in a period of relative peace and prosperity in Nauvoo, Joseph said:

---

[15]Joseph Smith, *DHC,* Vol. 3, pp. 390-391, July 2, 1839. (Italics added)
[16]George Albert Smith, *Conference Report,* October, 1941, p. 99.

I prophesied that the Saints would continue to suffer much affliction and would be driven to the Rocky Mountains, many would apostatize, others would be put to death by our persecutors or lose their lives in consequence of exposure or disease, and some of you will live to go and assist in making settlements and build cities and see the Saints become a mighty people in the midst of the Rocky Mountains.[17]

Wilford Woodruff bore witness just prior to his death that Joseph Smith had foreseen the destiny of the Church in the Rocky Mountains even earlier than 1842. In 1834 when the saints had been driven out of Independence, Missouri, the Prophet organized an army to bring about the redemption of Zion. Some two hundred young men gathered together and under the leadership of the Prophet marched to Missouri. This army became known as "Zion's Camp." Wilford Woodruff was one of the young men who accompanied the Prophet on that march. As the preparations were going forward for that great rescue effort, Joseph met with some of the men in a log cabin just prior to their departure. Many of the brethren stood and bore testimony to the truthfulness of the work. It was then that the Prophet Joseph responded with some rather startling predictions. In the words of Wilford Woodruff:

... The Prophet said, "Brethren, I have been very much edified and instructed in your testimonies here tonight, but I want to say to you before the Lord, that you know no more concerning the destinies of this Church and kingdom than a babe upon its mother's lap. You don't comprehend it." I was rather surprised. He said, "It is only a handful of Priesthood you see here tonight, but *this Church will fill North and South America—it will fill the world.*" Among other things he said, "*It will fill the Rocky Mountains.* There will be tens of thousands of Latter-day Saints who will be gathered in the Rocky Mountains, and there they will open the door for the establishing of the gospel among the Lamanites, who will receive the gospel and their endowments and the blessings of God. This people will go unto the Rocky Mountains; they will there build temples to the Most High. They will raise up a posterity there, and the Latter-day Saints who dwell in these mountains will stand in the flesh until the coming of the Son of Man. The Son of Man will come to them while in the Rocky Mountains."

---

[17]Joseph Smith, *DHC,* Vol. 5, p. 85, August 6, 1842.

> . . . I never expected to see the Rocky Mountains when I listened to that man's voice, but I have, and do today. I will say here that I shall not live to see it, you may not live to see it; *but these thousands of Latter-day Saint children that belong to the Sabbath schools, I believe many of them will stand in the flesh when the Lord Jesus Christ visits the Zion of God here in the mountains of Israel.*[18]

The succeeding hundred and thirty years have proven the great prophetic wisdom of the remarkable Joseph Smith. The great wave of apostasy which came upon the Church after the martyrdom, the subsequent expulsion from Nauvoo and the now-famous crossing of the plains and colonization of the Great Basin all bear witness that there indeed was a prophet of God.

Later history also showed that the removal to the Rocky Mountains was an important step in providing the saints with a place of refuge. Had they still been in the state of Missouri during the Civil War, they would no doubt have had to endure much suffering, for the fighting in Missouri was bitter and devastating.

Brigham Young described the mountains as the most ideal location for the saints in the entire world. He was speaking shortly after the outbreak of the Civil War.

> We are not now mingling in the turmoils of strife, warring, and contention—that we would have been obliged to have mingled in, had not the Lord suffered us to have been driven to these mountains—one of the greatest blessings that could have been visited upon us. *It has been designated, for many generations, to hide up the Saints in the last days, until the indignation of the Almighty be over. . . .*
>
> We are blessed in these mountains; this is the best place on the earth for the Latter-day Saints. Search the history of all the nations and every geographical position on the face of the earth, and you cannot find another situation so well adapted for the Saints as are these mountains. *Here is the place in which the Lord designed to hide his people.* Be thankful for it; be true to your covenants, and be faithful, each and every one.[19]

---

[18]Wilford Woodruff, *Conference Report,* April, 1898, p. 57. (Italics added)
[19]Brigham Young, *Deseret Evening News,* Vol. 11, May 1, 1861, p. 1. (Italics added)

Elder Melvin J. Ballard also spoke of these valleys as being places of refuge from previous and future storms.

> *Do you not know, my brethren and sisters, that God knew what was coming; that he brought this people into these mountain valleys as a place of refuge when the storm shall come.* We only hear the beginning of that storm. Dismal and distressful as has been its approach, while its thunders and its flashings have filled our hearts with terror, it is but the beginning of the storm. Oh, that it were passed, and that it were gone; but it is not, it is not![20]

Other Places of Refuge

Unquestionably, the valleys of the Rocky Mountains have provided a place for the Church to be protected from some of the judgments and also to grow into a world-wide organization. The present state of The Church of Jesus Christ of Latter-day Saints amply testifies that the prophecies have been fulfilled in that respect. One of the things that made this phenomenal growth possible was the fact that thousands upon thousands of faithful saints from all over the world gathered to Utah and its surrounding areas to help in the building of the kingdom.

After arriving in the Salt Lake Valley, the call went out from the headquarters of the Church over and over to come and join with the main body of the Church. This great gathering resulted in the building of a western empire and the expansion of the Church into spheres of world influence.

However, after the turn of the century, the needs of the Church gradually changed. Members of the Church all over the world were no longer encouraged to leave their homes, but rather to stay and build the Church in their own localities. It was still to be a gathering of the saints, but now they were to gather together wherever they lived. It was this foresighted decision by the leadership of the Church that has made possible the Church today, a Church with stakes, wards, and branches virtually all over the free world.

For some reason, however, the idea still persists in the minds of some people that as conditions worsen in the United

---

[20]Melvin J. Ballard, *Conference Report,* October, 1922, p. 59. (Italics added)

States and other countries, the members of the Church will be called back to Utah for peace and safety. People anxiously wonder if they should leave the confines of "Mormon Territory" for better job opportunities, schooling, or various other reasons, if they may have to "return to Utah when things really get bad." Statements by early prophets in this dispensation are read which stress the importance of being close to the heart of the Church, and these are interpreted to mean that safety in the crises to come lies only in the environs of Salt Lake City.

Such conclusions are the result of two basic errors: First, some do not realize that the times of the Church and its needs have changed. Second, they disregard the true spirit of the gathering that is to take place in preparation for the coming of the Lord. The prophets of this dispensation, both those early in the history of the Church and those today have explained that the gathering to places of refuge is much more than a simple relocation of the saints to Utah.

In a reference previously cited, Joseph Smith warned that the time was coming when there would be no peace on the earth except in Zion AND HER STAKES! He said:

> There will be here and there a Stake (of Zion) for the gathering of the Saints. Some may have cried peace, but the Saints and the world will have little peace from henceforth. *Let this not hinder us from going to the Stakes; for God has told us to flee,* not dallying, or we shall be scattered, one here, and another there. There [Where? In the stakes of Zion!] your children shall be blessed. . . .[21]

In the general conference just before his death, Joseph Smith made another important proclamation.

> You know there has been great discussion in relation to Zion—where it is, and where the gathering of the dispensation is, and which I am now going to tell you. The prophets have spoken and written upon it; but I will make a proclamation that will cover a broader ground. *The whole of America is Zion itself from north to south, and is described by the Prophets, who declare that it is the Zion where the mountain of the Lord should be, and that it should*

---

[21]Joseph Smith, *DHC*, Vol. 3, p. 390, July 2, 1839. (Italics added)

be in the center of the land. When Elders shall take up and examine the old prophecies in the Bible, they will see it. . . .

I have received instructions from the Lord that from henceforth wherever the Elders of Israel shall build up churches and branches unto the Lord throughout the States, there shall be a stake of Zion. In the great cities, as Boston, New York, etc., there shall be stakes. It is a glorious proclamation. . . .[22]

Brigham Young often spoke of the mountains as being a place of refuge, but he also said: "The time is nigh when every man that will not take up his sword against his neighbor must needs flee to Zion. *Where is Zion? Where the organization of the Church of God is.* And may it dwell spiritually in every heart; and may we so live as to always enjoy the Spirit of Zion!"[23]

President Joseph Fielding Smith quoted a prophecy by Wilford Woodruff wherein he said that the time was coming when Utah would be a pretty good place in which to live. Then President Smith said:

Now, I can't take time to read more of it, but he raised this warning voice, and I believe Utah will be a pretty good place to live in, *and other stakes of Zion, for I don't believe President Woodruff intended to confine this to the borders of Utah, but to the stakes of Zion.* But the judgments of the Almighty are being poured out, and they shall continue, for the Prophet of God has said it. We shall not escape unless we repent, turn to the Lord, honor our Priesthood and our membership in this Church, and be true and faithful to our covenants.[24]

Elder John A. Widtsoe put it this way:

. . . There is safety wherever the people of the Lord live so worthily as to claim the sacred title of citizens of the Zion of our Lord. Otherwise the name Zion is but an empty sound. The only safety that we can expect in this or any other calamitous time lies in our conformity to gospel requirements.[25]

---

[22]Joseph Smith, *ibid.*, Vol. 6, pp. 318-319, April 8, 1844. (Italics in original)
[23]Brigham Young, *Journal of Discourses,* Vol. 8, p. 205. October 8, 1860. (Italics added)
[24]Joseph Fielding Smith, *Conference Report,* April, 1937, p. 62. (Italics added)
[25]John A. Widtsoe, *Conference Report,* April, 1942, p. 33. (Italics added)

President Harold B. Lee has spoken several times against the false assumption that the only place of safety in the last days will be in the Rocky Mountains. During the great calamity of World War II he spoke of the anxiety some members of the Church had about living away from "Zion."

> I was down in Kelsey, Texas, last November, and I heard a group of anxious people asking, "Is now the day for us to come up to Zion, where we can come to the mountain of the Lord, where we can be protected from our enemies?" I pondered that question, I prayed about it. What should we say to those people who were in their anxiety? I have studied it a bit, I have learned something of what the Spirit has taught, *and I know now that the place of safety in this world is not in any given place; it doesn't make so much difference where we live; but the all-important thing is how we live, and I have found that the security can come to Israel only when they keep the commandments, when they live so that they can enjoy the companionship, the direction, the comfort, and the guidance of the Holy Spirit of the Lord, when they are willing to listen to these men whom God has set here to preside as His mouthpieces, and when we obey the counsels of the Church.*[26]

Five years later President Lee expanded the idea of the importance of giving heed to those men God has chosen to guide his people through times of trouble. After speaking of "gathering places" he said:

> The spirit of gathering has been with the Church from the days of that restoration. Those who are of the blood of Israel have a righteous desire after they are baptized, to gather together with the body of the Saints at the designated place. . . .
>
> After designating certain places in that day where the Saints were to gather, the Lord said this:
>
> "Until the day cometh when there is found no more room for them; and then I have other places which I will appoint unto them." (D&C 101:21)
>
> *Thus, clearly, the Lord has placed the responsibility for directing the work of gathering in the hands of the leaders of the Church to whom he will reveal his will where and when such gatherings would take place in the future. It would be well before the frightening events concerning the fulfillment of all God's promises and*

---

[26]Harold B. Lee, *Conference Report*, April, 1943, p. 129. (Italics added)

predictions are upon us, that the Saints in every land prepare
themselves and look forward to the instruction that shall come
to them from the First Presidency of this Church as to where they
shall be gathered and not be disturbed in their feelings until such
instruction is given to them as it is revealed by the Lord to the
proper authority.[27]

This is, of course, in exact agreement with what Joseph
Smith meant when he said, after speaking of gathering to the
stakes of Zion, "You must make yourselves acquainted with
those men who like Daniel pray three times a day toward the
house of the Lord. *Look to the presidency and receive instruc-*
tion."[28]

In his great address in general conference of 1970 President Lee again taught this same idea.

One of our brethren was reported to have said that the people
of California should move up to the tops of the Rocky Mountains,
that only there would be safety. *Contrary to that, we are constantly*
saying to our people that safety is where the pure in heart are, and
that there is just as much safety wherever you are, if you are living
and keeping the commandments of God.[29]

It is possible that in the calamitous times to come, some
may gather to the main headquarters of the Church in Utah,
but it is evident that this is not necessarily the expected course
for all members of the Church. The important thing is for a
person to so live that when the instructions come from the
Lord through his servants, he will be ready to heed them and
to gather to the designated places, be it Salt Lake City, the
outlying stakes, or wherever.

Like a Flowing Stream

Another assumption that is often made that should be
avoided is that only members of The Church of Jesus Christ
of Latter-day Saints will be protected and saved from the
judgments of God. Several prophecies already cited have

---

[27] Harold B. Lee, *The Improvement Era,* June, 1948, p. 320. (Italics added)
[28] Joseph Smith, *DHC,* Vol. 3, p. 391, July 2, 1839. (Italics added)
[29] Harold B. Lee, *Conference Report,* April, 1970, p. 56. (Italics added)

indicated that many who will not participate in the bloodshed and mobocracy will flee to Zion for peace and safety. This, of course, seems to indicate others besides members of the Church. Many of the prophets have told of the time when thousands of the "Gentiles" would come to us for protection. They seem to indicate that the crises in the nation will tend to shut off the Church from the rest of the United States, and thus leave us with the only peaceful organization in the world. For example, Brigham Young spoke of the time when there would be a great gulf between the righteous and the wicked.

> *By and by there will be a gulf between the righteous and the wicked so that they can not trade with each other, and national intercourse will cease.*[30]

Heber C. Kimball, first counselor to President Young for many years, described it as being like a curtain which would drop between the Church and the United States.

> Lay up your stores, and take your silks and fine things, and exchange them for grain and such things as you need, and the time will come when we will be obliged to depend upon our own resources; for *the time is not far distant when the curtain will be dropped between us and the United States.* When the time comes, brethren and sisters, you will wish you had commenced sooner to make your own clothing. I tell you, God requires us to go into home manufacture; and, prolong it as much as you like, you have got to do it.[31]

On two different occasions President Kimball also described the conditions that would prevail when the people came to the Church for protection. Speaking of the recent arrival of some handcart companies, he said:

> Is this the end of it? *No; there will be millions on millions that will come much in the same way, only they will not have hand carts, for they will take their bundles under their arms, and their children on their backs, and under their arms, and flee; and Zion's*

---

[30]Brigham Young, *Journal of Discourses,* Vol. 12, p. 284, October 8, 1868. (Italics added)

[31]Heber C. Kimball, *Journal of Discourses,* Vol. 5, p. 10, July 5, 1857. (Italics added)

people will have to send out relief to them, for they will come when the judgments come on the nation.[32]

The day will come when the people of the United States will come lugging their bundles under their arms, coming to us for bread to eat.[33]

Orson Pratt also spoke about these future times on several different occasions. For example, in 1855 he spoke of the time when the Gentiles would come to the Church as a flowing stream, not because they will want to join the Church but simply to escape the disastrous conditions that will prevail in the world.

Now how do we know, but when the gates of Zion shall be open to the nations, that the Gentiles will come flocking in, like a flowing stream? A flowing stream is one that runs continually: and the Gentiles will, in that day, come to us as a flowing stream, and we shall have to set our gates open continually, they will come as clouds and as doves in large flocks. . . .

Those nations are trembling and tottering and will eventually crumble to ruin, and those men of wealth will come here, not to be baptized, but many of them will come that have never heard the servants of God; but they will hear that peace and health dwell among us, and that our officers, and our tax-gatherers men of righteousness.[34]

George Q. Cannon explained that the non-members would flock to the Church in those trying times so that they could enjoy a peaceful government.

We are not alone in the thought that the republic is drifting steadily in that direction; that we are leaving the old constitutional landmarks, and that *the time is not far distant when there will be trouble in consequence of it, when there will be civil broils and strife; and, to escape them, we believe, men will be compelled to flee to the "Mormons," despised as they are now.*[35]

[32]*Ibid.*, Vol. 4, p. 106, September 28, 1856. (Italics added)
[33]*Ibid.*, Vol. 5, p. 10, July 5, 1857. (Italics added)
[34]Orson Pratt, *Journal of Discourses*, Vol. 3, p. 16, May 20, 1855.
[35]George Q. Cannon, *Journal of Discourses*, Vol. 18, p. 10, April 8, 1875. (Italics added)

God Watches Over His Own

The times which are coming will, indeed, be such that many wonder how anyone could survive. But as was pointed out in the introduction to this book, the Lord has extended his hand to us so that we may walk through the times of darkness with confidence and assurance that his will will prevail. He has abundantly testified that one of the great works which he will accomplish will be to gather his children into places of refuge so that they may be sheltered from the storms of his wrath.

The primary task of each member of the Church today is to make sure that he has placed his own hand in the hand of God. Only thus will a person be guided into those places of safe harbor. Zion is *the* place of refuge, and Zion is the pure in heart. For those who can truly qualify as "living in Zion" there will be no terror in the days to come.

President Brigham Young summed up the proper attitude most adequately in an address to the Quorum of the Twelve in Boston (the minutes of which Joseph Smith included in his *History of the Church*):

> The Lord does not require every soul to leave his home as soon as he believes. Some may be wanted to go to the isles of the sea, and some to go north, and some south. *But He does require them to hearken to counsel, and follow that course which He points out, whether to gather or stay to do some other work. . . .*
>
> Perhaps some of you are ready to ask, "Cannot the Lord save us as well where we are as to gather together?" Yes, if the Lord says so. *But if He commands us to come out and gather together, He will not save us by staying home. . . .*[36]

---

[36]Joseph Smith, *DHC*, Vol. 6, p. 12, September 9, 1843. (Italics added)

Faces Eastward

A Holy City

Many years before Christ, one of the great prophets to the nation of the Jaredites foresaw much of the destiny of the land on which his people dwelt. He saw the days of Christ, and far beyond them into our own dispensation. Moroni, the final scribe for the Book of Mormon, records the words of the Prophet Ether and his startling prediction concerning a city to be built upon this land. That city was to be called the New Jerusalem.[1]

It is not hard to imagine the excitement such a prophecy caused among the early members of the Church as they read this part of the Book of Mormon. John, the Revelator, had also spoken of the New Jerusalem,[2] but no one had ever dared suppose that it would be built here in America. The saints became eager to know of its location so that they might have a part in the building of this great city. In response to their questions and to his own, Joseph Smith asked the Lord for revelation that they might know where this remarkable city was to be built. In September, 1830, the Lord made it clear that no one knew yet where the city (also called the city of Zion) was to be located, but finally, in July, 1831, the Lord revealed that the center place for the city of Zion was in the small town of Independence, Jackson County, Missouri.[3]

Although the Prophet Joseph and many of the saints were by that time settled in Kirtland, Ohio, many other members

---

[1]Ether 13:4, 6, 8.
[2]Revelation 21:2.
[3]*Doctrine and Covenants* 57:1-4.

of the Church earnestly desired to live in the city so long promised by the Lord, and as a consequence moved their families to Zion. But their hopes of living in the holy city of Zion were frustrated, for history proved that the saints were not yet ready to establish the New Jerusalem. They were driven first from Jackson County and later from Missouri altogether. After all of the divine promises that had been made concerning the great destiny of this special city, the expulsion of the saints must have caused much consternation. However, the Lord made it clear that no change in location had been made, but only that the redemption of Zion would have to wait for a season, evidently until he had a people worthy to build and possess a city of such special nature.[4]

Salt Lake City Not the Permanent Headquarters

In the thirteen decades that have followed the abandonment of the land designated by the Lord as the land of Zion, the Church moved west, colonized hundreds of cities in the western half of the North American Continent, and grew into a world-wide organization with a membership of three million. From that first hot day when the pioneers entered the valley of the Great Salt Lake to the present when thousands of chapels, seminaries, temples, welfare farms and other Church properties dot the Intermountain West, Salt Lake City has been the headquarters of the Latter-day Saints. The vast, global organization which at the end of 1970 included some 537 stakes, 4,800 wards and branches and 93 missions,[5] has all been administered from the site laid out by Brigham Young a few days after arriving in Salt Lake Valley.

The amount of capital investment the Church has in the West is enough to stagger the mind, but even more impressive is the realization of the tremendous cost in human toil and sacrifice it has taken to move the Church from the barren existence of 1847 to its present stature. It is inconceivable that after so much investment of time, labor, and money that the Church should ever want to leave its headquarters. And yet, during the one hundred thirty years that the Church has been exiled from the lands of Jackson County, Missouri, the saints have ever been taught that Jackson County, not Utah, is to be their final, permanent headquarters.

Elder George Q. Cannon explained that this longing for Zion is not due to a dissatisfaction with the lands in which the saints presently find themselves, for Utah and its environs have been a happy home for the saints.

> We do not wish to leave this land, because it is not fertile, or because it is not a favoured land. We appreciate the home that God has given us here, so fruitful in blessings to the Saints; but *we look forward to that land with indescribable feelings, because it is the place where God has said His City shall be built.*[6]

Orson F. Whitney stated the case in the most explicit terms:

> Will our mission end here (in Utah)? Is the State of Utah the proper monument of the Mormon people? No . . . *the monument to Mormonism will stand in Jackson County, Missouri.* There the great city will be built: There Zion will arise and shine, "the joy of the whole earth," and there the Lord will come to his temple in his own time, when his people shall have made the required preparation.[7]

In his three-volume work, *Doctrines of Salvation,* President Joseph Fielding Smith also clearly stated the belief of the Church that Missouri is to be the location of the city of Zion.

> We accept the fact that the *center place* where the City New Jerusalem is to be built, is in Jackson County, Missouri. It was never the intention to substitute Utah or any other place for Jackson County. But we do hold that Zion, when reference is made to the land, is as broad as America, both North and South—*all of it is Zion.*[8]

---

[6]George Q. Cannon, *Journal of Discourses,* Vol. 11, pp. 336-337, March 3, 1867. (Italics added)

[7]Orson F. Whitney, An address given in Salt Lake City, April 9, 1916. Recorded in Hyrum M. Smith and Janne M. Sjodahl, *Doctrine and Covenants Commentary* (Deseret Book Co.: Salt Lake City, 1967), p. 147. (Italics added)

[8]Joseph Fielding Smith, *Doctrines of Salvation* (Bruce R. McConkie, comp.), Vol. 3, (Bookcraft: Salt Lake City, 1956) p. 72. (Italics in original)

President Lorenzo Snow cautioned the saints against feeling that the return to Jackson County was so close that they should not try and build up the area in which they were presently living, but he made it clear that the day was coming when the worthy members of the Church would return to build the city there.

> The time is speedily coming—we do not want to talk very much, though, about going to Jackson County, Missouri, because through our weakness we would not care anything about building houses and making ourselves comfortable here. I know when we first started a colony in Brigham City, the people generally thought it was nonsense, perfectly useless, to plant peach trees, currant bushes and the like, because we were going to Jackson County so speedily; and it was with the utmost effort that we were enabled to discourage them of this idea. *We are not going tomorrow, nor next day, this week or next week; but we are going, and there are many—hundreds and hundreds within the sound of my voice that will live to go back to Jackson County and build a holy temple to the Lord our God. . . .*[9]

President Brigham Young spoke of a vision he had received before the saints were driven from Missouri. In the vision he saw the members of the Church scattered in every direction, but saw them returning to Jackson County *from the west*. Said he: "When this people return to the Center Stake of Zion, they will go from the west."[10] On another occasion, President Young said:

> Suppose we are ready for it, and a great Temple is built at the central point, in Jackson County. Gentlemen, don't be startled; for if we don't go back there, our sons and daughters will; and a great Temple will be built upon the consecrated spot, and a great many more besides that.[11]

Orson Pratt also spoke at some length on our future destiny.

> *Is God limited to this little narrow spot, called the great basin of North America? Why, no. It is only for the present, for the time being that we dwell here.* Where will we dwell in the future?

---

[9]Lorenzo Snow, *Conference Report,* April, 1898, p. 64. (Italics added)
[10]Brigham Young, *Journal of Discourses,* Vol. 11, p. 17, December 11, 1864.
[11]*Ibid.,* Vol. 6, p. 296, August 15, 1852.

What is our future destiny? It is not on the Sandwich Islands, it is not in New Zealand, it is not in Australia, it is not in any of the islands of the sea, but I will tell you the future destiny of this people in a very few words. *Not many years hence—I do not say the number of years—you will look forth to the western counties of the State of Missouri, and to the eastern counties of the State of Kansas, and in all that region round about you will see a thickly populated country, inhabited by a peaceful people, having their orchards, their fruit trees, their fields of grain, their beautiful houses and shade trees, their cities and towns and villages.* And you may ask — Who are all these people? And the answer will be—Latter-day Saints.[12]

The Center "Place" of Zion

The reader may have noticed that the site for the city of Zion or the New Jerusalem is variously referred to by some Church authorities as the "Center Stake of Zion" and by others as the "center place of Zion." The former term was more often used by earlier members of the Church, and as Elders Smith and Sjodahl explain, it is not as accurate as the latter. In a footnote to a quotation from Brigham Young wherein he calls it the "Center Stake of Zion," they say:

> It has become customary to speak of the "Center Stake of Zion." It might, therefore, be well to remember that no Stake was ever organized in Jackson County. Following the figure given by Isaiah Ch. 33:20 and 54:2, we cannot speak of a "center stake of Zion." The term "Stake of Zion" was first used in a revelation given in November, 1831. (Sec. 68) It is a comparison to the stakes which bind a tent. Isaiah says: "Look upon Zion, the city of our solemnities; thine eyes shall see Jerusalem a quiet habitation, a tabernacle that shall not be taken down; not one of the stakes thereof shall ever be removed, neither shall any of the cords thereof be broken." Again, "Enlarge the place of thy tent and let them stretch forth the curtains of thine habitations; spare not, lengthen thy cords, and strengthen thy stakes." Zion is the tent, and how can the tent be a stake?[13]

It is not a serious error but the difference is worth noting since both phrases will be found in the statements of various Church leaders in this and following chapters.

[12]Orson Pratt, *Journal of Discourses,* Vol. 21, p. 135, September 7, 1879. (Italics added)
[13]Smith and Sjodahl, *op. cit.,* p. 189.

Not All Shall Return

"But," says one, "why then does the Church continue to build up the areas around Utah if we are just going to desert them?" The answer to that question is twofold. First, and most obvious, the call to return to Jackson County has not been given to the Church as yet; until it is the Church is expected to build Zion in the hearts of its people wherever they are located. This could not be done if further growth and development of the Church was curtailed in anxious anticipation of the call to Missouri. No one yet knows exactly when the call will come; until it does come the Church will continue to build Zion and the kingdom of God in that location in which they find themselves. For only in this way will they be prepared to build up the center place of Zion.

However, that still leaves a second and more important reason. The investment in time, energy, and money which the Church and its members have made in the building up of the Western Empire is not simply to be abandoned. When one considers the massive expenditures which have recently gone into the new temples in Utah, the new Church office building, the granite vaults in Little Cottonwood Canyon, the new Visitors' Center and many other new buildings and programs inaugurated by the leaders of the Church, it would indeed seem tragic to abandon the present headquarters of the Church.

Such will not be the case, for the prophets have amply testified that although the majority of the Church will move to Missouri, that in no way implies that every member will. Just a few years after coming to Utah, President Brigham Young said:

> Remarks have been made as to our staying here in the Rockies. I will tell you how long we shall stay here. If we live our religion, we shall stay here in these mountains for ever and for ever, worlds without end, *and a portion of the Priesthood will go and redeem and build up the Center Stake of Zion.*[14]

---

[14]Brigham Young, *Journal of Discourses,* Vol. 11, p. 16, December 11, 1864. (Italics added)

Shortly before his death, President Young put it even more clearly:

> Are we going back to Jackson County? Yes. When? As soon as the way opens up. Are we all going? Oh no! Of course not. The country is not large enough to hold our present numbers. *When we do return there, will there be any less remaining in these mountains than we number today? No, there may be a hundred then for every single one that there is now. It is folly in men to suppose that we are going to break up these our hard earned homes to make others in a new country.* We intend to hold our own here, and also penetrate the north and the south, the east and the west, there to make others and to raise the ensign of truth.[15]

In his conference address to the Church in 1900 concerning the return to Zion, President Lorenzo Snow described it as "a large portion" who would return.

> Now the time is fast approaching when a large portion of the people that I am now addressing will go back to Jackson County. . . . A large portion of the Latter-day Saints that now dwell in these valleys will go back to Jackson County to build a holy city to the Lord, as was decreed by Jehovah and revealed through Joseph Smith.[16]

Orson Pratt made it evident that it was his belief that some would remain in the areas already organized and built up by the Church.

> We expect that these mountains will not be the residences of all the Latter-day Saints; we expect that *the great majority* of the people will emigrate.[17]

All of the efforts of building and the great sacrifices that have been made down through the years are not simply to be left behind. As Zion expands to encompass all of North and South America the great building effort of generations of saints will be put to valuable use. However, the work of the

---

[15]*Ibid.,* Vol. 18, pp. 355-356, April 6, 1877. (Italics added)
[16]Lorenzo Snow, *Conference Report,* October, 1900, p. 61.
[17]Orson Pratt, *Journal of Discourses,* Vol. 24, p. 23, October 26, 1879. (Italics added)

Lord and his kingdom will be headquartered in the city of Zion which will be built in Jackson County, Missouri. It is for this reason that the Church still looks to the east.

The Army of the Lord

As one contemplates this great return to the center place of Zion, many questions flood into the mind. Who will go? How soon will it be? What will conditions be like? What mode of transportation will be used? Will there be any problems en route which will hinder the return? These and many other intriguing problems cry for an answer. Of course, not all of the answers are known. The Lord has left some of these questions as yet unanswered, but from all that he has revealed through his prophets it can be safely said that the return to the east will be a marvelous manifestation of the Lord's power. Those privileged to be in that great company will have much to tell their children and grandchildren.

When the saints were driven from Jackson County in the last months of 1833, the Lord revealed to Joseph Smith what has now become the 101st section of the Doctrine and Covenants. He explained that the saints were driven out because of transgression but were reassured of God's love and concern for them. Other stakes of Zion were promised. Then the Lord gave an interesting parable in order that the Church would know his will concerning the redemption of Zion.[18] In the parable, a nobleman sent his servants to a "very choice" spot of land to plant some olive trees. They were commanded to set watchmen around the grove and to build a tower to guard against enemies coming in to destroy the trees. At first the servants were faithful and planted the trees and set watchmen over them, but soon they began to be slothful and rationalized concerning their duties, failing to complete the tower. During the night, the enemy broke down the hedge of the grove and destroyed the trees.

When the nobleman heard of what had happened he was understandably wroth with his servants and rebuked them

---

[18]*Doctrine and Covenants* 101:43-62.

severely for their slothfulness. Then a most significant part of the parable follows. The nobleman called one of his servants and gave him special instructions, telling him to gather an army to reclaim the vineyard from the enemy.[19]

With the perspective of history, the meaning of the first part of the parable is quite clear. The choice piece of land chosen by the Lord for his work was Zion—Independence, Missouri, and its surrounding areas. The Lord's people were sent there with the instructions to build up a great work unto the Lord, but with a special caution to be particularly watchful so that the enemy did not destroy the work. But the saints were slothful in keeping the Lord's commandments in Zion. They were selfish, petty, eager to follow their own counsel over that of Joseph's, and thus they were not watchful and were driven from the choice land.

At first, it looked as though the last part of the parable would have its fulfillment in the small army Joseph Smith organized and started toward Missouri to redeem Zion. But "Zion's Camp" as it was called, was disbanded before it ever reached Jackson County and the mission was not completed. The saints moved to the northern counties of Missouri and then eventually left the state completely, so this part of the parable dealing with the redemption of Zion still awaits fulfillment.

Other scriptures and statements by the prophets indicate that the redemption of Zion must indeed come by power as the parable said. In February, 1834, the Lord spoke of the future redemption of Zion, and said:

> Behold, I say unto you, the redemption of Zion must needs come by power;
>
> Therefore, I will raise up unto my people a man, who shall lead them like as Moses led the children of Israel.
>
> For ye are the children of Israel, and of the seed of Abraham, and ye must needs be led out of bondage by power, and with a stretched-out arm.

---

[19]*Ibid.,* 101:55-62.

And as your fathers were led at the first, even so shall the redemption of Zion be.[20]

Of the man "like unto Moses" more shall be said later in the chapter, but the entire promise is a thrilling one, for what power can withstand the power of the Lord?

Four months after this revelation was given, the Lord again spoke of the redemption of Zion, but explained that his "army" was not yet worthy to do so. He spoke of the time when the army would be sanctified and thus in their righteousness become terrible to behold.[21]

The use of the term "army" invokes pictures of great battles and actual combat in the redemption of Zion but this does not seem to be the case here. The Lord's "army" is an army of an unusual nature. In 1831, the Lord warned the saints that they must purchase the land of Zion and not obtain it through the shedding of blood, for if they did shed blood they would be scourged from city to city.[22] President Lorenzo Snow referred to this scripture in speaking of the redemption of Zion.

> *We will not take possession of the land of Zion by force.*
> If we should do, it would turn out to us as it did with the people who were upon the land of Zion when this revelation was given. As the Lord here tells us, there are only two ways in which we can come in possession of that land. One way is by purchase, "and if by purchase, behold you are blessed." The other way is by blood, "and if by blood, as you are forbidden to shed blood, lo, your enemies are upon you, and ye shall be scourged from city to city and from synagogue to synagogue, and but few shall stand to receive an inheritance." These are the words of God.[23]

In section 103 of the Doctrine and Covenants the Lord spoke of his presence going up before his people. Orson Pratt described this presence as being the thing that would strike terror into the hearts of the people.

---

[20]*Ibid.*, 103:15-18.
[21]*Ibid.*, 105:29, 32.
[22]*Ibid.*, 63:29-31.
[23]Lorenzo Snow, *Conference Report*, October, 1900, p. 63. (Italics added)

We shall go back to Jackson County. Not that all this people will leave these mountains, or all be gathered together in a camp, but when we go back there will be a very large organization consisting of thousands, and tens of thousands, and they will march forward, the glory of God overshadowing their camp by day in the form of a cloud, and a pillar of flaming fire by night, the Lord's voice being uttered forth before his army. . . .

Will not this produce terror upon all the nations of the earth? *Will not armies of this description, though they may not be as numerous as the armies of the world, cause a terror to fall upon the nations?* The Lord says the banners of Zion shall be terrible. If only one or two millions of this people were to go down and build the waste places of Zion, would it strike the people of Asia and Europe with terror? Not particularly, unless there was some supernatural power made manifest. *But when the Lord's presence is there, when his voice is heard, and his angels go before the camp, it will be telegraphed to the uttermost parts of the earth and fear will seize upon all people, especially the wicked,* and the knees of the ungodly will tremble in that day, and the high ones that are on high, and the great men of the earth.[24]

Another testimony of the divine protection to be given to that group on their way to Jackson County came during the dedication of the Kirtland Temple. During that great spiritual occasion many members of the Church had marvelous experiences. Joseph Smith spoke of some of these and then told of a vision which his scribe had.

Many of my brethren who received the ordinance with me saw glorious visions also. Angels ministered unto them as well as to myself, and the power of the Highest rested upon us, the house was filled with the glory of God, and we shouted Hosanna to God and the Lamb. My scribe also received his anointing with us, and *saw, in a vision, the armies of heaven protecting the Saints in their return to Zion, and many things which I saw.*[25]

Not So Much as a Yellow Dog

There seems to be another reason why the saints will not have to redeem the land of Zion by actual combat and war-

[24]Orson Pratt, *Journal of Discourses,* Vol. 15, p. 364, March 9, 1873. (Italics added)
[25]Joseph Smith, *DHC,* Vol. 2, p. 381, January 21, 1836. (Italics added)

fare. It must be remembered that the United States will see great chaos and destruction in the form of mobs and anarchy. It is not clear from the prophecies just exactly when the return to Missouri will take place in relationship to this time of civil destruction, but Heber C. Kimball spoke of a prophecy made by President Brigham Young in which he said that upon the return of the saints there would be no inhabitants in that area of Missouri to plague the Church.

> The western boundary of the State of Missouri will be swept so clean of its inhabitants that as President Young tells us, when you return to that place, *there will not be left so much as a yellow dog to wag his tail.*[26]

One can only speculate on how such devastation might come about. In any case, this desolation would allow the saints to possess the land without having to contest for it. Two separate statements by Orson Pratt also suggest that the return would be after or at least during this great period of chaos. In 1875 he said:

> Well then, to return to the prophesying, when the time shall come that *the Lord shall waste away this nation,* he will give commandment to this people to return and possess their own inheritance which they purchased some forty-four years ago in the state of Missouri.[27]

Then four years later he told the saints:

> Now, there are a great many cities in the United States that will not be totally destroyed when the inhabitants are swept off the surface of the earth. Their houses, their desolate cities will still remain unoccupied until Zion in her glory and strength shall enlarge the place of her tents, and stretch forth the curtains of her habitations. That is the destiny of this nation, and the destiny of the Latter-day Saints.[28]

---

[26]Heber C. Kimball, *Deseret News, Church Department,* May 23, 1931, p. 3. (Italics added)
[27]Orson Pratt, *Deseret Evening News,* Vol. 8, No. 265, October 2, 1875, p. 1. (Italics added)
[28]Orson Pratt, *Journal of Discourses,* Vol. 24, pp. 31-32, October 26, 1879.

Although the saints may not have to fight to reclaim the center place of Zion, this does not imply that they will necessarily return in peace. If anarchy and mobs are still sweeping the nation when the Church returns there will certainly be problems in moving a group of people as large as the prophecies indicate without some conflict. In a most interesting sermon by Joseph F. Smith, this is substantiated. His statement is also significant for it is one of the few prophecies that talks about the transportation on the way back to the East.

> . . . When God leads the people back to Jackson County, how will he do it? Let me picture to you how some of us may be gathered and led to Jackson County. *I think I see two or three hundred thousand people wending their way across the great plain, enduring the nameless hardships of the journey, herding and guarding their cattle by day and by night, and defending themselves and little ones from foes on the right hand and on the left, as when they came here. They will find the journey back to Jackson County will be real as when they came out here.* Now, mark it. And though you may be led by the power of God "with a stretched-out arm," it will not be more manifest than the leading the people out here to those that participate in it. They will think there are a great many hardships to endure in this manifestation of the power of God, and it will be left, perhaps to their children to see the glory of their deliverance, just as it is left for us to see the glory of our former deliverance, from the hands of those that sought to destroy us. This is one way to look at it. It is certainly a practical view. Some might ask, what will become of the railroads? I fear that the sifting process would be insufficient were we to travel by railroads. We are apt to overlook the manifestations of the power of God to us because we are participators in them, and regard them as commonplace events. *But when it is written in history—as it will be written—it will be shown forth to future generations as one of the most marvelous, unexampled and unprecedented accomplishments that has ever been known to history.*[29]

Destruction or collapse of the great transportation network of the United States could easily be the result of widespread war and mobocracy. Unquestionably, the return of the saints to Jackson County, Missouri, will require the power

---

[29]Joseph F. Smith, *Journal of Discourses*, Vol. 24, pp. 156-157, December 3, 1882. (Italics added)

of the Lord, both in the preparation of the area round about and also in the actual journey itself.

A Man Like unto Moses

As was mentioned earlier, when the Lord spoke of the redemption of Zion coming by power, he promised that he would "raise up unto my people a man, who shall lead them like as Moses led the children of Israel."[30] This promise has caused a great deal of speculation in the Church since that time. Many people wondered just who that man might be. Brigham Young was a man very much like Moses in his leading of the saints to Utah and some have speculated that this passage might have referred to him. Some have also felt that Joseph Smith would be resurrected and return to lead the people back. The great prophecy by Joseph of Egypt, as recorded in Nephi's writings, referred to Joseph Smith as a man like unto Moses.[31] The Lord also compared Joseph to Moses in Section 28 of the Doctrine and Covenants.[32]

Orson Pratt discussed this man "like unto Moses" at some length in a sermon delivered to the saints in 1873.

> Whether that man is now in existence, or whether it is some one yet to be born; or whether it is our present leader who has led us forth into these valleys of the mountains, whether God will grant unto us the great blessing to have his life spared to lead forth his people like a Moses, we perhaps may not all know. . . . *But be this as it may, whether he [Joseph Smith] is the man, whether President Young is the man, or whether the Lord shall hereafter raise up a man, for that purpose, we do know that when that day comes the Lord will not only send his angels before the army of Israel, but his presence will also be there.*[33]

One of the most definitive statements on the "man like unto Moses" is that given by Elder John A. Widtsoe in his work, *Evidences and Reconciliations.* In answer to the question, "Who is the man like unto Moses?" he writes:

---

[30]*Doctrine and Covenants* 103:16.
[31]2 Nephi 3:9.
[32]*Doctrine and Covenants* 28:2.
[33]Orson Pratt, *Journal of Discourses,* Vol. 15, pp. 362-363, March 9, 1873. (Italics added)

There have been many conjectures concerning this statement. There have even been misguided men who have declared themselves to be this man "like as Moses." Yet, the meaning as set forth in the scriptures, is very simple. In modern revelation the President of the Church is frequently compared to Moses. Soon after the organization of the Church, the Lord said, "no one shall be appointed to receive commandments and revelations in this church excepting my servant Joseph Smith, Jun., for he receiveth them even as Moses" (D.&C. 28:2). In one of the great revelations upon Priesthood, this is more specifically expressed: "the duty of the President of the office of the High Priesthood is to preside over the whole church, and to be like unto Moses" (D.&C. 107:91).

The discussion of this question among the Saints led to the following statement in the *Times and Seasons* (6:922) by John Taylor, then the editor: *"The President* (of the Church) *stands in the Church as Moses did to the children of Israel, according to the revelations."*

The man like unto Moses in the Church is the President of the Church.[34]

The important fact to remember is that there will be a mighty prophet of God, raised up by the Lord to deliver his people back to the site of the New Jerusalem.

Only the Worthy

One last important consideration remains in the discussion of the return to Jackson County, viz., who will be allowed to go and on what basis will the determination be made? The answer, of course, is the same as the answer to such questions as how one avoids the judgments of God, how one escapes from the desolating scourge that is to come, and so on. The answer is simply this: Only the worthy will be called on to return to build up that great city.

Brigham Young said:

Now, it is for you and me to prepare to return back again; not to our fatherland, in many cases, but to return east, and by-and-by to build up the Centre Stake of Zion. *We are not prepared*

---

[34]John A. Widtsoe, *Evidences and Reconciliations,* (Bookcraft: Salt Lake City, 1943), p. 197. (Italics added)

to do this now, but we are here to learn until we are of one heart and of one mind in things of this life.[35]

Joseph F. Smith said that the return to Missouri could not come before the people were prepared to go.

> . . . No man, so far as I know, can foretell the day or the hour, the month or the year when the people of God are prepared to go back, and not before. Whether it be in this generation or in the next generation, it matters not; *it will only be when the people have prepared themselves to do it by their faithfulness and obedience to the commands of God. I prophesy to you, in the name of the Lord, that when the Latter-day Saints have prepared themselves through righteousness to redeem Zion, they will accomplish that work;* for the Lord has said it shall be done, and it will be done in the due time of the Lord, when the people are prepared for it.[36]

On another occasion Brigham Young warned that the Church must hasten its preparation or the Lord would be ready for the return before the saints were.

> *Just as soon as the Latter-day Saints are ready and prepared to return to Independence, Jackson County, in the State of Missouri, North America, just so soon will the voice of the Lord be heard, "Arise now, Israel, and make your way to the centre stake of Zion."*
>
> Do you think there is any danger of our being ready before the Lord prepares the other end of the route? Do you believe that we, as Latter-day Saints, are preparing our own hearts, our own lives, to return to take possession of the centre Stake of Zion, as fast as the Lord is preparing to cleanse the land from those ungodly persons who dwell there? You can read, reflect, and make your own calculations. *If we are not very careful, the earth will be cleansed from wickedness before we are prepared to take possession of it.* We must be pure to be prepared to build up Zion. To all appearance, the Lord is preparing that end of the route faster than we are preparing ourselves to go there.[37]

---

[35]Brigham Young, *Journal of Discourses,* Vol. 11, p. 324, February 10, 1867. (Italics added)

[36]Joseph F. Smith, *Millennial Star,* Vol. 56, p. 385, June 18, 1894. (Italics added)

[37]Brigham Young, *Journal of Discourses,* Vol. 9, p. 137, July 28, 1861. (Italics added)

Wilford Woodruff explained that the Lord will give us power to accomplish his work just as fast as we prepare ourselves to receive his aid.

> We are called upon to work with the Lord just as fast as we are prepared to receive the things of his kingdom. But I am satisfied there has got to be a great change with us in many respects before we are prepared for the redemption of Zion and the building up of the New Jerusalem. I believe the only way for us is to get enough of the Spirit of God that we may see and understand our duties and comprehend the will of the Lord.[38]

And Lorenzo Snow asked:

> Do you suppose that the Lord would ever send you and me back to Jackson County until He could feel perfectly assured that we would do those things which the people of Jackson County failed to do for lack of experience and faith?[39]

Worthiness—first, last and always—is the criteria for serving the Lord and enjoying the great blessings he has prepared for his children.

All That I Have Is Thine

However, in the case of the saints turning their faces eastward and returning to Jackson County, a special kind of worthiness will be required. When the members of the Church were first sent to inhabit the land of Independence, Missouri, they were also given a law to live that was to prepare them to be a "Zion people" in a "Zion place." This law was the Law of Consecration and Stewardship, sometimes also called the United Order. It was a law designed to provide for God's children in such a way that poverty would be eliminated and all members would live together in perfect harmony and brotherhood.

To enter this order, a member of the Church had to make solemn covenants to consecrate everything to the Lord. It was evidently a failure on the part of the saints to live up to these

---

[38]Wilford Woodruff, *Journal of Discourses,* Vol. 16, p. 36, April 7, 1873.
[39]Lorenzo Snow, *Conference Report,* October, 1900, p. 62.

covenants that made them unworthy to stay and build up the city of Zion.[40]

Therefore, as Lorenzo Snow stated in the reference cited above, before the saints today can expect to return they must be willing to do more than those early saints did. In other words, anyone returning to Jackson County must be able and willing to live the principles of the Law of Consecration. This is testified to abundantly by many of the leaders of the Church. The following is just a sampling of those testimonies.

> We have had a great deal said about the United Order, and about our becoming one. And some people would wish—Oh, how they do wish, they could get around that principle, if they could! But you Latter-day Saints, you cannot get around it; you cannot dig around it; it will rise before you every step you take, for God is determined to carry out his purposes, and to build up his Zion; *and those who will not walk into line he will move out of the way and no place will be found for them in Israel. Hear it, you Latter-day Saints for I say to you in the name of Israel's God that it is a revelation from the Most High, and you cannot get around it.*[41]

> But when shall I be prepared to go there? Not while I have in my heart the love of this world more than the love of God. Not while I am possessed of that selfishness and greed that would induce me to cling to the world or my possessions in it, at the sacrifice of principle or truth. *But when I am ready to say, "Father, all that I have, myself included, is Thine; my time, my substance, everything that I possess is on the altar, to be used freely, agreeable to Thy holy will, and not my will, but Thine, be done," then per-haps I will be prepared to go and help to redeem Zion.* For Zion can only be built up by the law that God revealed for that purpose, which is the law of consecration—not the law of tithing. . . .

> *It behooves us, therefore, my brethren and sisters, to look to ourselves, turning the eye of scrutiny in upon our own souls, and to ask ourselves, "Am I preparing to help redeem Zion and to build up the waste places thereof?" "Am I shaping my conduct so that when the Lord shall call upon the people to do this, I will be one that will be chosen for the work?"*[42]

---

[40]See for example *Doctrine and Covenants* 97:21-26; 101:1-8; 103:4; 104:5-9.

[41]John Taylor, *Journal of Discourses,* Vol. 20, p. 43, August 4, 1878. (Italics added)

[42]Joseph F. Smith, *Millennial Star,* Vol. 56, pp. 385-387, June 18, 1894. (Italics added)

These are things for the Latter-day Saint and for every man and woman to think about, *and we should commence to prepare and fit ourselves for the United Order.* As far as spiritual things are concerned we are pretty well united, but when it comes to temporalities we often differ. But you will see the day, if you live properly, observe the Word of Wisdom and do that which is required, you will go back to Jackson county, many of you whom I am addressing this afternoon. I am sure of this.[43]

You may ask, in what respect we shall differ in settling up those countries when we go there to fulfill the commandments of the Lord? *I will tell you. No man in those localities will be permitted to receive a stewardship on those lands, unless he is willing to consecrate all his properties to the Lord.*[44]

Jesus will never receive the Zion of God unless its people are united according to celestial law, for all who go into the presence of God have to go there by this law. Enoch had to practice this law, and *we shall have to do the same if we are ever accepted of God as he was. It has been promised that the New Jerusalem will be built up in our day and generation, and it will have to be done by the United Order of Zion and according to celestial law.*[45]

Terror or Anticipation?

Up to this chapter, much of the prophecies have dealt with the terrible calamities which are coming upon the world. The days ahead as described by these prophecies are to be grim ones indeed, and it is little wonder that people should look upon the future with dread and uncertainty. The carnage and the bloodshed described so vividly as coming upon the United States and the world are enough to make one cry out for deliverance from such days of terror. The sentiments of the young college girl who stated that she would rather die before Christ comes so that she would not have to endure such times are understandable.

However, these chapters and the foreboding picture that they paint are not the complete story. It is true that the wicked have much reason to fear, if they do not repent.

---

[43]Lorenzo Snow, *Conference Report,* April, 1898, p. 14. (Italics added)
[44]Orson Pratt, *Journal of Discourses,* Vol. 21, p. 149, November 1, 1879. (Italics added)
[45]Wilford Woodruff, *Journal of Discourses,* Vol. 17, p. 250, October 9, 1874. (Italics added)

But this chapter and the following ones present the other half of the future scene, viz., the great blessings and experiences that await those who are prepared and waiting for the coming of the Lord. Those saints who qualify in the latter category find that the overwhelming emotion when contemplating the future is not one of terror, but rather that of anticipation.

Some would argue that the most powerful motivating factor which comes from studying the prophecies of the coming of the Lord is fear, but it is hoped that before the complete picture is finished, the reader may come to feel that poignant longing to be worthy enough to participate in the great events of these last days. For this anticipation can be an even stronger motivation than fear.

"A Land of Peace, a City of Refuge"

We Are the Favored People

What is it about the City of Zion that will inspire the saints to leave comfortable homes, that will thrust the main body of the Church from its present headquarters, that will cause vast numbers of people to risk a long and probably very hazardous journey? What enticement could cause generations of faithful members to keep their sights turned to the east? How could any location initiate such a tremendous expenditure in human toil and sacrifice? Why has the New Jerusalem been so much a part of the dreams of the Church membership for thirteen decades?

Elder George Q. Cannon, later a counselor in the First Presidency to President John Taylor, stated the answer very simply. Speaking of Zion, he said:

> We do not wish to leave this land, because it is not fertile, or because it is not a favoured land. We appreciate the home that God has given us here, so fruitful in blessings to the Saints; but *we look forward to that land with indescribable feelings, because it is the place where God has said His City shall be built.*[1]

It is hard for the finite mind to comprehend what a magnificent experience it will be to live in the City of God with a people who can be truly classified as the people of Zion—

---

[1]George Q. Cannon, *Journal of Discourses,* Vol. 11, pp. 336-337, March 3, 1867. (Italics added)

the pure in heart. Little wonder that the Lord described it in such overwhelming terms when he said:

> *And it shall be called the New Jerusalem, a land of peace, a city of refuge, a place of safety for the saints of the Most High God. . . .*
>
> And it shall come to pass that *the righteous shall be gathered out from among all nations, and shall come to Zion, singing with songs of everlasting joy.*[2]

What a special privilege it will be for those so chosen to return to the city of the Most High God and there participate in the great works necessary to prepare the world for the coming of the Lord. How blessed that generation of saints fortunate enough to witness these events. Little wonder that the person who sees prophecy in its fullest scope looks forward to that return to Jackson County with fervent longing rather than with fear or dread.

Let us now turn to the prophetic promises concerning the City of Zion so that we, too, may come to understand this great future heritage of the Church which is yet to unfold.

The Grandeur of Zion

In the parable of the redemption of Zion discussed in the previous chapter, the Lord spoke of the site for the grove of olive trees as a "very choice piece of land."[3] In August, 1831, the Prophet Joseph Smith visited the land of Zion in Jackson County, and there dedicated the temple site. In his history he wrote a description of the land as it appeared then, describing the rich soil, mild climate, shrubbery, etc. The Prophet spoke briefly of the disadvantages there, all of which were due to its uncivilized state at that time, and then went on to say:

> But all these impediments vanish when it is recollected what the Prophets have said concerning Zion in the last days; how the glory of Lebanon is to come upon her; the fir tree, the pine tree, and the box tree together, to beautify the place of His sanctuary,

---

[2]*Doctrine and Covenants* 45:66, 71. (Italics added)
[3]*Ibid.*, 101:44.

that He may make the place of His feet glorious. Where for brass, He will bring gold; and for iron, He will bring silver; and for wood, brass; and for stones, iron; and where the feast of the fat things will be given to the just; yea, when the splendor of the Lord is brought to our consideration for the good of His people, the calculations of men and the vain glory of the world vanish, and we exclaim, "Out of Zion the perfection of beauty, God hath shined."[4]

Elder Orson Pratt also described this "perfection of beauty" that would glorify the city of the Lord.

The cities and temples which we are now engaged in building, we expect to decay; we expect the rock and the various building materials will in time waste away, according to natural laws. *But when we build that great central city, the New Jerusalem, there will be no such thing as the word decay associated with it; it will not decay any more than the pot of manna which was gathered by the children of Israel and put into a sacred place in the ark of the covenant. It was preserved from year to year by the power of God;* so will he preserve the city of the New Jerusalem, the dwelling houses, the tabernacles, the Temples, etc., from the effects of storms and time.[5]

And on another occasion, he said:

Therefore, Latter-day Saints, when you return to build up the waste places of Zion, and when you build up the New Jerusalem upon the place that he has appointed, *whatever materials shall be used, by the blessing of the Priesthood, which God has ordained, these materials will endure forever: they will continue during the thousand years, without waste, and when they shall be caught up to heaven, when the earth flees away, they will still endure in all their perfection and beauty.* When these cities shall descend again upon the new earth, in its immortal and eternal state, they will still be as endurable as the earth itself, no more to be subject to the curse, and therefore, will no more waste; death is gone—everything that is corruptible in its nature has ceased, so far as this habitable globe is concerned, and all sorrow and mourning are done away.[6]

---

[4]Joseph Smith, *DHC,* Vol. 1, p. 198, August 2, 1831.
[5]Orson Pratt, *Journal of Discourses,* Vol. 21, p. 153, November 1, 1879. (Italics added)
[6]*Ibid.,* Vol. 18, p. 348, February 25, 1877. (Italics added)

President David O. McKay, who was then second counselor to President Heber J. Grant, spoke to a Brigham Young University Leadership Assembly on the subject of Zion in 1935. In the address he spoke of building Zion, both spiritually and physically. He suggests from his remarks that the City of Zion will be great, temporally as well as spiritually — a city of scientific and cultural advancement.

> If we have in mind the physical Zion, then we must strive for more fertile acres; bring from the mountains gold and silver in abundance; found factories to furnish more employment; extend in length and width our concrete public highways; build banks to protect, or to dissipate, as has been the case recently, the wealth we accumulate; transform our vast coal fields into electricity that will furnish light, heat and power to every family; improve the means of communication until with radio in our pockets we may communicate with friends and loved ones from any point at any given moment.
>
> Is it these physical phases of Zion which we are to build? *Certainly it is difficult to picture the City of Zion without at least some—if not all—such modern necessities and luxuries.*[7]

He goes on to indicate that such material conveniences are only one aspect of Zion and will accompany the children of Zion only if they are spiritually prepared.

Built by Revelation

Obviously, the city thus described by the various prophets will not be standing waiting for the saints to inhabit it, nor will such a city build itself. This is to be one of the great tasks of the saints who are privileged to return to the land of Zion. A city of such marvelous construction cannot be built after earthly patterns and the prophets have made it most evident that the Lord's servants will complete this work through revelation which he gives to them.

President Brigham Young explained that this was one of the basic reasons for the gathering of the saints that has been taking place in the Church. Until they were gathered, they

---

[7] David O. McKay, "Zion Shall Flourish," *The Improvement Era,* April, 1935, p. 229. (Italics added)

could not prepare themselves to build up Zion in all of its power and glory.

> *Not a man in all the realms and kingdoms that exist knows how to commence the foundation of the Zion of God in the latter days without revelation. If the people in the world could sanctify themselves and prepare themselves to build up Zion they might remain scattered, but they cannot, they must be gathered together to be taught, that they may sanctify themselves before the Lord and become of one heart and of one mind.*[8]

Elder Orson Pratt also spoke of the important role direct revelation will play in the building of the City of Zion. In a sermon in 1873 he said:

> *God intends to have a city built up that will never be destroyed nor overcome, but that will exist while eternity shall endure; and he will point out the pattern and show the order of architecture; he will show unto his servants the nature of the streets and the pavement thereof, the kind of precious stones that shall enter into the buildings, the nature of the rock and precious stones that will adorn the gates and the walls of that city; for the gates will be open continually* says the Prophet Isaiah, that men may bring in the force of the Gentiles. . . .
>
> Suffice it to say that *God by revelation will inspire his servants and will dictate to them the order of the buildings of that city*— the number and width of the streets, the kind of houses, the character of the Temple that is to be built therein, the kind of rock, timber and the various materials that will have to be brought from a distance to enter into the composition of that beautiful city.[9]

President John Taylor said essentially the same thing in one of the general conferences of the Church.

> *The architectural designs of those splendid edifices, cities, walls, gardens, bowers, streets, etc., will be under the direction of the Lord, who will control and manage all these matters; and the people, from the President down, will all be under the guidance and direction of the Lord in all the pursuits of human life,* until

---

[8]Brigham Young, *Journal of Discourses,* Vol. 12, p. 38, April 14, 1867. (Italics added)
[9]Orson Pratt, *Journal of Discourses,* Vol. 15, p. 365, March 9, 1873. (Italics added)

eventually they will be enabled to erect cities that will be fit to be caught up—that when Zion descends from above, Zion will also ascend from beneath, and be prepared to associate with those from above.[10]

Part of the design for the city is already known, for it was given through revelation to the Prophet Joseph Smith in 1833. The saints in Missouri were sent a city plat which included detailed instructions for laying out the city itself, and also for the building of homes, buildings, etc.[11] Although the Prophet did not explain in his history how he had received these plans, Wilford Woodruff testified later that they had been given in a vision.

> *The plan which he presented was given to him by vision,* and the future will prove that the visions of Joseph concerning Jackson County, all the various stakes of Zion and the redemption of Israel will be fulfilled in the time appointed of the Lord.[12]

It is not the purpose of the present study to consider those plans in detail, but a careful scrutiny shows clearly the inspiration behind them. Many of the ideas were later incorporated in the cities of Nauvoo, Salt Lake, and many other towns in the West. When the New Jerusalem is built it is very likely that Joseph's plans will be used once again as the model for its construction.

Built Through Effort and Obedience

The fact that the city will be built under the inspiration and revelations of God does not in any way imply that there will not be a great labor to perform. A city of such magnificence will not rise of itself. It is for this exact reason that the saints shall return to Jackson County, so that this place of refuge and peace may be built before the Savior returns as Lord of lords and King of kings.

---

[10]John Taylor, *Journal of Discourses,* Vol. 10, p. 147, April 6, 1863. (Italics added)

[11]Joseph Smith, *DHC,* Vol. 1, pp. 357-362, June 25, 1833.

[12]Wilford Woodruff, *Journal History,* April 6, 1837. (Italics added)

President Young cautioned the saints about expecting the Lord to do the work for them in building this eternal city.

> Are we prepared now to establish the Zion that the Lord designs to build up? I have many times asked the questions, "Where is the man that knows how to lay the first rock for the wall that is to surround the New Jerusalem, or the Zion of God on the earth? Where is the man who knows how to construct the first gate of the city? Where is the man who understands how to build up the kingdom of God in its purity and to prepare for Zion to come down to meet it?" "Well," says one, "I thought the Lord was going to do this." So He is if we will let Him. That is what we want; we want the people to be willing for the Lord to do it. But He will do it by means. He will not send His angels to gather the rock to build up the New Jerusalem. *He will not send His angels from the heavens to go to the mountains to cut the timber and make it into lumber to adorn the city of Zion. He has called upon us to do this work; and if we will let Him work by, through, and with us, He can accomplish it; otherwise we shall fall short, and shall never have the honor of building up Zion on the earth.* Is this so? Certainly. Well, then, let us keep the commandments[13]

President John Taylor also spoke in this vein while at a conference in Malad, Idaho, in 1881.

> Shall we build up a Zion? We shall; but we shall not, every one of us, have our own way about it. We shall feel that we need the will of God; and we shall feel that we require the Priesthood, under His direction, to guide and direct us, not men who are seeking to aggrandize themselves; but men who are seeking to build up the Church and Kingdom of God upon the earth; men of clean hands and pure hearts, every one honoring his Priesthood and magnifying it.[14]

Others to Come to Zion Besides Latter-day Saints

Sometimes as the great worthiness required of those who are to build up Zion is discussed it leaves the impression that only the members of The Church of Jesus Christ of Latter-day Saints will be privileged to live in Zion. Several state-

---

[13]Brigham Young, *Journal of Discourses,* Vol. 13, p. 313, April 7, 1870. (Italics added)
[14]John Taylor, *Journal of Discourses,* Vol. 26, p. 109, October 20, 1881.

ments by the prophets indicate that this is not so. The scripture wherein Zion is described as a place of refuge has already been cited. In that same reference, the Lord indicated that those who would not take up the sword against their neighbor would flee to this place of refuge.[15]

President Brigham Young described the freedom of religion which would exist after Zion became the ruling power in the world.

> They will ask, "If I bow the knee and confess that he is that Saviour, the Christ, to the glory of the Father, will you let me go home and be a Presbyterian?" "Yes." "And not persecute me?" "Never." "Won't you let me go home and belong to the Greek Church?" "Yes." "Will you allow me to be a Friend Quaker, or a Shaking Quaker?" "O yes, anything you wish to be, but remember that you must not persecute your neighbors, but must mind your own business, and let your neighbors alone, and let them worship the sun, moon, a white dog, or anything else they please, being mindful that every knee has got to bow and every tongue confess. When you have paid this tribute to the Most High, who created you and preserves you, you may then go and worship what you please, or do what you please, if you do not infringe upon your neighbors."[16]

President John Taylor spoke of those whose motivation would be to simply find a place where just and equitable laws were administered.

> Those who will not take up their sword to fight against their neighbor must needs flee to Zion for safety. *And they will come, saying, we do not know anything of the principles of your religion, but we perceive that you are an honest community; you administer justice and righteousness, and we want to live with you and receive the protection of your laws,* but as for your religion we will talk about that some other time. Will we protect such people? Yes, all honorable men. When the peoples shall have torn to shreds the Constitution of the United States the Elders of Israel will be found holding it up to the nations of the earth and proclaiming liberty and equal rights to all men, and extending the hand of fellowship to the oppressed of all nations. This is part of the programme, and

---

[15]*Doctrine and Covenants* 45:68.
[16]Brigham Young, *Journal of Discourses,* Vol. 2, p. 317, July 8, 1855

as long as we do what is right and fear God, he will help us and stand by us under all circumstances.[17]

Life in the City of Zion

As one considers the great prophetic promises about the New Jerusalem, one cannot help but wonder what it would be like to live in such a city. Will life consist of the normal day-to-day things which make up existence now? Will we continue to work at occupations? Go to school? Seek recreation? Such fascinating questions have fortunately been answered to some degree by the prophets of our times.

John Taylor described the city as being one of excellence in all respects, a city that would indeed be a joy to its inhabitants.

> . . . We believe that we shall rear splendid edifices, magnificent temples and beautiful cities that. shall become the pride, praise and glory of the whole earth. *We believe that this people will excel in literature, in science and the arts and in manufacture.* In fact, there will be a concentration of wisdom, not only of the combined wisdom of the world as it now exists, but men will be inspired in regard to all these matters in a manner and to an extent that they have never been before, and we shall have eventually, when the Lord's purposes are carried out, the most magnificent buildings, the most pleasant and beautiful gardens, the richest and most costly clothing, and be the most healthy and the most intellectual people that will reside upon the earth. This is part and parcel of our faith.[18]

In a discourse given in 1879, Orson Pratt explained that education would play a major role in the activities of the New Jerusalem.

> *We expect to be farmers, a great many of us. We expect to introduce all kinds of machinery and manufactures. We expect to build mills. We expect to have our merchandise and our stores and storehouses in that land.* We expect to build a great many hundred school-houses in that country, just the same as we have

---

[17]John Taylor, *Journal of Discourses,* Vol. 21, p. 8, August 31, 1879. (Italics added)
[18]John Taylor, *ibid.,* Vol. 10, p. 147, April 6, 1863. (Italics added)

already done in this country and in the two adjacent Territories, Idaho in the north and Arizona in the south. We do not calculate to neglect our children in regard to their education. We expect to build a great number of academies or the higher schools, and besides a great many school-houses. We expect to erect universities for the still higher branches to be taught. We expect to build many hundreds of meeting-houses, and we expect to be a people very densely located there—not one man taking up six or eight miles of land, and calling it his farm; we don't expect to live in that way, but we expect to settle a very dense settlement in that region of country.[19]

Such excellence will attract the attention of the learned and wise over all the earth and attract them to Zion according to both Elders Pratt and Taylor. Said President Taylor:

> When Zion is established in her beauty and honor and glory, the kings and princes of the earth will come, in order that they may get information and teach the same to their people. They will come as they came to learn the wisdom of Solomon.[20]

Elder Pratt referred to a prophecy in Isaiah that describes that light that will emanate from the city and the remarkable effect this will have on others.

> . . . That true light which is of God will be rendered visible to the eyes of all the inhabitants of that city. And shall I limit it there? No. The light will shine so conspicuously from that city, extending to the very heavens, that it will in reality be like unto a city set upon a hill that cannot be hid, and it will have quite a tendency to strike terror to all the nations of the earth. Will all see it? No, some may be too far off, beyond the ocean, to behold that miraculous light that will shine forth in this city, but I will tell you the effect it will have upon the kings, queens, rulers, congressmen and judges of the earth—they will hear of it by telegraph; the news will be flashed over the civilized nations of the earth, but they will not believe it. They will say, "Let us cross the ocean, and let us see this thing that is reported to us by telegraph; let us see whether it is so or not." Well, when they get within a day or two's journey of the city they will be alarmed. Some of these kings and nobles, when they see the light shining forth like the northern lights in the

---

[19]Orson Pratt, *Journal of Discourses,* Vol. 24, p. 23, October 26, 1879. (Italics added)

[20]John Taylor, *Journal of Discourses,* Vol. 6, p. 169, January 17, 1858.

arctic regions, illuminating the whole face of the heavens—when they see this light shining forth long before they reach the city, fear will take hold of them, says the Psalmist, in the 48th Psalm, they will become weak, and their knees will smite together like the knees of Belshazzar. They will try to haste away from the glory of God and from the power of God, and to get out of the country as soon as possible. Fear and terror will be upon them. It will have an effect upon many other kings and nobles, more pure in heart, more honest, that are willing to receive the truth; it will have a different effect upon them. . . .[21]

It will, without question, be a highly privileged people fortunate enough to live in such a city. Little wonder that an editorial quoted by the Prophet Joseph Smith said that the prophets down through history looked upon our own day "with peculiar delight."[22]

Inheritances in the Land of Zion

In the previous chapter it was made clear that the Law of Consecration and Stewardship will be the basic social order lived in New Jerusalem.[23] When the saints were driven from Jackson County they were forbidden by revelation to sell their inheritances even though they were not permitted to dwell on them at that time.[24] Not only that, but the saints were commanded to continue to purchase lands there, even after their expulsion.[25] This, the Lord explained, was so that the armies of the Lord would be justified in reclaiming the land of Zion when the time of its redemption would come.

And after these lands are purchased, I will hold the armies of Israel guiltless in taking possession of their own lands, which they have previously purchased with their moneys, and of throwing down the towers of mine enemies that may be upon them, and scattering their watchmen, and avenging me of mine enemies unto the third and fourth generation of them that hate me.[26]

---

[21]Orson Pratt, *Journal of Discourses,* Vol. 24, p. 29, October 26, 1879.
[22]Joseph Smith, *DHC,* Vol. 4, p. 609, May 2, 1842.
[23]For the revelations on the Law of Consecration see especially sections 42, 51, 58, 85, and 104 of the *Doctrine and Covenants.*
[24]*Doctrine and Covenants* 101:96-101.
[25]*Ibid.,* 105:28-29.
[26]*Ibid.,* 105:30.

Thus, evidently an important part of the return to build up Zion will be the assigning out of inheritances to the saints. In section 85 of the Doctrine and Covenants a very unusual prophecy is recorded. The Lord explained the importance of keeping a record of all those who had consecrated their properties and received legal inheritances from the bishop. Those that did not receive their inheritances through consecration were to be blotted from the records and history of the Church. Then follows the prophecy:

> And it shall come to pass that I, the Lord God, will send one mighty and strong, holding the scepter of power in his hand, clothed with light for a covering, whose mouth shall utter words, eternal words, while his bowels shall be a fountain of truth, to set in order the house of God, and to arrange by lot the inheritances of the saints whose names are found, and the names of their fathers, and of their children, enrolled in the book of the law of God;
>
> While that man, who was called of God and appointed, that putteth forth his hand to steady the ark of God, shall fall by the shaft of death, like as a tree that is smitten by the vivid shaft of lightning.[27]

Of the "one mighty and strong" more will be said shortly, but note that the inheritances are to be given out by this person to those saints whose names are found written in "the book of the law of God." According to President Joseph F. Smith, those whose names would be written in this book originally were those who were living true to the covenants they had made in the Law of Consecration. However, when the saints did not prove themselves capable of living that order, the Lord substituted the law of tithing, and so those who are now recorded in that book *are those who are faithfully paying their tithes.* This will be the basis for determining the inheritances in Zion, according to President Smith. He quotes verses 9-12 of section 85 and then states:

> This is the position the people will be in when they come to claim an inheritance in Zion, if their names are not found recorded in the book of the law of God. *And I want to tell you that this*

---

[27]*Ibid.,* 85:7-8.

refers directly to the law of tithing. In the first place it referred to the law of consecration, but that law, as has been explained, was not properly kept, and inasmuch as people are under greater condemnation when they keep not the laws that are given them, the Lord in His mercy withdrew from the Latter-day Saints the law of consecration, because the people were not prepared to live it, and as long as it was in force and they kept it not they were under condemnation. The law of tithing was given in its place.[28]

In general conference the year following President Smith's address, President Lorenzo Snow also spoke of tithing and its relationship to the Law of Consecration and of those who would receive an inheritance in the city of Zion.

Joseph tried to develop them [the saints] so that they would conform to the law of consecration, which is in advance of the law of tithing, *and is a principle which, as sure as I am speaking, you and I will one day have to conform to. When that day comes we will be prepared to go to Zion. . . .*

But there is this about it: the Latter-day Saints in these valleys have had an experience that the Saints then didn't have. We have learned that which they did not learn. They were badly persecuted and driven from the land of Zion, and as the revelation says, "But few shall stand to receive an inheritance." There are some perhaps within the sound of my voice who will receive an inheritance in Jackson county, before they pass into the next life.[29]

"The One Mighty and Strong"

Perhaps no other scripture has caused so much controversy as verses seven and eight of section 85. Down through the years many men have arisen and claimed they were "the one mighty and strong" who is to "set in order the house of God." Apostasy in the present or past leadership of the Church is generally cited by such individuals as the reason for their "special calling" and they seek to identify various presidents of the Church with the man who is "called of God" who shall "fall by the shaft of death."

Presidents Joseph Smith, Brigham Young, Wilford Woodruff (for issuing the Manifesto banning plural marriages in the

---

[28]Joseph F. Smith, *Conference Report,* October, 1899, p. 42. (Italics added)
[29]Lorenzo Snow, *Conference Report,* October, 1900, pp. 61-62. (Italics added)

Church) and nearly every other president have been identified by such apostate groups as being the fulfillment of that prophecy. Some recent groups have even claimed President McKay to be the one, although they do not explain how a man who was president for nineteen years, lived to be ninety-six, and then died peacefully in his sleep could be described as falling "like a tree that is smitten by the vivid shaft of lightning."

In 1905, the First Presidency (Joseph F. Smith, John R. Winder, and Anthon H. Lund) issued an official statement explaining the two verses in question. This was first printed in the *Deseret News* and then was reprinted two years later in *The Improvement Era*. Such a statement clears up many of the questions that have arisen, and as the beginning paragraph makes it clear, is to be viewed as an authoritative one. Space here will not permit quoting the entire statement but pertinent sections clear up the question of who is "the one mighty and strong."

> The following has been issued by the Presidency of the Church of Jesus Christ of Latter-day Saints in explanation of verses 7 and 8 of section 85 of the *Doctrine and Covenants, and is to be received as authoritative.*[30]

The two verses are quoted and then the statement goes on:

> One would think in such a matter as this that sufficient native modesty would assert itself to restrain a man from announcing himself as the one upon whom such high honors are to be conferred, and who is to exercise such great powers in establishing the Saints in their inheritances; and that even if one suspected, for any reason, that such a position, and such exceptional powers were to be conferred upon him, he would wait until the Lord would clearly indicate to the Church, as well as to himself, that he had indeed been sent of God to do the work of so noble a ministry, as is described in the passage under question. Those, however, who have so far proclaimed themselves as being the one "mighty and strong," have manifested the utmost ignorance of the things of God and the order of the Church. Indeed their insufferable ignorance and egotism have been at the bottom of all their pretensions, and the cause of

---

[30]"One Mighty and Strong," Official statement by the First Presidency, *The Improvement Era,* October, 1907, p. 929. (All italics in this statement are added)

all the trouble into which they have fallen. They seem not to have been aware of the fact that the Church of Christ and of the Saints is completely organized, and that *when the man who shall be called upon to divide unto the Saints their inheritances comes, he will be designated by the inspiration of the Lord to the proper authorities of the Church, appointed and sustained according to the order provided for the government of the Church.* So long as that Church remains in the earth—and we have the assurance from the Lord that it will now remain in the earth forever—the Saints need look for nothing of God's appointing that will be erratic, or irregular, or that smacks of starting over afresh or that would ignore or overthrow the established order of things.[31]

Some discussion is given in the statement of the speculation that has gone on in the Church concerning who the man is, indicating that the martyrdom of the Prophet Joseph has led some to suggest that it was he who fell "by the shaft of death." Then the statement explains the context in which the revelation was originally given. It was part of a letter written by Joseph Smith to William W. Phelps who was at that time living in Independence, Missouri. The entire letter to Phelps is quoted and also several revelations that substantiate the fact that Bishop Partridge was the man called to act as the Bishop in the land of Zion. Then the First Presidency continue:

This much, then, we have learned, viz., that Edward Partridge, the Bishop of the Church, was the one "called and appointed, to divide by lot unto the Saints their inheritances." *But was Edward Partridge the one in 1832 who was "putting forth his hand to steady the ark," and threatened with falling "by the shaft of death like as a tree that is smitten by the vivid shaft of lightning?"* Undoubtedly.[32]

The First Presidency go to some lengths in discussing Edward Partridge and his calling in Zion. During the Jackson County experience Bishop Partridge went through a period of apostasy, as did many other of the brethren in Missouri during those difficult days of persecution and bitter hatred. Correspondence from Joseph to these brethren attempting to alleviate the strong hostility is quoted in the statement which indicates

[31]*Ibid.,* pp. 929-931.
[32]*Ibid.,* p. 934.

that it was Bishop Partridge who was "called and appointed" and out of favor with God.

The First Presidency then indicate that Bishop Partridge went on to repent and served a faithful and noble role in the later persecutions in Northern Missouri. This repentance appeased the dissatisfaction of the Lord and the threatened punishment was avoided.

Thus, the First Presidency puts to rest all of the speculation concerning he "who is to fall by the shaft of death." They then turn their attention in this document to the other important aspect of the prophecy, viz., "the one mighty and strong." They first call attention once again to the fact that the section as originally given referred to Edward Partridge. They discuss at some length the possibility that the whole prophecy was set aside upon the repentance of the man to whom it was directed. But then they say:

> If, however, there are those who will still insist that the prophecy concerning the coming of "one mighty and strong" is still to be regarded as relating to the future, let the Latter-day Saints know that *he will be a future bishop of the Church who will be with the Saints in Jackson county, Missouri, when the Lord shall establish them in that land; and he will be so blessed with the spirit and power of his calling that he will be able to set in order the house of God, pertaining to the department of the work under his jurisdiction; and in righteousness and justice will "arrange by lot the inheritances of the Saints."* He will hold the same high and exalted station that Edward Partridge held; for the latter was called to do just this kind of work—that is, to set in order the house of God as pertaining to settling the Saints upon their inheritances. . . .
>
> This future bishop will also be called and appointed of God as Aaron of old, and as Edward Partridge was. *He will be designated by the inspiration of the Lord, and will be accepted and sustained by the whole Church, as the law of God provides. His coming will not be the result of a wild, erratic movement, or the assumption of authority by a self-appointed egotist seeking power that he may lord it over the people; God's house is one of order, and admits no such irregular procedure.*
>
> *Certainly this prophecy does not allude in any way to any President of the Church, past, present, or to come.* The revelation under consideration does not relate to matters that especially con-

cern the duties of the President of the Church: but to the arranging "by lot the inheritances of the Saints," and that is the whole substance of the revelation, a matter distinctly placed under the jurisdiction of the Bishop of the Church. . . .[33]

The Great Temple of Zion

Once the saints have returned to the center place of Zion and begin to settle into the routine of living, they will turn their hearts to one of the most remarkable projects ever undertaken by man—the building of the temple of Zion. The privilege of engaging in such a work is enough to make the mind reel, for the task will be completed with the divine help of the Lord. President Wilford Woodruff had an unusual dream in 1877 in which he saw the temple under construction and the divine help given to those engaged in building it.

> *I saw people coming from the river and from distant places to help build the Temple. It seemed as though there were hosts of angels helping to bring material for the construction of that building. Some were in Temple robes, and the pillar-like cloud continued to hover over the spot.*[34]

When the Prophet Joseph first sent the plat for the model city of Zion to the brethren in Missouri, he spent some time in describing the temple that would be built.[35] Actually, a better phrase to use would be "temple complex," for it is a series of buildings, all of which have differing purposes in the work of the Lord. Elder Orson Pratt spoke in greater detail of these various sections described by Joseph Smith.

> There will be 24 different compartments in the Temple that will be built in Jackson County. The names of these compartments were given to us some 45 or 46 years ago; the names we still have, *and when we build these 24 rooms, in a circular form and arched over the centre, we shall give the names to all these different compartments just as the Lord specified through Joseph Smith.* . . . Perhaps you may ask for what purposes these 24 compartments

---

[33]*Ibid.*, pp. 940-942.
[34]Matthias F. Cowley, *Wilford Woodruff, History of His Life and Labors,* (Bookcraft: Salt Lake City, 1964), p. 505. (Italics added)
[35]Joseph Smith, *DHC,* Vol. 1, pp. 359-362, June 25, 1833.

are to be built. I answer not to assemble the outside world in, nor to assemble the Saints all in one place, but *these buildings will be built with a special view to the different orders, or in other words the different quorums or councils of the two Priesthoods that God has ordained on the earth. That is the object of having 24 rooms so that each of these different quorums, whether they be High Priests, or Seventies, or Elders, or Bishops, or lesser Priesthood, or Teachers, or Deacons, or Patriarchs, or Apostles, or High Councils, or whatever may be the duties that are assigned to them, they will have rooms in the Temple of the Most High God, adapted, set apart, constructed, and dedicated for this special purpose.* Now, I have not only told you that we shall have these rooms, but I have told you the object of these rooms in short, not in full. But will there be any other buildings excepting those 24 rooms that are all joined together in a circular form and arched over the center—are there any other rooms that will be built—detached from the Temple? Yes. There will be tabernacles, there will be meeting houses for the assembling of the people on the Sabbath day. There will be various places of meeting so that the people may gather together: but the Temple will be dedicated to the Priesthood of the Most High God, and for most sacred and holy purposes.[36]

Elder Alvin R. Dyer also spoke of the temple in Zion and described it as an "administrative temple complex."[37]

It is evident from the various names given to the 24 compartments or separate buildings of this temple complex that there is yet much to be revealed concerning God's work during this period. But some few hints have been given by the prophets concerning some activities there.

The Prophet Joseph, for example, stated in an article on the priesthood which he wrote in 1840 that one of the things that would be restored in the time prior to Christ's coming would be the law of sacrifice. This is somewhat surprising as many people have long considered sacrifice to be part of the Mosaic law and thus done away with under Christ. But this is not so, according to the Prophet. He quotes Malachi 3:3, and then explains its significance for our day.

[36]Orson Pratt, *Journal of Discourses,* Vol. 24, pp. 24-25, October 26, 1879. (Italics added)
[37]Alvin R. Dyer, "The Center Place of Zion," (BYU Press: Provo, 1968), pp. 9-10.

These sacrifices, as well as every ordinance belonging to the Priesthood, will, when the Temple of the Lord shall be built, and the sons of Levi be purified, be fully restored and attended to in all their powers, ramifications, and blessings. This ever did and ever will exist when the powers of the Melchizedek Priesthood are sufficiently manifest; else how can the restitution of all things spoken of by the holy Prophets be brought to pass? It is not to be understood that the law of Moses will be established again with all its rites and variety of ceremonies; this has never been spoken of by the Prophets; but those things which existed prior to Moses' day, namely, sacrifice, will be continued.[38]

Most likely this restoration of sacrifices would center in the temple. Orson Pratt, as another example, spoke of the time when all of the records that Mormon and Moroni had in their trust would be transferred to the temple in Zion.

But the grand depository of all the numerous records of the ancient nations of the western continent was located in another department of the hill, and its contents under the charge of Holy angels, until the day should come for them to be transferred to the sacred temple of Zion.[39]

We Shall See Him Face to Face

In the Beatitudes given to the people in Palestine and also to the Nephites on this continent, the Savior said: "Blessed are the pure in heart: for they shall see God."[40] The implications of that scripture have been much discussed in the Church and out, but one of the most exciting implications is brought to mind when that statement is coupled with another of the Lord's. "Blessed are the pure in heart: for they shall see God," and "For this is Zion—THE PURE IN HEART."[41]

One of the most sublime of all privileges awaiting those worthy enough to participate in the building of Zion is the promise that they shall be visited by the Savior in all of his glory and majesty. What a staggering thought that the saints there might be privileged to see and converse with the Savior!

[38]Joseph Smith, *DHC*, Vol. 4, pp. 211-212, October 5, 1840. (Italics added)
[39]Orson Pratt, *Millennial Star*, Vol. 28, p. 417, July 7, 1866. (Italics added)
[40]Matthew 5:8; 3 Nephi 12:8.
[41]*Doctrine and Covenants* 97:21.

Brigham Young testified that those so blessed, even though they would be comparatively few, would see him face to face.

> Jesus has been upon the earth a great many more times than you are aware of. When Jesus makes his next appearance upon the earth, but few of this Church will be prepared to receive him and *see him face to face and converse with him; but he will come to his temple.*[42]

Orson Pratt explained that a change would have to be wrought in the faithful before they could endure the presence of Christ, but then they would be able to stand in his presence and behold his face.

> . . . *All of them who are pure in heart will behold the face of the Lord and that too before he comes in his glory in the clouds of heaven, for he will suddenly come to his Temple,* and he will purify the sons of Moses and of Aaron, until they shall be prepared to offer in that Temple an offering that shall be acceptable in the sight of the Lord. *In doing this, he will purify not only the minds of the Priesthood in that Temple, but he will purify their bodies until they shall be quickened, renewed and strengthened, and they will be partially changed, not to immortality, but changed in part that they can be filled with the power of God, and they can stand in the presence of Jesus, and behold his face in the midst of that Temple.*[43]

Charles W. Penrose, of the First Presidency, described it as an opportunity which the Lord would use to instruct his faithful saints in the building of his kingdom.

> They [the saints] will come to the Temple prepared for him, and his faithful people will behold his face, hear his voice, and gaze upon his glory. *From his own lips they will receive further instructions for the development and beautifying of Zion and for the extension and sure stability of his Kingdom.*[44]

---

[42]Brigham Young, *Journal of Discourses,* Vol. 7, p. 142, May 22, 1859. (Italics added)

[43]Orson Pratt, *Journal of Discourses,* Vol. 15, pp. 365-366, March 9, 1873. (Italics added)

[44]Charles W. Penrose, *Millennial Star,* Vol. 21, pp. 582-583, September 10, 1859. (Italics added)

President Lorenzo Snow, who had himself seen the Savior in the Salt Lake Temple, spoke of this future appearance as being a most personal and thrilling experience and even suggested that some might be privileged to invite the Master into their homes for a visit. Speaking to a reunion of priesthood authorities of the Weber Stake just a short time before his death, he said:

> Many of you will be living in Jackson County and there you will be assisting in building the Temple; *and if you will not have seen the Lord Jesus at that time you may expect Him very soon, to see Him, to eat and drink with Him, to shake hands with Him and to invite Him to your houses as He was invited when He was here before. I am saying things to you now, which I know something of the truth of them.*[45]

The Greek word which is translated "blessed" in the New Testament, means literally "happy." And how better could it be summed up than that? Happy are the pure in heart—the people of Zion—for they shall see God.

Seek to Be Found Worthy

Now it becomes more evident why The Church of Jesus Christ of Latter-day Saints looks to Missouri with eager eyes and joyful hearts. When the blessings of those who dwell in Zion are enumerated, what heart does not long to join with that chosen company? The desire to repent in order to escape the fearful judgments of God is swallowed up in the poignant longing to be found worthy for such distinctive blessings. How accurately the Lord predicts the feelings of the heart when he says: "And it shall come to pass that the righteous shall be gathered out from all nations, and shall come to Zion, singing with songs of everlasting joy."[46]

---

[45]Lorenzo Snow, *Deseret News,* June 15, 1901, p. 1. (Italics added)
[46]*Doctrine and Covenants* 45:71.

The Hour Approaches

As the righteous begin to gather to Zion with songs of everlasting joy and the great city's construction is undertaken, those who are eagerly watching the signs of the times may know that the hour of the coming of the Lord is drawing near. However, the building of the New Jerusalem will not signal the end of the world as we know it, but will only indicate that the final preparations are about to begin. From the prophetic promises which have been given through scripture and the living oracles, it is clear that there are other signs of the times which must also be fulfilled before Christ can come to claim his kingdom.

Of these harbingers, five are of such significance that a large body of prophecy has accrued concerning their eventual fulfillment. Although it is difficult to place any chronological order to their occurrence, the prophets have spoken of them in such a way that it seems apparent that they will take place either during the establishment of Zion or shortly thereafter.

These five important events are (1) the establishment of the kingdom of God, (2) the restoration of the Lamanite peoples, (3) the return of the lost tribes of Israel, (4) the great council that is to take place at Adam-ondi-Ahman, and (5) the last great missionary call to all the world. The order in which they will be treated in this chapter is an arbitrary one and in no way is meant to imply that this will be the order of their fulfillment.

THE KINGDOM OF GOD

Some six hundred years before the Savior came to earth, one of the great Old Testament prophets was called upon to interpret a dream of Nebuchadnezzar, king of Babylon. The king had forgotten what the content of the dream was, and when his astrologers and soothsayers could not tell him he swore in his wrath that all the wise men of Babylon should die. Daniel and three other Hebrew slaves had been especially selected to be trained in the learning of the Babylonians, so they, too, were classed as part of the "wise men" and came under the sentence of death. Daniel appealed to the Lord for help, and then gained audience with the king to reveal the dream and its interpretation.[1]

The dream is one of great significance, for Daniel was told by the Lord that before the king had gone to sleep that night he had been troubled about what should come to pass in the future. The Lord responded by giving Nebuchadnezzar a dream symbolizing "what shall be in the latter days."[2] Then Daniel told the king of the great image he had seen in his dream, an image with head of gold, breast and arms of silver, belly and thighs of brass, legs of iron, and feet of iron and clay. Then in the dream the king saw a stone cut out from a mountain without hands that smote the feet of the great image and broke it into pieces.[3]

Interpreting the dream, Daniel explained that the differing ingredients of the statue represented various kingdoms which would come out of Nebuchadnezzar's own kingdom which was symbolized by the head of gold.[4] Then Daniel explained to the king the significance of the stone breaking the image into pieces. "And in the days of these kings [represented by the toes of iron and clay] shall the God of heaven set up a kingdom, which shall never be destroyed: and the kingdom shall not be left to other people, but it shall break

---

[1]Daniel 2:1-26.
[2]*Ibid.*, 2:28-29.
[3]*Ibid.*, 2:31-35.
[4]*Ibid.*, 2:36-45.

in pieces and consume all these kingdoms, and it shall stand forever."[5]

It is one of the beliefs of the Mormon faith that The Church of Jesus Christ of Latter-day Saints is that kingdom which Daniel foresaw more than two thousand years ago. Through the restoration of the authority of God through the Prophet Joseph Smith the kingdom was cut out of the mountain "without hands," i.e., it is not man-made, and is rolling forth to fill the whole earth.

The prophets of this dispensation have abundantly testified that the Church is the kingdom of God. At present this kingdom is only ecclesiastical but in the future it will be a political one also. In 1866, for example, President Brigham Young bore witness that the Church is the kingdom which Daniel saw.

> It may be asked what I mean by the kingdom of God. The Church of Jesus Christ has been established now for many years, and the kingdom of God has got to be established, even that kingdom which will circumscribe all the kingdoms of this world. It will yet give laws to every nation that exists upon the earth. *This is the kingdom that Daniel, the prophet, saw should be set up in the last days.*[6]

In our own time, President Joseph Fielding Smith stated this fact very clearly.

> Now, let us speak plainly and clearly in relation to this remarkable vision and Daniel's interpretation.
>
> *This great kingdom is verily the Church of Jesus Christ,* which has been established in the earth for the last time. It is not to be destroyed but is to continue to endure and increase until it shall fill the earth in the due time of the Lord. . . .
>
> This remarkable prophetic vision that was interpreted by Daniel is bound to be fulfilled. The Lord set up his kingdom, or divine Church, through the ministry of the Prophet Joseph Smith. *The stone cut out of the mountain is indeed The Church of Jesus*

---

[5]*Ibid.,* 2:44.
[6]Brigham Young, *Journal of Discourses,* Vol. 11, p. 275, December 23, 1866. (Italics added)

Christ of Latter-day Saints, which is to endure through all time, or "stand forever."[7]

On another occasion Brigham Young explained that the political aspects of the kingdom would act as a shield and protection to the ecclesiastical Church.

> The Church of Jesus Christ will produce this government, and cause it to grow and spread, and it will be a shield round about the Church. And under the influence and power of the Kingdom of God, the Church of God will rest secure and dwell in safety, without taking the trouble of governing and controlling the whole earth. The Kingdom of God will do this, it will control the kingdoms of the world. . . .

> And you may pile on state after state, and kingdom after kingdom, and all hell on top, and we will roll on the Kingdom of our God, gather out the seed of Abraham, build the cities and temples of Zion, and establish the Kingdom of God to bear rule over all the earth, and let the oppressed of all nations go free.[8]

In 1859, Charles W. Penrose wrote an article entitled "The Second Advent" wherein he discussed the signs of the times and the coming of the Lord. He spoke of those who would embrace the gospel and be led to forsake the erroneous traditions of their fathers and become part of the people of God. Then he went on to say:

> Of necessity some form of government must be set up among them, as they will exist in a national as well as an ecclesiastical capacity. This government will be a theocracy, or, in other words, the kingdom of God. The laws, ordinances, regulations, etc., will be under the direction of God's priesthood, and the people will progress in arts, sciences, and everything that will produce happiness, promote union, and establish them in strength, righteousness, and everlasting peace.[9]

The kingdom of God was a favorite theme of President John Taylor, and he spoke of it often. He, too, makes it clear

---

[7]Joseph Fielding Smith, "What Is the Status of the 'Fundamentalists'?", *The Improvement Era*, February, 1967, p. 4. (Italics added)

[8]Brigham Young, *Journal of Discourses*, Vol. 2, p. 317, July 8, 1855. (Italics added)

[9]Charles W. Penrose, "The Second Advent," *Millennial Star*, Vol. 21, p. 582, September 10, 1859.

that this kingdom will have this dual capacity.

> But not only will the everlasting Gospel be again restored, and be preached in its fulness as formerly, and go as a messenger to all the world; not only will there be a spiritual kingdom and organization; but *there will also be a literal kingdom,* a nation, or nations, a Zion, and the people will gather to that.[10]

In the same work which he entitled *The Government of God,* after saying that the kingdom would be literally established on the earth, President Taylor continued:

> The Lord will be king over all the earth, and all mankind literally under his sovereignty, and every nation under the heavens will have to acknowledge his authority, and bow to his sceptre. Those who serve him in righteousness will have communications with God, and with Jesus; will have the ministering of angels, and will know the past, the present, and the future.[11]

Obviously, as President Taylor indicates, such a kingdom will be a marvelous blessing to those so privileged to live under its jurisdiction.

The Kingdom of God Will Govern All People

President Taylor spoke of those who served God in righteousness and the blessings that would come to them because of it. This implies that there are some who will not so serve him. Others of the prophets have made it clear that this is true in the spiritual sense, that is, not all people at that time will be members of the Church of Jesus Christ, but all people will be subject to this kingdom in the political sense.

Brigham Young, for instance, made it very explicit that it is an error to suppose that all people will belong to the Church.

> If the Latter-day Saints think, when the kingdom of God is established on the earth, that all the inhabitants of the earth will

---

[10]John Taylor, *The Government of God,* (S. W. Richards: Liverpool, England, 1852), p. 97. (Italics added)

[11]*Ibid.,* pp. 87-88.

join the church called Latter-day Saints, they are egregiously mistaken. I presume there will be as many sects and parties then as now. Still, when the kingdom of God triumphs, every knee shall bow and every tongue confess that Jesus is the Christ, to the glory of the Father. Even the Jews will do it then; but will the Jews and Gentiles be obliged to belong to the Church of Jesus Christ of Latter-day Saints? No; not by any means.[12]

More recently President Joseph Fielding Smith explained the relationship between the two aspects of the kingdom and how the people of the world would be affected by them.

After Christ comes, all the peoples of the earth will be subject to him, but there will be multitudes of people on the face of the earth who will not be members of the Church; yet all will have to be obedient to the laws of the kingdom of God, for it will have dominion upon the whole face of the earth. These people will be subject to the *political government,* even though they are not members of the *ecclesiastical kingdom which is the Church.*

This government which embraces all the peoples of the earth, both in and out of the Church, is also sometimes spoken of as the kingdom of God, because the people are subject to the kingdom of God which Christ will set up; but they have their agency and thousands will not be members of the Church until they are converted; yet at the same time they will be subject to the theocratic rule.[13]

What Is "The Kingdom of God"?

As President Joseph Fielding Smith pointed out, sometimes both the political kingdom and the ecclesiastical kingdom are called the "kingdom of God," and confusion may result. One of the great scholars of the Church, Brigham H. Roberts, who was also a member of the First Council of Seventy, explained in a footnote to the last volume of the *History of the Church* that sometimes the scriptures use the terms "Church of God," and "Kingdom of God," interchangeably. However, this does not mean that the Church and the political kingdom

---

[12]Brigham Young, *Journal of Discourses,* Vol. 11, p. 275, December 23, 1866. (Italics added)

[13]Joseph Fielding Smith, *Doctrines of Salvation* (Bruce R. McConkie, comp.), Vol. 1, (Bookcraft: Salt Lake City, 1954) p. 229. (Italics are partially in original and partially added)

are the same, even though they may both sometimes be referred to as the "kingdom of God." Roberts cites George Q. Cannon and then summarizes.

> The late President George Q. Cannon while editor of the *Juvenile Instructor* said: "We are asked, Is the Church of God, and the Kingdom of God the same organization? and we are informed that some of the brethren hold that they are separate.
>
> "This is the correct view to take. *The Kingdom of God is a separate organization from the Church of God. There may be men acting as officers in the Kingdom of God who will not be members of the Church of Jesus Christ of Latter-day Saints.* On this point the Prophet gave particular instructions before his death, and gave an example, which he asked the younger elders who were present to always remember. It was to the effect that men might be chosen to officiate as members of the Kingdom of God who had no standing in the Church of Jesus Christ of Latter-day Saints. *The Kingdom of God when established will not be for the protection of the Church of Jesus Christ of Latter-day Saints alone, but for the protection of all men, whatever their religious views or opinions may be. Under its rule, no one will be permitted to overstep the proper bounds or to interfere with the rights of others. . . ."*
>
> However, it is proper to note that sometimes these terms "the Church of Christ," "the Kingdom of God" and "the Kingdom of Heaven" are used interchangeably in the scriptures and hence the confusion in these terms sometimes obtains.[14]

Part of the confusion arises because the political kingdom grows out of the Church, and is centered around Christ, but as one can see from this note the political kingdom involves more than just the Church. In the same discourse cited above, President Joseph Fielding Smith goes on to make this point evident.

> When our Saviour comes to rule in the millennium, all governments will become subject unto his government, and this has been referred to as the Kingdom of God, which it is; but this is the *political kingdom* which *will embrace all people whether they are in the Church or not.* Of course, when every kindred, tongue and people become subject to the rule of Jesus Christ such will be

---

[14]Note by Brigham H. Roberts, *DHC*, Vol. 7, p. 382. (Italics added)

in that political kingdom. We must keep these two thoughts in mind. *But the kingdom of God is the Church of Jesus Christ, and it is the kingdom that shall endure forever. . . .*

When Christ comes, the political kingdom will be given to the Church. [Here President Smith cites Daniel 7:27] The Lord is going to make an *end* to all nations; that means this nation as well as any other. The kingdom of God is the Church, but during the millennium, the multitudes upon the face of the earth who are not in the Church will have to be governed, and many of *their officers,* who will be elected, may not be members of the Church.[15]

The reader need not be overly concerned with the shades of differences in the various meanings, but should be aware that the terms are used to signify different things at different times, and should be read in context of the quote. The important thing to remember is that the kingdom will be set up, both religiously and politically, and all things will center in Christ, the King.

A Theocracy

In ancient Greece, *theos* was the word for God, and the infinitive "to rule" was *kratein.* Thus, the Greeks formed a word—*theokratia*—which meant, literally, "God rules." That is the present meaning of the word "theocracy" which we borrowed from the Greeks. Once the kingdom of God—in the political sense—is established upon the earth it shall be a true theocracy, a government where God rules. Christ will be the head of the government and all laws will emanate from him. Such a government would incorporate many democratic principles, but the authority will lie in that holy and perfect being who earned, by right of his divine sacrifice and perfect life, the title of "King of kings, and Lord of lords."

President Young described this form of government in glowing terms.

When the kingdom of God is established upon the earth, people will find it to be very different from what they now imagine. Will it

---

[15]Joseph Fielding Smith, *op. cit.,* pp. 229-230. (Italics in original)

be in the least degree tyrannical and oppressive towards any human being? No, it will not; for such is not the kingdom of God.

I believe in a true republican theocracy, and also in a true democratic theocracy, as the term democratic is now used; for they are to me, in their present use, convertible terms.

What do I understand by a theocratic government? *One in which all laws are enacted and executed in righteousness, and whose officers possess that power which proceedeth from the Almighty.* That is the kind of government I allude to when I speak of a theocratic government, or the kingdom of God upon the Earth. It is, in short, the eternal powers of the Gods.[16]

When one contemplates the billions of peoples down through history who have wept and suffered and died under the hands of unrighteous and cruel leaders, it is not difficult to comprehend why the setting up of the government of God is one of the great signs of the times and a necessary step for the ushering in of the millennial era.

To Blossom as the Rose

Another of the great signs that will herald the approaching end concerns the restoration of the Lamanite people. Undoubtedly, that work has now been undertaken by The Church of Jesus Christ of Latter-day Saints, and like the return of the Jews to Palestine, is in the process of being fulfilled.

This great work actually commenced before the Church was organized with the translation of the Book of Mormon. This ancient record was written especially so that it could be brought forth in the latter days to the Lamanite people. Shortly after the work of translation had begun, Joseph Smith foolishly yielded to the pressure of Martin Harris and allowed him to take the 116 pages of manuscript they had completed thus far to show his family and friends. The sacred pages were lost and the young prophet was severely chastised by the Lord. In that message of rebuke, now recorded in section 3 of the Doctrine and Covenants, the Lord stated that the Book of

---

[16]Brigham Young, *Journal of Discourses,* Vol. 6, pp. 346-347, July 31, 1859. (Italics added)

Mormon was to be a major tool in bringing about the restoration of the Lamanites—a people who had sunk to such a level that they were commonly called "the American Aborigines."

> *And for this very purpose are these plates preserved, which contain these records*—that the promises of the Lord might be fulfilled, which he made to his people;
>
> *And that the Lamanites might come to a knowledge of their fathers, and that they might know the promises of the Lord, and that they may believe the gospel and rely upon the merits of Jesus Christ,* and be glorified through faith in his name, and that through their repentance they might be saved.[17]

The very title page of the Book of Mormon states the same purpose and in many other places throughout the book it is reiterated.[18] As "Gentiles" who have been greatly blessed by the Book of Mormon, members of the Church should recognize that they have a great obligation to help bring about the great promises of the Lord to his people.

The Savior, himself, foretold that the Gentiles would be established in the land of America and be the means of bringing the word to the remnant of Israel left in the land.[19] And several Book of Mormon prophets described this future work of the Gentiles as being like unto nursing fathers and mothers.

> And after our seed is scattered the Lord God will proceed to do a marvelous work among the Gentiles, which shall be of great worth unto our seed; *wherefore, it is likened unto being nourished by the Gentiles and being carried in their arms and upon their shoulders.*[20]

The latter-day prophets have abundantly testified of the coming reclamation of this downtrodden remnant of the House of Israel and of the role that the Church of Jesus Christ will play in that restoration. Through the Prophet Joseph Smith,

[17]*Doctrine and Covenants* 3:19-20. (Italics added)
[18]For examples see Enos 11-18; Jarom 2; 2 Nephi 3:19-20; Mormon 7:1-9; Moroni 1:4.
[19]3 Nephi 21:4-6.
[20]1 Nephi 22:6, 8. (Italics added) See also 2 Nephi 10:9, 18.

the Lord emphatically declared: "But before the great day of the Lord shall come, Jacob shall flourish in the wilderness, *and the Lamanites shall blossom as the rose.*"[21] Wilford Woodruff recalled the time when Joseph said:

> It is only a handful of priesthood you see here tonight, but this Church will fill North and South America—it will fill the world.

> It will fill the Rocky Mountains. There will be tens of thousands of Latter-day Saints who will be gathered in the Rocky Mountains, and there they will open the door for the establishing of the gospel *among the Lamanites, who will receive the gospel and their endowments and blessings of God.*[22]

On another occasion, the Prophet Joseph said:

> . . . One of the most important points in the faith of the Church of the Latter-day Saints, through the fulness of the everlasting Gospel, is the gathering of Israel (*of whom the Lamanites constitute a part*) that happy time when Jacob shall go up to the house of the Lord, to worship Him in spirit and in truth, to live in holiness. . . .[23]

In 1845, the Twelve Apostles wrote a proclamation to all the leaders of the nations of the world. It is a very unusual document and foretells the great destiny of the Church in preparing the world for the coming of the Lord. The future destiny of the Lamanites was foretold by these men in some detail.

> He will assemble the natives, the remnants of Joseph in America, and make of them a great, and strong and powerful nation; and he will civilize and enlighten them, and will establish a holy city, and temple, and seat of government among them, which shall be called Zion. . . .

> The despised and degraded son of the forest, who has wandered in dejection and sorrow, and suffered reproach, shall then drop his disguise and stand forth in manly dignity, and exclaim to the Gentiles who have envied and sold him—"I am Joseph;

---

[21]*Doctrine and Covenants* 49:24. (Italics added)
[22]Wilford Woodruff, *Conference Report,* April, 1898, p. 57. (Italics added)
[23]Joseph Smith, *DHC,* Vol. 2, p. 357, January 6, 1836. (Italics added)

does my father yet live?" or, in other words, I am a descendant of that Joseph who was sold into Egypt. You have hated me, and sold me, and thought I was dead; but lo! I live and am heir to the inheritance, titles, honours, priesthood, sceptre, crown, throne, and eternal life and dignity of my fathers, who live for evermore.

He shall then be ordained, washed, anointed with holy oil, and arrayed in fine linen, even in the glorious and beautiful garments and royal robes of the high priesthood, which is after the order of the Son of God; and shall enter into the congregation of the Lord, even into the Holy of Holies, there to be crowned with authority and power which shall never end.

The spirit of the Lord shall then descend upon him like the dew upon the mountains of Hermon, and like refreshing showers of rain upon the flowers of Paradise.

His heart shall expand with knowledge, wide as eternity, and his mind shall comprehend the vast creations of his God, and his eternal purpose of redemption, glory, and exaltation, which was devised in heaven before the worlds were organized; but made manifest in these last days, for the fulness of the Gentiles, and for the exaltation of Israel.

He shall also behold his Redeemer, and be filled with his presence, while the cloud of his glory shall be seen in his temple.[21]

Elder Spencer W. Kimball, an apostle who has labored much among the Lamanite people, spoke of the great improvements that would come upon this people once they began to accept the gospel of Jesus Christ.

Historians have written about your past; poets have sung of your possibilities; prophets have predicted your scattering and your gathering; and your Lord has permitted you to walk through the dark chasms of your ancestor's making, but has patiently waited for your awakening, and now smiles on your florescence, and points the way to your glorious future as sons and daughters of God. You will arise from your bed of affliction and from your condition of deprivation if you will accept fully the Lord, Jesus Christ, and his total program. You will rise to former heights in culture and education, influence and power. You will blossom as the rose upon the mountains. Your daughters will be nurses, teachers, and social

---

[21]"Proclamation of the Twelve Apostles of the Church of Jesus Christ of Latter-day Saints," October 22, 1845, pp. 8-10. Note: This Proclamation is included in Vol. 6 of the *Millennial Star* at the end of the volume, but the page numbers are separate. (Italics added)

workers, and, above all, beloved wives and full-of-faith mothers of a righteous posterity.

Your sons will compete in art, literature, and medicine, in law, architecture, etc. They will become professional, industrial and business leaders, and statesmen of the first order. *Together you and we shall build in the spectacular city of New Jerusalem the temple to which our Redeemer will come.* Your hands with ours, also those of Jacob, will place the foundation stones, raise the walls, and roof the magnificent structure. Perhaps your artistic hands will paint the temple and decorate it with a master's touch, and together we shall dedicate to our Creator Lord the most beautiful of all temples ever built in his name.[25]

Nourished by the Gentiles

As was indicated above, the prophecies in the Book of Mormon speak of the important role the Gentiles will have in bringing about the purposes of the Lord in respect to the remnant of Jacob. Part of that could refer to the role the United States government has played in the care of the American Indian, but a greater part of the prophecies are to be fulfilled by the Church of Jesus Christ and its members. Elder Kimball spoke of when the members of the Church would work side-by-side with the Lamanites to accomplish great works. Earlier presidents of the Church explicitly described the responsibility that rests on the saints to bring about these future conditions. President John Taylor put it most unequivocally when he said: *"The work of the Lord among the Lamanites must not be postponed, if we desire to retain the approval of God. . . ."*[26] Wilford Woodruff stated that he was speaking by the power of the Holy Ghost when he said: "Those who will feed and clothe these Lamanites and see to their wants, as our President has told us, they shall be blessed and prosper, *while those who despise them shall go down and shall not stand in the kingdom of God."*[27]

---

[25]Spencer W. Kimball, "To You, Our Kinsmen," *The Improvement Era,* December, 1959, pp. 938-939. (Italics added)

[26]John Taylor, *Millennial Star,* Vol. 44, p. 733, October 18, 1882. (Italics added)

[27]Wilford Woodruff, *Journal of Discourses,* Vol. 9, p. 222, July 15, 1855. (Italics added)

This nourishing role of the Church in the restoration of the Lamanites was described by Spencer W. Kimball in a picturesque analogy of a glider plane and a tow plane, the sailplane—the Lamanite—being given the initial lift by the tow plane of the Church and its people.[28]

It is an exciting concept to see the future of this people who for so long have been despised and rejected; even more fascinating is to imagine one's own possible role in the fulfillment of such prophecies.

As a Young Lion

If, however, the Gentiles do not fulfill their responsibilities to these downtrodden people, another prophetic promise shall come into play, namely, the destruction of the Gentile nations. The Lord made it clear to the Nephites when he visited among them that if the Gentiles did not repent they would be destroyed *by a remnant of the people to which he was speaking!*

> And I say unto you, that *if the Gentiles do not repent,* after the blessings which they shall receive, after they have scattered my people—
>
> *Then shall ye, who are a remnant of the house of Jacob, go forth among them; and ye shall be in the midst of them who shall be many; and ye shall be among them as a lion among the beasts of the forest, and as a young lion among the flocks of sheep, who, if he goeth through both treadeth down and teareth in pieces, and none can deliver.*[29]

In the Doctrine and Covenants the great prophecy on war found in section 87 speaks again of this remnant and their future conflict with the Gentiles. "And it shall come to pass also that the remnants who are left of the land will marshal themselves, and shall become exceedingly angry, and shall vex the Gentiles with a sore vexation."[30] This remnant may include other parts of the House of Israel besides the descend-

---

[28]Spencer W. Kimball, "The Lamanites: Their Burden—Our Burden," an address given to the Brigham Young University, April 25, 1967, (BYU Press: Provo, Utah, 1967), pp. 15-16.

[29]3 Nephi 20:15-16. (Italics added)

[30]*Doctrine and Covenants* 87:5.

ants of Lehi, but that they are included as part of that group seems clearly indicated. Joseph Smith, for example, in the dedicatory prayer on the Kirtland Temple, spoke of them in terms that clearly suggest the Indian peoples.[31] And Daniel H. Wells, of the First Presidency under Brigham Young, was even more explicit.

> There are some very important portions of this prophecy, [section 87] however, which yet remain to be fulfilled. To add to the sufferings and great calamities of the American nation, *they will be greatly distressed by the aborigines,* who will "marshall themselves, and become exceeding angry," and vex them "with a sore vexation." This event, we believe, may not take place in its fulness until the nation has been greatly weakened by the death of millions in their own revolutionary battles. To what extent the Indians will have power over the nation is not stated in this revelation; but from what Jesus informed their forefathers at the time of his personal ministry among them, as recorded in the Book of Mormon, they will have power in a great measure of the whole nation. . . . [He then quotes 3 Nephi 9:8-12 and also cites other *Book of Mormon* references] . . . . It appears more improbable, now, to the people of the United States, that the Indians should ever become so powerful an enemy and so dreadful a scourge to them, than it did before the commencement of the rebellion, [the Civil War] that they would ever engage in so dreadful a civil war as that now raging. Yet this will as surely be fulfilled as have the other portions of the prophecy.[32]

Evidently, this is not the remnant of the Lamanites that are converted to the gospel and participate with the members of the Church in the building up of Zion; rather, they seem to be a majority of the Lamanites which have not yet come into the gospel fold. Orson Pratt explained it in this manner:

> Do not misunderstand me, do not think that all the Lamanite tribes are going to be converted and receive this great degree of education and civilization before we can return to Jackson County. Do not think this for a moment, it will only be a remnant; for when we have laid the foundation of that city and have built a portion of it, and have built a Temple therein, there is another

---

[31]*Ibid.,* 109:65.
[32]Daniel H. Wells, *Millennial Star,* Vol. 27, pp. 186-187, March 25, 1865. (Italics added)

work which we have got to do in connection with these remnants of Jacob whom we shall assist in building the city. What is it? *We have got to be sent forth as missionaries to all parts of this American continent. Not to the Gentiles, for their times will be fulfilled; but we must go to all those tribes that roam through the cold regions of the north—British America, to all the tribes that dwell in the Territories of the United States, also to all those who are scattered through Mexico, and Central and South America, and the object of our going will be to declare the principles of the Gospel unto them, and bring them to a knowledge of the truth.* "Then shall they assist my people who are scattered on all the face of the land, that they may be gathered in to the New Jerusalem."[33]

Earlier, Elder Pratt stated:

It is true, so says the Book of Mormon, that inasmuch as the Gentiles receive the Gospel, they shall assist my people the remnant of Jacob, saith the Lord, to build the New Jerusalem. And when they have got it built, then we are told that they shall assist my people who are of Jacob to be gathered unto the New Jerusalem.

Only a few thousand or hundreds of thousands, then, are to be engaged in this work, and then, *after it is done, we are to assist the Lamanites to gather in;* and then shall the powers of heaven be in your midst; and then is the coming of Christ.[34]

It is a distinct possibility, then, that the descendants of Lehi shall play a major role in the wars and destruction that will rage in the United States and other countries and with such ferocity that they are vividly described as being like a lion rampaging through a flock of sheep. Such is the promise if the Gentiles do not repent.

Building the City and the Temple with the Lamanites

The statement of the Savior concerning the future of the unrepentant Gentiles is grim, but likewise is the promise a glorious one to those Gentiles who do repent.

But *if they will repent* and hearken unto my words, and harden not their hearts, I will establish my church among them, and they

[33]Orson Pratt, *Journal of Discourses,* Vol. 17, p. 301, February 7, 1875. (Italics added)
[34]*Ibid.,* Vol. 3, p. 18, May 20, 1855. (Italics added)

shall come in unto the covenant and be numbered among this remnant of Jacob, unto whom I have given this land for their inheritance;

And they shall assist my people, the remnant of Jacob, and also as many of the house of Israel as shall come, that they may build a city, which shall be called the New Jerusalem.[35]

Several of the prophets quoted above have referred to the partnership of the Lamanites and the Church in building the city of Zion and the temple there. Lorenzo Snow also referred to it in a general conference address shortly before his death. He had been speaking about some of the apostate groups then living in Jackson County, Missouri, and then said:

. . . The time is arriving when that Temple should be built, but it will not be built by that class of people [the Josephites and Hedrickites]. It will be built by the Latter-day Saints *in connection with the Lamanites.*[36]

What grand and glorious fulfillment of the promises of the Lord, that this people so long despised of men should have the privilege of engaging in this great work of the last days!

As one reads through the prophecies concerning the "remnant of Jacob" and the future destiny of the Lamanites, there is one point that may be misinterpreted. Many people have assumed that the "remnant of Jacob" spoken of by the Lord during his visit to the Nephites must refer exclusively to the descendants of Lehi which would, of course, be the Lamanites. But as was indicated above, even though the evidence is clear that the Lamanites form a part of this group known as the "remnant of Jacob," that does not imply that they alone constitute the remnant. When the prophets speak of the Church assisting the Lamanites in the building of Zion, some picture, because of this misconception, the members of the Church taking a secondary role once "Israel gets back in the driver's seat."

President Joseph Fielding Smith has discussed the scriptures from which this concept comes. He clearly shows that

---

[35]3 Nephi 21:22-23. (Italics added)
[36]Lorenzo Snow, *Conference Report,* October, 1900, p. 63. (Italics added)

the intent of these passages is broader than many think. He explains that the whole house of Israel who have been scattered qualify as being a part of the "remnant of Jacob" and will all be gathered in and assist in the building of Zion and the other great works of the last great day of preparation.[37] The Lamanites constitute a definite part of this promise, but so do members of the Church, according to President Smith.

> I take it we, the members of the Church, most of us of the tribe of Ephraim, are of the remnant of Jacob. We know it to be the fact that the Lord called upon the descendants of *Ephraim to commence his work* in the earth in these last days. We know further that he has said that he set Ephraim, according to the promises of his birthright, at the head. Ephraim receives the *"richer blessings,"* these blessings being those of *presidency* or *direction. The keys are with Ephraim.* It is Ephraim who is to be endowed with *power to bless and give to the other tribes, including the Lamanites,* their blessings. All the other tribes of Jacob, including the Lamanites, are to be crowned with glory in Zion *by the hands of Ephraim.*
>
> Now do the scriptures teach that Ephraim, after doing all of this is to abdicate, or relinquish his place, and give it to the Lamanites and then receive orders from this branch of the "remnant of Jacob" in the building of the New Jerusalem? This certainly is inconsistent with the whole plan and with all that the Lord has revealed in the *Doctrine and Covenants* in relation to the establishment of Zion and the building of the New Jerusalem. . . .
>
> That the remnants of Joseph, found among the descendants of Lehi, will have *part* in this great work is certainly consistent, and the great work of this restoration, the building of the temple and the City of Zion, or New Jerusalem, will fall to the lot of the descendants of Joseph, but it is *Ephraim* who will stand at the head and direct the work.[38]

And what a day of rejoicing it shall be when the descendants of Ephraim join with the descendants of Manasseh and the other tribes to fulfill the great covenants made with their fathers centuries before!

---

[37]Joseph Fielding Smith, *Doctrines of Salvation* (Bruce R. McConkie, comp.), Vol. 2, (Bookcraft: Salt Lake City, 1955), pp. 247-250.
[38]*Ibid.,* pp. 250-251. (Italics added)

FROM OUT OF THE NORTH

This discussion of the "remnants of Jacob" naturally leads one to inquire of the prophesied destiny of the other tribes of Israel and of the part they shall play in the final scenes of the earth's history. Probably best known of the remaining tribes is the tribe of Judah, or, as they are commonly known in today's world, the Jews. The prophecies concerning Judah are rich and plentiful and will be discussed in the following chapter. But equally fascinating, though more mysterious, is the other great body of Israelites commonly known today as the "Ten Lost Tribes."

They are so named for they were lost to history more than seven centuries before the birth of Christ and have been an enigma ever since. During the reign of King Solomon, the people of Israel grew very weary of the heavy burden of taxation the king had levied on them to finance his fabulously rich empire. At his death the people pleaded with his son, Rehoboam, to lessen the burden or lose their allegiance. Rehoboam arrogantly refused, and the northern tribes split off and formed their own kingdom called Israel, leaving the followers of Rehoboam to form their own kingdom. It was called Judah, for it consisted primarily of the tribe of Judah. The Northern Kingdom of Israel rapidly became a wicked and degenerate people until finally in 721 B.C. they were besieged and conquered by the Assyrians under Shalmaneser and were led away captive to Assyria.[39] How long the Israelites remained in Assyria is not known. It is likely that some became assimilated into the Assyrian culture; but evidently, some time after the captivity of their kingdom, a group of Israelites left Assyria, traveling northward and were lost to history.[40] Thus, today they are called the "lost ten tribes."

---

[39]2 Kings 17:18, 20-23.

[40]The Old Testament makes mention of the scattering of Israel quite frequently and several prophets refer to their being brought back from the "north countries." (See for example Jeremiah 23:8; 31:8; Zechariah 2:6.) But the course which they took is not given anywhere in the canonical books of the Bible. However, in the Apocrypha, an account of their movement is given in the second book of Esdras. It should be remembered that Joseph Smith was told not to revise the Apocrypha while he was working on the rest of the Bible. The Lord explained that there were "many things contained therein that are true" but there were also "many

Down through the centuries there have been innumerable speculations as to where the lost ten tribes are. These speculations have ranged all the way from a planet somewhere in outer space to exotic hidden places under the ice cap of the Arctic regions. Some have speculated that they went into present-day Europe, and became the various present nations of that continent. Some Church members seek to support this latter idea with the fact that many patriarchal blessings state that an individual is of the tribe of Ephraim (one of those lost), and also because of the great gathering of converts that has taken place since the early history of the Church out of the nations of Europe. (Since Europe is north of Palestine and Assyria in latitude, they feel this geographical location qualifies in the sense of being gathered from the lands of the north.)

They Shall Come as a Body

All such speculation as to the whereabouts of this group of Israelites is strictly that—only speculation. As yet, their specific location has not been revealed to the Church. But the idea that the gathering has already been fulfilled in the great missionary efforts of the Church is in error, for the prophets have definitely stated that they shall come *as a body;* their

---

things contained therein that are not true." (*Doctrine and Covenants* 91:1, 2) Which of these two headings this particular account in Esdras would fall under is, of course, not known, so it must be read with that in mind. The account is of interest, nevertheless. It is given in 2 Esdras 13:39-50, and reads:

"And whereas thou sawest that he gathered another peaceable multitude unto him; those are the Ten Tribes which were carried away prisoners out of their own land in the time of Osea the king, whom Salmanasar, the King of Assyria, led away captive, and he carried them over the waters, and so they came into another land. But they took this counsel among themselves, that they would leave the multitude of the heathen, and go forth into a further country, where never mankind dwelt, that they might there keep their statutes, which they never kept in their own land. And they entered Euphrates by the narrow passages of the river, for the Most High then showed signs for them, and held still the floods till they were passed over. For through that country there was a great way to go, *viz.*, of a year and a half; and the same region is called Arsareth. Then dwelt they there until the latter time; and now when they shall begin to come, the Highest shall stay the springs of the streams again, that they may go through; therefore sawest thou the multitude with peace. But those that he left behind of thy people are they that are found within my borders. Now when he destroyeth the multitude of the nations that are gathered together, he shall defend his people that remain. And then shall he show them great wonders."

coming shall be so miraculous that it could not be mistaken for a gradual response to missionary work.

On the 3rd day of November, 1831, Joseph Smith received a revelation which the Lord designated should be the Appendix to the compilation of revelations later known as the Doctrine and Covenants. In that revelation, the Lord spoke of the return of the ten tribes from out of the north.

> And they who are in the north countries shall come in remembrance before the Lord; and their prophets shall hear his voice, and shall no longer stay themselves; and they shall smite the rocks, and the ice shall flow down at their presence.
>
> And an highway shall be cast up in the midst of the great deep.
>
> And their enemies shall become a prey unto them.
>
> And in the barren deserts there shall come forth pools of living water; and the parched ground shall no longer be a thirsty land.
>
> And they shall bring forth their rich treasures unto the children of Ephraim, my servants.
>
> And the boundaries of the everlasting hills shall tremble at their presence.
>
> And there shall they fall down and be crowned with glory, even in Zion, by the hands of the servants of the Lord, even the children of Ephraim.
>
> And they shall be filled with songs of everlasting joy.[41]

As one contemplates the full import of those prophetic statements, it is not hard to understand why Jeremiah says:

> Therefore, behold, the days come, saith the Lord, that they shall no more say, The Lord liveth, which brought up the children of Israel out of the land of Egypt;
>
> But, *The Lord liveth, which brought up and which led the seed of the house of Israel out of the north country, and from all countries whither I had driven them;* and they shall dwell in their own land.[42]

Several of the latter-day prophets have made it clear that the return of the ten tribes is not to be some figurative event

---

[41]*Doctrine and Covenants* 133:26-33.
[42]Jeremiah 23:7-8. (Italics added)

but an actual return of the group so long lost. President Charles W. Penrose explained why many members of the Church are of the lineage of Ephraim or other tribes and shows how this cannot be construed to mean that the ten tribes have already returned.

> There is no doubt in the minds of those who have investigated this subject, that when traveling northward, as described by Esdras, the tribes of Israel mingled on the way with Gentile nations, and that numbers of their posterity are to be found in the various provinces of Germany, in Switzerland, in Holland, in Sweden, Denmark, Norway, Finland, Iceland, and the numerous islands in the far north.

> Much of the blood of Israel is, doubtless, to be found in the British Isles. It was obtained, in all probability, by the admixture of Saxon, Danish, Norwegian and Swedish blood with that of the ancient Britons and the Picts and Scots, who inhabited those islands and were subject to the incursions and conquests of the peoples mentioned, among whose ancestors the Israelites mingled in their journey of a year and a half towards the extreme north. Thus the nations here mentioned became impregnated with the seed of Israel, and their descendants who came to this country, bringing the principles of religious freedom and planting the standard of liberty, were also of the lineage to whom many blessings were promised, and from among all these, many who are of Israel embrace the gospel of the latter-day dispensation. The gathering of some of their descendants to Zion is in part fulfillment of the prophecies in regard to the gathering, but there are revelations which cannot be said to be literally fulfilled in this movement. Some of these are here cited: [Here he quotes *Doctrine and Covenants* 133:26-34.]

> *This indicates the coming of a body of these Israelites, with prophets at their head, from regions of ice and rocks, under Divine direction, to receive blessings on this land where are the "everlasting hills," and the gathering place for Israel and the keys of power and authority in the hands of the "children of Ephraim." It is evident, also, that they have important records, containing accounts of the dealings of the Lord with them, and his word concerning them, which they are to bring with them, that they may be joined with the record of the Jews—the Bible—and the record of the Nephites—the Book of Mormon (see 1 Nephi 15:12, 13.)*[43]

---

[43]Charles W. Penrose, "Something About the 'Lost Tribes'," *The Improvement Era*, October, 1910, pp. 1087-1088. (Italics added)

In both of the general conferences in 1916, Elder James E. Talmage warned against trying to water down the prophecies concerning the ten tribes by interpreting them figuratively. In April conference he said:

> There is a tendency among men to explain away what they don't wish to understand in literal simplicity, and we, as Latter-day Saints are not entirely free from the taint of that tendency. . . . Some people say that prediction is to be explained in this way: A gathering is in progress, and has been in progress from the early days of this Church; and thus the "Lost Tribes" are now being gathered; but that we are not to look for the return of any body of people now unknown as to their whereabouts. True, the gathering is in progress, this is a gathering dispensation; *but the prophecy stands that the tribes shall be brought forth from their hiding place bringing their scriptures with them, which scriptures shall become one* with the scriptures of the Jews, the holy Bible, and with the scriptures of the Nephites, the Book of Mormon, and with the scriptures of the Latter-day Saints as embodied in the volumes of modern revelation.[44]

In the October conference Elder Talmage added a startling and marvelous promise:

> The tribes shall come; they are not lost unto the Lord; they shall be brought forth as hath been predicted; *and I say unto you, there are those now living—aye, some here present—who shall live to read the records of the Lost Tribes of Israel,* which shall be made one with the record of the Jews, or the Holy Bible, and the record of the Nephites, or the Book of Mormon, even as the Lord hath predicted.[45]

President Joseph Fielding Smith also explained that the gathering of Israel from among the Gentiles was not the same as the gathering of the lost tribes.

> We discover from the declaration by the Prophet to the people of the world, that the cleansing of the earth of much of its iniquity, by blood, fire, earthquake, pestilence and the display of angry elements, was to assist in preparing the way for the return of the lost tribes of Israel. We should not be confused. The call for the

---

[44]James E. Talmage, *Conference Report*, April, 1916, p. 130. (Italics added)
[45]*Ibid.*, October, 1916, p. 76. (Italics added)

gathering of scattered Israel had been proclaimed three years earlier and the missionaries had been hard at work gathering into the fold those of Israel who had scattered themselves among the Gentiles. *The great day of the coming of the lost tribes would be after the preparatory work had been accomplished in the destruction of the wickedness in very great measure, and the way prepared in part for the coming of the Lord also and the building of his Holy City and Temple.*[46]

Elder Orson Pratt described their coming as being after the building of the New Jerusalem, also, and explained that it would be such a marvelous event that even the mountains would tremble at their coming.

After Zion is built in Jackson County, and after the Temple is built upon that spot of ground where the corner stone was laid in 1831; after the glory of God in the form of a cloud by day shall rest upon that Temple, and by night the shining of a flaming fire that will fill the whole heavens round about; after every dwelling place upon Mount Zion shall be clothed upon as with a pillar of fire by night, and a cloud by day, about that period of time, the ten tribes will be heard of, away in the north, a great company, as Jeremiah says, coming down from the northern regions, coming to sing in the height of the latter-day Zion. Their souls will be as a watered garden, and they will not sorrow any more at all, as they have been doing during the twenty-five hundred long years they have dwelt in the Arctic regions. They will come, and the Lord will be before their camp, he will utter his voice before that great army, and he will lead them forth as he led Israel in ancient days. *This long chain of Rocky Mountains, that extends from the cold regions of the north away into South America, will feel the power of God, and will tremble before the hosts of Israel* as they come to sing on the heights of Zion. In that day the trees of the field will clap like hands, says the Prophet, and in that day the Lord will open waters in the wilderness, and streams in the desert, to give drink to his chosen, his people Israel. And when they come to the height of Zion they shall be crowned with glory under the hands of the servants of God living in those days, the children of Ephraim, crowned with certain blessings that pertain to the Priesthood, that they could not receive in their own lands.[47]

---

[46]Joseph Fielding Smith, *Church History and Modern Revelation,* Melchizedek Priesthood Course of Study, Published by the Council of the Twelve Apostles of The Church of Jesus Christ of Latter-day Saints, Salt Lake City, Utah, 1948, Vol. 2, p. 141. (Italics added)
[47]Orson Pratt, *Journal of Discourses,* Vol. 18, p. 68, July 25, 1875. (Italics added)

Blessings and Counter-Blessings

As can be seen from the statements of the Lord and the various prophets, this will be one of the great events of the entire world's history and one that should be inspiring indeed to those privileged to witness it. The promises speak of these lost peoples coming to be "crowned with glory, even in Zion, by the hands of the servants of the Lord, even the children of Ephraim."[48] As was discussed in the previous section, the children of Ephraim include the faithful members of the Church. This crowning of the children of Israel by the children of Ephraim will consist in part of helping them to come to a fulness of the gospel and obtain the blessings of the temple.

President Wilford Woodruff explained in detail what this "crowning" would consist of.

> Again, here are the ten tribes of Israel, we know nothing about them only what the Lord has said by His Prophets. There are Prophets among them, and by and by they will come along, and they will smite the rocks, and the mountains of ice will flow down at their presence, and a highway will be cast up before them, and *they will come to Zion, receive their endowments, and be crowned under the hands of the children of Ephraim, and there are persons before me in this assembly today, who will assist to give them their endowments.*[49]

The blessings will not flow in one direction only, however. The children of Ephraim shall receive many blessings from these children of God so long lost to us. The Doctrine and Covenants states that they will bring their rich treasures to the members of the Church awaiting them in Zion.[50] Part of these riches will undoubtedly consist of a new book of scripture—sacred records of God's dealings with this group of people equal to our own present standard works. Elder Talmage and others already cited have referred to these records. What a record it must be! It will probably contain

---

[48]*Doctrine and Covenants* 133:32.
[49]Wilford Woodruff, *Journal of Discourses,* Vol. 4, pp. 231-232, February 22, 1857. (Italics added)
[50]*Doctrine and Covenants* 133:30.

the account of their original journey to the location of their long concealment and of the prophets that have dealt with them down through the centuries. It, too, will act as another witness for Christ, just as our own Book of Mormon, for Christ told the Nephites that he would visit the lost tribes just as he had them.[51]

This fulfillment of the great prophecies concerning the lost ten tribes of Israel will provide one of the most sure and most impressive signs that the end of the world in its telestial state is about to draw to a close.

Adam-Ondi-Ahman

When Daniel interpreted the dream of Nebuchadnezzar, it was only the beginning of the prophetic vision he had of the last days. The last chapters of his writings are filled with the records of his visions and revelations. Many of these are couched in symbolic language and are difficult to interpret. In the seventh chapter, for example, Daniel speaks of one known as the "Ancient of Days," speaking at some length concerning him.

> I beheld till the thrones were cast down, and the Ancient of days did sit, whose garment was white as snow, and the hair of his head like the pure wool: his throne was like the fiery flame, and his wheels as burning fire.
>
> A fiery stream issued and came forth from before him: thousand thousands ministered unto him, and ten thousand times ten thousands stood before him: the judgment was set, and the books were opened. . . .
>
> I saw in the night visions, and behold, one like the Son of man came with the clouds of heaven, and came to the Ancient of days, and they brought him near before him.
>
> And there was given him dominion, and glory, and a kingdom, that all people, nations, and languages, should serve him: his dominion is an everlasting dominion, which shall not pass away, and his kingdom that which shall not be destroyed.[52]

[51]3 Nephi 15:19-20; 16:1-3; 17:4.
[52]Daniel 7:9-10, 13-14.

To many people of the world these verses are no more clear in their meaning than are the other symbolical verses recorded by Daniel. But fortunately, the Lord revealed to the Prophet Joseph Smith the meaning of these verses and thus provided information about another great sign of the approaching return of Jesus Christ. Joseph Smith spoke of this "Ancient of Days" in his *History of the Church.*

> Daniel in his seventh chapter speaks of the Ancient of Days: *he means the oldest man, our Father Adam, Michael, he will call his children together and hold a council with them to prepare them for the coming of the Son of Man.* He (Adam) is the father of the human family, and presides over the spirits of all men, and *all that have had the keys must stand before him in this grand council. This may take place before some of us leave this stage of action.* The Son of Man stands before him, and there is given him glory and dominion. Adam delivers up his stewardship to Christ, that which was delivered to him as holding the keys of the universe, but retains his standing as head of the human family.[53]

Orson Pratt commented further on the Prophet's statement:

> We are told by this Prophet that the Ancient of days is the most ancient personage that ever had an existence in days here on the earth. And who was he? *Why, of course, old father Adam,* he was the most ancient man that lived in days that we have any knowledge of. *He comes, then, as a great judge, to assemble this innumerable host of which Daniel speaks. He comes in flaming fire. The glory and blessing and greatness of this personage it would be impossible even for a man as great as Daniel to fully describe. He comes as a man inspired from the eternal throne of Jehovah himself. He comes to set in order the councils of the Priesthood pertaining to all dispensations, to arrange the Priesthood and the councils of the Saints of all former dispensations in one grand family and household.*
>
> What is all this for? Why all this arrangement? Why all this organization? Why all this judgment and the opening of the books? It is to prepare the way for another august personage whom Daniel saw coming with the clouds of heaven, namely the Son of Man, and these clouds of heaven brought the Son of Man near before the Ancient of days. *And when the Son of Man came to the*

---

[53]Joseph Smith, *DHC,* Vol. 3, pp. 386-387, July 2, 1839. (Italics added)

> *Ancient of days, behold a kingdom was given to the Son of Man,* and greatness and glory, that all people, nations and languages should serve him, and his kingdom should be an everlasting kingdom, a kingdom that should never be done away.[54]

Thus, what Daniel foresaw was a great meeting of all the righteous holders of priesthood keys in the various dispensations. At this great meeting they each in turn stand before Adam to report their labors to him. Not only were the purposes and participators in this great event shown to Joseph Smith, but also he was given the location of that great council. In the spring of 1838, Joseph walked with some of the brethren to a place in Northern Missouri with the intent of selecting a site for a city. He records in his journal:

> In the afternoon I went up the river about half a mile to Wight's Ferry, accompanied by President Rigdon, and my clerk, George W. Robinson, for the purpose of selecting and laying claim to a city plat near said ferry in Daviess County, township 60, ranges 27 and 28, and sections 25, 36, 31, and 30, which the brethren called "Spring Hill," but by the mouth of the Lord it was named Adam-ondi-Ahman, because, said He, it is the place where Adam shall come to visit his people, or the Ancient of Days shall sit, as spoken of by Daniel the Prophet.[55]

Not only is this the place for a future visit of Adam, but the Prophet also gave the startling information that it was in this same general area that Adam lived during his mortal life. In the Valley of Adam-ondi-Ahman, three years previous to his death, Adam called his righteous posterity together and blessed them with his last blessing. The Lord appeared to the gathering and Adam was filled with the Holy Ghost and predicted the future of his posterity right down to the last generation.[56]

The Great Priesthood Council

The meeting that Adam had with his righteous posterity in the Valley of Adam-ondi-Ahman must surely have been a

---

[54]Orson Pratt, *Journal of Discourses*, Vol. 17, pp. 185-186, October 11, 1874. (Italics added)
[55]Joseph Smith, *DHC*, Vol. 3, p. 35, May 19, 1838. (See also D&C 116)
[56]*Doctrine and Covenants* 107:53-57.

marvelous one to all those in attendance. But just as surely, this great future meeting at the same location will be one of the greatest events to transpire in the preparation of the world for the coming of the Lord. President Joseph Fielding Smith vividly described what would take place at this council:

> Not many years hence there shall be another gathering of high priests and righteous souls in this same valley of Adam-ondi-Ahman. At this gathering Adam, the Ancient of Days, will again be present. At this time the vision which Daniel saw will be enacted. The Ancient of Days will sit. *There will stand before him those who have held the keys of all dispensations, who shall render up their stewardships to the first Patriarch of the race, who holds the keys of salvation.* This shall be a day of judgment and preparation. . . .
>
> It was in the night vision that all this was shown to Daniel, and he saw the Son of Man come to the grand council, as he did to the first grand council in the valley of Adam-ondi-Ahman, and there he received the keys from Adam. . . .
>
> This council in the valley of Adam-ondi-Ahman is to be of the greatest importance to this world. At that time there will be a transfer of authority from the usurper and impostor, Lucifer, to the rightful King, Jesus Christ. Judgment will be set and *all who have held keys will make their reports and deliver their stewardships, as they shall be required. Adam will direct this judgment, and then he will make his report, as the one holding the keys for this earth, to his Superior Officer, Jesus Christ. Our Lord will then assume the reins of government; directions will be given to the Priesthood there assembled.* This grand council of priesthood will be composed, not *only of those who are faithful who now dwell on this earth, but also of the prophets and apostles of old,* who have had directing authority. Others may also be there, but if so they will be there by appointment, for this is to be an official council called to attend to the most momentous matters concerning the destiny of this earth.[57]

Orson Pratt also spoke of this great meeting in the most glowing terms:

> *. . . All the various quorums and councils of the Priesthood in every dispensation that has transpired since the days of Adam until the present time will find their places, according to the call-*

---

[57]Joseph Fielding Smith, *The Way to Perfection*, (Genealogical Society: Salt Lake City, 1931), pp. 289-291. (Italics added)

*ings, gifts, blessings, ordinations and keys of Priesthood which the
Lord Almighty has conferred upon them in their several generations.
This, then, will be one of the grandest meetings that has ever
transpired upon the face of our globe.* What manner of person
ought you and I, my brethren and sisters, and all the people of God
in the latter days to be, that we may be counted worthy to participate in the august assemblies that are to come from the eternal
worlds, whose bodies have burst the tomb and come forth immor-
talized and eternal in their nature?[58]

The mind is nearly incapable of comprehending such a
meeting and the feelings of those privileged to be in attendance. It calls to mind again why the prophets from earliest
times have looked down to the present dispensation and envied
the saints who were blessed to live in it.

This great meeting of the priesthood there in Northern
Missouri is a clear and definite sign that the end is approaching although the majority of the world shall not know when
it is fulfilled. President Joseph Fielding Smith indicated above
that only those appointed to be there would be privileged to
attend. In the same discourse he indicates that the meeting
will generally be a secret and will fulfill the Lord's promise
that he would come as a thief in the night.

> When this gathering is held, the world will not know of it;
> the members of the Church at large will not know of it, yet it shall
> be preparatory to the coming in the clouds of glory of our Savior
> Jesus Christ as the Prophet Joseph Smith has said. *The world
> cannot know of it. The Saints cannot know of it—except those who
> officially shall be called into this council—for it shall precede the
> coming of the Jesus Christ as a thief in the night, unbeknown to all
> the world.*[59]

Elder Alvin R. Dyer said essentially the same thing, and
further suggested that some presently living would participate
in that meeting.[60] That naturally brings up the question:
"If it is a secret, how can we be sure that it has not already
taken place?" Three things suggest an answer. First, the

---

[58]Orson Pratt, *Journal of Discourses,* Vol. 17, pp. 187-188, October 11, 1874.
(Italics added)
[59]Joseph Fielding Smith, *op. cit.,* p. 291. (Italics added)
[60]Alvin R. Dyer, "The Millennium," *The Instructor,* June, 1970, pp. 196-197.

General Authorities who speak of it, still speak of it as being in the future. Second, it is a council of vast proportions that is to be held in the state of Missouri. That would seem to indicate that it might take place after the Church returns to claim the land of Zion. But the third and most definite of all was given by Daniel himself. He said that the Ancient of Days would sit after earthly thrones "were cast down." He went on to say that he beheld the "horn" making war against the saints, *"until the Ancient of Days came,* and judgment was given to the saints of the most High; and the time came that the saints possessed the kingdom."[61] Joseph Fielding Smith explained it in this way: "Until this grand council is held, Satan shall hold rule in the nations of the earth; but at that time thrones are to be cast down and man's rule shall come to an end."[62] Obviously, Satan still rules in the nations of the world in many respects and so the Grand Council of Adam-ondi-Ahman seems to be one of the last events and one of the great signs of the times which is yet to be fulfilled.

THE LAST CALL

In his book entitled *The Government of God,* John Taylor wrote of the coming judgments on the earth and the mistaken idea that they will come instantaneously upon the world. Said he:

> Some people talk about the world being burned up, about plagues, pestilence, famine, sword, and ruin, and all these things being instantaneous. *Now it would not be just for the Lord to punish the inhabitants of the earth without warning. For if the world are ignorant of God, they cannot altogether be blamed for it; if they are made the dupes of false systems, and false principles, they cannot help it. . . .* Before the Lord destroyed the inhabitants of the old world, he sent Enoch and Noah to warn them. Before the Lord destroyed Sodom and Gomorrah, he sent Lot into their midst. Before the Children of Israel were carried captive to Babylon, they were warned of it by the Prophets; and before Jerusalem was destroyed, the inhabitants had the testimony of our Lord, and

---

[61]Daniel 7:21-22. (Italics added)
[62]Joseph Fielding Smith, *op. cit.,* p. 290.
[63]*Ibid.,* 88:88-90.

his Disciples. *And so will it be in the last days; and as it is the world that is concerned, the world will have to be warned.*[63]

To raise the warning voice to the world has been a major mission of The Church of Jesus Christ of Latter-day Saints since its earliest beginnings. In the preface to the Doctrine and Covenants, the Lord explicitly stated that this was his purpose in calling Joseph Smith to be a prophet and his reason for restoring the gospel.[64] Missionary work has been a divine injunction upon the Church since that time and thousands of faithful members of the Church through the years have heeded, and are still heeding, that call. Literally millions of people have been gathered into the Church through this great effort.

In chapter 3, prophecies were cited of the time when the missionaries of the Church would be called home because of the spreading war and chaos in the United States and other countries. The Lord indicated this same thing when he spoke of "preaching his own sermons."[65] So it appears as though there may be a time when normal missionary work will not take place in the world. But the Lord is long-suffering and ever merciful to his children and seeks to give them every chance to repent and return to him.

Thus it is that one of the final things to be done prior to the return of the Savior and the beginning of the Millennium will be a last great missionary effort designed to gather out the righteous from all nations before the earth is cleansed by fire. This last great call will come from a force of missionaries the likes of which the world has never before known. In all of its history, the Church has never had more than about 15,000 missionaries in the field at one time; most of the time much less than that amount were missionaries. In the last call, the force shall be nearly ten times that number—a vast army of missionaries numbering 144,000 men.

---

[63]John Taylor, *The Government of God,* (S. W. Richards: Liverpool, England, 1852), p. 95. (Italics added)

[64]*Doctrine and Covenants* 1:17, 35-36.

[65]*Ibid.,* 88:88-90.

John the Revelator was shown this great body of missionaries in his visions of the latter days and described them as servants whom were sealed by the angels: "And I heard the number of them which were sealed: and there were sealed an hundred and forty and four thousand of all the tribes of the children of Israel." He then goes on to explain that 12,000 were chosen from each of the twelve tribes of Israel.[66] The Lord spoke of these special servants in the Appendix to the Doctrine and Covenants also: ". . . For the hour of his coming is nigh—When the Lamb shall stand upon Mount Zion, and with him a hundred and forty-four thousand, having his Father's name written on their foreheads."[67]

While working on the revision of the King James Version in the spring of 1832, Joseph Smith asked several questions concerning the revelations of John. One of those questions pertained to the verses cited above.

Q. What are we to understand by sealing the one hundred and forty-four thousand, out of all the tribes of Israel—twelve thousand out of every tribe?

A. *We are to understand that those who are sealed are high priests, ordained unto the holy order of God, to administer the everlasting gospel; for they are they who are ordained out of every nation, kindred, tongue, and people, by the angels to whom is given power over the nations of the earth, to bring as many as will come to the Church of the Firstborn.*[68]

A statement as clearly put as that leaves little room for debate as to the mission and purpose of these special servants.

President Joseph Fielding Smith spoke of these high priests and the privilege it would be to be included in that group.

This certainly is a great honor to be one of the 144 thousand who are specially called by the power of "the angels to whom is

---

[66]Revelation 7:3-8.
[67]*Doctrine and Covenants* 133:17-18.
[68]*Ibid.*, 77:11. (Italics added)

given power over the nations of the earth" to bring souls unto Christ. John the Apostle, had the great desire to bring souls to Christ. The Three Nephite Disciples likewise sought this great honor and it was granted to them. It is one of the noblest desires that a man can have. It will be a wonderful blessing to those who are called in this great group.[69]

It is difficult to say when the actual calling of these men will take place. Some prophets have spoken as though it would be after the return of the ten tribes. But whether it would happen before, after, or during the Council of Adam-ondi-Ahman is not clear. Joseph Smith once indicated to some holders of the priesthood that the selection for that group of high priest-missionaries had already commenced even then.

> I attended prayer-meeting with the quorum in the assembly room, and made some remarks respecting the hundred and forty-four thousand mentioned by John the Revelator, *showing that the selection of persons to form that number had already commenced.*[70]

The question of "when" is an interesting one but not a critical one. What *is* comforting is the knowledge that one last great and final call shall go out before the cleansing fire sweeps the world. Then, indeed, will John's vision of the angel flying through the midst of heaven be fulfilled.[71]

The Hour Approaches

The last days prior to Christ's great advent shall be momentous ones for those worthy to stand. It is marvelous to consider how much information concerning the last days the Lord has given his children. *There is no reason why any person should be caught unaware as the end of the world approaches.* Well did the Lord speak when he promised:

---

[69]Joseph Fielding Smith, *Church History and Modern Revelation, op. cit.,* Vol. 2, pp. 71-72.

[70]Joseph Smith, *DHC,* Vol. 6, p. 196, February 4, 1844. (Italics added)

[71]Revelation 14:6.

*And unto you it shall be given to know the signs of the times,
and the signs of the coming of the Son of Man.*[72]

The establishment of the kingdom of God, the blossoming
of the Lamanite people, the return of the ten tribes, the great
priesthood meeting at Adam-ondi-Ahman and the last call to
the nations of the earth are five of those signs and will signal
the approaching hour of the coming of the Lord.

---

[72]*Doctrine and Covenants* 68:11. (Italics added)

The House of Judah

On the one hundred and thirtieth anniversary of the organization of the Church, Elder George Q. Morris, of the Council of Twelve, said:

> . . . I thought I would like to mention three signs that the Lord gave that we might observe and know when we saw them that he had set his hand again to accomplish *final preparatory work for the coming of the millennium.*
>
> The first of these was to be the restoration of the gospel of Jesus Christ. . . .
>
> Another sign of great importance was the rise of an evil power. . . .
>
> *A third item is God's promise that he would gather Jews to Jerusalem,* and I think perhaps we may well now not continue saying the Jews are going to gather in Jerusalem. *I think now we may well say they have gathered.* The ultimate returns will come later as they develop this land and are joined by others.[1]

When the independent state of Israel was created in 1948, the words of prophets long dead were fulfilled and a new era in the long and troubled history of the House of Israel was born. With it one of the great signs of the Lord's coming, predicted by prophets many centuries before, entered the final stages of its fulfillment.

Israel the Unfaithful

Several thousand years before the birth of the Savior, Abraham was promised that the hand of Jehovah would be

---

[1]George Q. Morris, *Conference Report*, April, 1960, pp. 100-101. (Italics added)

over him and his posterity. Through the chosen, or covenant, people which came from this great patriarch, were all the nations of the earth to be blessed.[2] As part of that covenant, Abraham was told that he and his posterity would be given a promised land as their "everlasting possession" and, said Jehovah, "I will be their God."[3]

Abraham, Isaac and Jacob were men of high spiritual stature, and well earned their right to the covenant. Unfortunately, as time passed, much of their posterity were not as anxious to have Jehovah as their God, and, like an unfaithful spouse, turned to the gods of the heathen. Through succeeding generations, notwithstanding the efforts of mighty prophets like Moses, Samuel, Isaiah, Jeremiah, Daniel and others, the House of Israel turned to idolatry and wickedness. Whether it was unnamed golden calves or deities with strange names like Baal, Ashtoreth, Molech, or Chemosh didn't matter a great deal; the Israelites generally preferred them to the God of Abraham, Isaac, and Jacob. And thus the stage for the future tragedy of this nation was set.

The prophets of Israel began early in their history to predict the great scattering of this people. Before they even crossed the River Jordan to possess the promised land, Moses predicted the tragic consequences of Israel's idolatry.

> I call heaven and earth to witness against you this day, that ye shall soon utterly perish from off the land whereunto ye go over Jordan to possess it; ye shall not prolong your days upon it, but shall utterly be destroyed.
>
> And *the Lord shall scatter you among the nations,* and ye shall be left few in number among the heathen, whither the Lord shall lead you.[4]

Periodically during the reign of the judges and the long era of the kings, the covenant people would turn back to their God, but the repentance was never permanent enough to last for more than one or two generations.

---

[2]Abraham 2:8-11.
[3]Genesis 17:5-8.
[4]Deuteronomy 4:26-27. (Italics added) See also Leviticus 26:27-39.

So Jeremiah warned:

> *I will scatter them also among the heathen, whom neither they nor their fathers have known: and I will send a sword after them, till I have consumed them.*[5]

And Ezekiel promised:

> And I will scatter toward every wind all that are about him, to help him, and all his bands; and I will draw out the sword after them.
>
> And they shall know that I am the Lord, *when I shall scatter them among the nations, and disperse them in the countries.*[6]

With the added perspective of history, we today can see the literal fulfillment of these prophetic utterances. After Solomon's death, Israel was split into two kingdoms—the northern kingdom of Israel and the southern kingdom of Judah. In 721 B.C., the Assyrians under Shalmaneser swept the northern kingdom into captivity and those ten-and-a-half tribes were lost to history, and remain lost to this day. One hundred and thirty-four years later, King Nebuchadnezzar brought the Babylonians against Judah, and that kingdom too was carried away. Through the righteousness of men like Daniel, his three companions, and Ezra, the house of Judah was not destroyed, but seventy years later Cyrus freed them to return to Jerusalem. Even this did not change the hearts of the remaining Israelites for very long. Though the captivity corrected their tendency to worship idols, their hearts were still hardened away from "true worship" of their God. Soon the Jews were back in virtual slavery to a variety of conquering nations.

The Savior came into the Jewish nation at a time when they were nothing more than a vassal province of Rome. He, too, struggled to overcome the hypocrisy and pride of the Jewish nation, but had comparatively little success. So, sadly he mourned:

---

[5]Jeremiah 9:16. (Italics added)
[6]Ezekiel 12:14-15. (Italics added)

O Jerusalem, Jerusalem, thou that killest the prophets, and stonest them which are sent unto thee, how often would I have gathered thy children together, even as a hen gathereth her chickens under her wings, and ye would not!

Behold, your house is left unto you desolate.[7]

The final scattering of that royal tribe was completed less than forty years after Christ was crucified. Vespasian and Titus, Roman generals, brought in the mighty Roman legions to crush a Jewish revolt. The rebellion spread until Jerusalem itself came under siege, and, in one of the great catastrophes of the world's history the Jewish nation ceased to exist. Elder Ezra Taft Benson referred to that tremendous final blow and later persecutions in a conference address in 1950.

I think one of the saddest chapters in history is the account of the dispersion and suffering of Judah.

I have before me a quotation of Will Durant in his book, *The Story of Civilization,* in which he states that "no people in history fought so tenaciously for liberty as the Jews, nor any other people against such odds." He says further, "No other people has ever known so long an exile, or so hard a fate."

Then referring to the siege of Jerusalem under Titus, lasting for 134 days, during which 1,110,000 Jews perished and 97,000 were taken captive; he states that the Romans destroyed 987 towns in Palestine and slew 580,000 men, and a still larger number, we are told, perished through starvation, disease, and fire.

"Nearly all Judea was laid waste. So many Jews were sold as slaves that their price fell to that of a horse. Thousands hid in underground channels rather than be captured. Surrounded by Romans they died one by one of hunger while the living ate the bodies of the dead."

Scarcely eight thousand Jews were left in all of Palestine. And even their banishment and scattering didn't end their persecution. Efforts were made to drive them from various countries. Some nations made an effort to banish them completely. They were accused of causing the "Black Death" that spread through Europe in 1348, and many Jews were crucified therefor.

I have said nothing regarding the Crusades and the dastardly deeds perpetrated in the name of Christianity upon the remaining

---

[7]Matthew 23:37-38. (Italics added)

Jews in Palestine. *Yes, the prophecies regarding the dispersion and the suffering of Judah have been fulfilled.*[8]

Little wonder that Christ said: "Behold, your house is left unto you desolate." Little wonder that Hosea, speaking for the Lord, says: "Rejoice not, O Israel, for joy, as other people: for thou hast gone a whoring from thy God. . . ."[9]

Israel and Judah to Return

Ironically, even as the ancient prophets predicted the calamities that would befall their people, they often predicted their future restoration as well. The Lord promised Abraham that the covenant was to be an everlasting one, and the Lord's promises will be kept. This is why Elder Morris designated the restoration of the Jews as one of the signs that the preparatory work for the Millennium was begun. This is also why the Lord explained to the Nephites that the restoration of his people would be *the* sign to indicate when the end was drawing near.

> And verily I say unto you, I give unto you a sign, that ye know the time when these things shall be about to take place— *that I shall gather in, from their long dispersion, my people, O house of Israel, and shall establish again among them my Zion.*[10]

This great work of gathering Israel has been going on since the organization of the Church, but the gathering of the Jews back to the land of Jerusalem is a more recent phenomenon. On October 24, 1841, one of the Twelve Apostles of God returned to Jerusalem and specifically dedicated that land for the return of the Jews. The world took little note of that special mission of Elder Orson Hyde's, but the century following that solitary prayer has seen great changes upon the land so dedicated. The prayer of Orson Hyde has been abundantly answered, for in part he said:

---

[8]Ezra Taft Benson, *Conference Report,* April, 1950, pp. 74-75. (Italics added)
[9]Hosea 9:1.
[10]3 Nephi 21:1. (Italics added)

Grant, therefore, O Lord, in the name of Thy well-beloved Son, Jesus Christ, to remove the barrenness and sterility of this land, and let springs of living water break forth to water its thirsty soil. Let the vine and olive produce in their strength, and the fig tree bloom and flourish. Let the land become abundantly fruitful when possessed by its rightful heirs; let it again flow with plenty to feed the returning prodigals who come home with a spirit of grace and supplication; upon it let the clouds distil virtue and richness, and let the fields smile with plenty. Let the flocks and herds greatly increase and multiply upon the mountains and the hills; and let Thy great kindness conquer and subdue the unbelief of Thy people. Do Thou take from them their stony heart, and give them a heart fresh; and may the Sun of Thy favor dispel the cold mists of darkness which have beclouded their atmosphere. *Incline them to gather in upon this land according to Thy word. Let them come like clouds and like doves to their windows. Let the large ships of the nations bring them from the distant isles;* and let kings become their nursing fathers, and queens with motherly fondness wipe the tear of sorrow from their eye.[11]

With an additional one hundred and thirty years' perspective, it is not difficult to see the prophetic nature of Elder Hyde's prayer. The Jews have indeed been returning to their native land from which they have been dispersed for so many centuries. The land has indeed begun to be abundantly fruitful to these rightful heirs, and they have once again become a government worthy of identity. The Apostle's request that the large ships of the nations be used to return the Jews to their homeland brings forth the vivid pictures of refugee ships described in the novel *Exodus,* by Leon Uris.

In the talk previously referred to, Elder George Q. Morris went on to recount the great miracle of the return of the Jews.

In a writing issued recently this statement was made:

"About two million Jews have returned to restore land which has lain desolate for centuries. In little more than ten years fetid swamps have been transformed into fertile valleys. Orchards now blossom on stony hillsides. Farms have sprouted in the desert and towns and cities have been built on the site of ancient settlements." (*Know the World: Israel,* "Around the World Program" by Peggy Mann.) . . . .

---

[11]Joseph Smith, *DHC,* Vol. 4, p. 457, October 24, 1841. (Italics added)

In 1948, with a population of 600,000 the Declaration of Independence was issued, and the State of Israel was established. An army of 35,000 Jews was opposed by an army of nearly 80,000 Arabs. In about nine months peace was declared and they set up their government. They planted more than 53 million trees. Martyrs' Forest has six million trees, one for each Jewish life lost in Nazi Europe.

This statement by a writer is very interesting:

> "Strangely enough when the State of Israel was reborn in 1948, it was a nation of 600,000, the same number which the Bible reports that Moses led out of bondage in Egypt. It now numbers some two million, the same number which it is said populated the ancient Kingdom of Solomon, when Israel was in all its glory." (See above reference)

That is why we may now say that the Jews have returned to Palestine. On a land one-tenth the size of Utah they have nearly a half million more people than we have in our whole Church [1960]. They have about 258 people for each square mile in Palestine, which is a dense population. We have about ten a square mile in Utah.[12]

The continuing miracle of the Jewish tenacity for national life in the face of nearly overwhelming odds is yet another testimony that the promises of the Lord concerning this downtrodden people are being fulfilled.

The Great Gathering Home

It is exciting to know that prophecies that have stood unfulfilled for hundreds, even thousands of years are being fulfilled in one's own lifetime. That is the case with the gathering home of the Jews to their ancient homeland. The sufferings which this people have endured while awaiting their return are too numerous to recount. Fresh in the minds of most people are the terrible persecutions which raged against the Jews under Nazi Germany, but that was only one example out of many hundreds of scourges this people have undergone down through the centuries. Ezra Taft Benson of the Quorum of Twelve spoke of these devastating calamities and showed how they have worked to further the Lord's purposes

---

[12]George Q. Morris, *op. cit.*, p. 101.

in gathering these, his children, back home. He spoke of visiting the ruins of a Jewish ghetto in Warsaw, Poland, after World War II.

> As we stood on the crumbled brick and mortar and the rubble some fifteen feet deep, with only the spire of one burned synagogue showing—no other building in that vast area—we were told by the guide that some two hundred thousand bodies, it was estimated, still remained under the rubble of those once great buildings in this section of Warsaw.
>
> We visited some of the concentration camps and the crematoriums where it is estimated, six million of the sons and daughters of Judah lost their lives, reducing their world population from seventeen to eleven million.
>
> We were impressed almost to tears as we visited some of these wanderers, these persecuted and driven sons of our Heavenly Father, to find how doggedly they were determined to return to Palestine. Ofttimes, as they would come into relief agencies to get temporary help, we would ask them why they did not settle nearby. Sometimes they were invited to stay. *But they had one desire, and that was to return to the land of their fathers.*
>
> I recall that a survey was made by UNRRA, United Nations Relief and Rehabilitation Administration, in which they interviewed 3,629 Jews in displaced persons' camps to determine what they would like to do if they were given their freedom to move and locate as they pleased. *Of this number, 3,619 indicated that they would like to go back to Palestine.* Nine of them expressed a desire to come to the United States, and one to Australia. This desire—which is almost a passion—was so great that it was as strong as life itself. . . .
>
> *Yes, my brethren and sisters, this great drama goes on before our very eyes, in large measure unnoticed by the Christian world. One hardly ever hears reference to the prophecies regarding Judah's return. Yet, the promises are clear that it would be one of the great events of the last days. And, of course, we know from modern revelations and prophecies that much more is yet to occur.*[13]

It is equally exciting to see the words of our own latter-day prophets fulfilled through events that are transpiring in the world today. Joseph Smith clearly indicated, for example, that Christ could not come before the Jews were gathered

---

[13]Ezra Taft Benson, *op. cit.,* pp. 77-79. (Italics added)

home. In the general conference of the Church in April, 1843, he said:

> Judah must return, Jerusalem must be rebuilt, and the temple, and water come out from under the temple and the waters of the Dead Sea be healed. It will take some time to rebuild the walls of the city and the temple etc.; *and all this must be done before the Son of Man will make His appearance.*[14]

This statement was made while there was a great flurry in the United States over William Miller's predictions that the second advent would occur in that year. History has now shown the folly of those predictions and the accuracy of Joseph Smith's.

President Wilford Woodruff was also most explicit when he spoke of the gathering of the Jews as being one of the unfulfilled signs of the times. In 1875, speaking of Christ, he said: *"He will never come until the Jews are gathered home and have rebuilt their temple and city and the Gentiles have gone up there to battle against them."*[15] Four years later, after becoming president of the Church, Wilford Woodruff made another prediction:

> *The time is not far distant when the rich men among the Jews may be called upon to use their abundant wealth to gather the dispersed of Judah and purchase the ancient dwelling places of their fathers in and about Jerusalem and rebuild the holy city and temple.* For the fulness of the Gentiles has come in, and the Lord has decreed that the Jews should be gathered from all the Gentile nations where they have been driven, into their own land, in fulfillment of the words of Moses their law-giver.[16]

Elder Benson referred to this quote by President Woodruff in the conference talk referred to above and said: "It is rather significant that up to 1948 *more than seven hundred million dollars has been expended by American Jews alone* in helping

---

[14]Joseph Smith, *DHC,* Vol. 5, p. 337, April 6, 1843. (Italics added)
[15]Wilford Woodruff, *Journal of Discourses,* Vol. 18, p. 111, September 12, 1875. (Italics added)
[16]Wilford Woodruff, *Millennial Star,* Vol. 41, p. 244, April 21, 1879. (Italics added)

to bring about the fulfillment of this prophecy by President Wilford Woodruff."[17] In an interview in 1967, Israel's Prime Minister, Levi Eshkol explained Israel's magnificent progress as a nation as partially resulting from help given to the Jews by other Jews from all over the world who ". . . look upon this enterprise of the homecoming as a joint venture of the Jewish people throughout the world. They have helped with about 100 million dollars a year in donations to assist Jewish immigrants to Israel . . . including more than 90 per cent who came penniless."[18]

Jerusalem for the Jews and the Temple Rebuilt

One of the signs given by the Savior to his disciples concerning the end referred to the city of Jerusalem. Christ spoke of the time when Jerusalem would be encompassed about with armies, and warned the Jews to flee from these days of vengeance.[19] He then continued:

> But woe unto them that are with child, and to them that give suck, in those days! for there shall be great distress in the land, and wrath upon this people.
>
> And they shall fall by the edge of the sword, and shall be led away captive into all nations: *and Jerusalem shall be trodden down of the Gentiles, until the times of the Gentiles be fulfilled.*[20]

As was previously mentioned, that promise was fulfilled when the Roman legions besieged the city of Jerusalem and finally destroyed it (A.D. 70). Although the city itself was restored under the Emperor Hadrian about sixty-five years later, Jerusalem remained as a city of the Gentiles down through the centuries. Hadrian built a temple to Jupiter upon the site of the ancient temple; five hundred years later the city was taken by the Arab chieftain, Khalif Omar, in 637 A.D.; the European Christians held it for a few years after

---

[17]Ezra Taft Benson, *op. cit.*, pp. 76-77. (Italics added)
[18]*U.S. News and World Report,* April 17, 1967, p. 76. As quoted by Daniel H. Ludlow, "Israel Prophecies Being Fulfilled," BYU Summer Devotional, (BYU Press: Provo, Utah) August 8, 1967, p. 8.
[19]Luke 21:20-22.
[20]*Ibid.,* 21:23-24. (Italics added)

the Crusades, but the city soon fell into the possession of the Turks; it intermittently passed back and forth between various Arab and Turkish rulers until the British captured it under General Allenby in World War I. For more than 1800 years the prediction of the Master was literally fulfilled—Jerusalem was trodden down by the Gentiles.

Although the British set up Palestine as a homeland for the Jews and the Jewish people began to flock back to Jerusalem, the city of Jerusalem was still not completely controlled by the Jews. When Israel declared themselves to be a free and independent nation in 1948, the Arabs bitterly protested and war broke out. Peace was finally achieved through the United Nations, but Jerusalem was partitioned and became a divided city—half belonging to Israel, the other half to Jordan. Perhaps this is what Zechariah foresaw when he said that ". . . a line shall be stretched forth upon Jerusalem."[21] But finally, after nearly 1900 years, in June, 1967, the now-famous "six-day war" broke out and Israeli forces smashed through Jordanian defenses and captured all of Jerusalem. So as Christ, Joseph Smith, Wilford Woodruff, Orson Hyde, and others predicted, Jerusalem is being rebuilt and inhabited once again by those so long ago dispersed from its streets and dwelling places.

These prophets also spoke of the time when the temple would be constructed once more. As yet, that prophecy is unfulfilled, but the conditions are shaping up so as to bring about its fulfillment, perhaps in the next few years. Once again it seems as though the obstacles are insurmountable, but the prophets have spoken. The site of the temple is presently occupied by one of the holiest of Moslem shrines—the Mosque of Omar, also known as the Dome of the Rock. Tradition associates it with the spot where Abraham nearly offered up Isaac for sacrifice. But in addition, Moslems believe that it was from this site that their Prophet Mohammed ascended into heaven. Even though the site is now under Jewish control, the Jews are understandably reluctant to tear down a shrine

---

[21]Zechariah 1:16.

of such stature. If they were to do so, it would undoubtedly bring the rage of the Arab world into sharp focus, and aggravate matters far beyond their present tenuous limits.

But the obstacles against the Jews repossessing Palestine and the holy city also seemed insurmountable; yet the Lord brought about his work and fulfilled his word. So it is that it can be expected that the temple will also be rebuilt and the words of the Lord's servants vindicated. When that is accomplished, the world will have yet another indication that "God works in mysterious ways, his wonders to perform!"

As the promises concerning the Jews are fulfilled, it brings to mind President Woodruff's statement when he spoke of the future destiny of the Jews and warned the nations of the Gentiles to take heed of the Lord's promises so that they themselves might avoid his coming judgments.

> The gospel is now restored to us Gentiles, for we are all Gentiles in a national capacity, and it will continue with us, if we are faithful, until the law is bound, and the testimony sealed, and the times of the Gentiles are fulfilled, when it will again revert to the Jews, whom the Lord will have prepared to receive it. *They will gather to their own land, taking with them their gold and silver, and will rebuild their city and temple, according to the prediction of Moses and the prophets.* When this time arrives, which is nigh, even at our doors, let the Gentile nations who reject the gospel which is now sent to them, prepare to meet the judgments of an offended God! For when their cup is full even to the brim, the Lord will then remember the chastisements of the Jews, his favored people, and at whose hands they will have received double for their iniquities. Offenses must come, said the Savior, but woe unto them by whom they come. *Woe unto the Gentiles, who have administered afflictions to the Jews for these many years! Woe unto them if they now reject this only means of salvation, for the awful calamities spoken of in these books, the Bible and Book of Mormon will certainly befall them.*[22]

The Great War—The Jews Find Their Messiah

Since the June, 1967, war an uneasy and sporadic peace has hung over the nations of the Middle East. The large

---

[22]Wilford Woodruff, *Journal of Discourses*, Vol. 18, pp. 220-221, August 13, 1876. (Italics added)

political powers of the world have applied diplomatic pressures to bring about cease-fire agreements and treaties of peace. Some of the leading statesmen have predicted that the conflict in this area of the world can be resolved without further warfare. The ways of God are not the ways of men, however, and the decrees of God are often ignored by the "wise men" of the world. The prophecies clearly indicate that the troubled conflicts already witnessed in the Middle East are but a prelude to great catastrophic events yet to come. Especially is this true of war.

According to both the prophets of the Old Testament and those of the latter-day restoration, the Jews are yet to see a war of such staggering proportions that the mind finds it difficult to grasp. It seems clear from the description given by these prophets that none of the conflicts in Jerusalem's long and bloody history could qualify as being this predicted war. Ezekiel, for example, recorded the words of the Lord, wherein the great invading force was described. The leader, symbolically called Gog, prince of the land of Magog, was pictured as leading a great host of warriors from many lands.[23] Anciently, the land of Magog was a land to the north of the generally known world of the Israelites. Josephus identified it as the land of the Scythians, who were the people living in the regions north of the Black and Caspian Seas in present-day Russia. It was also used to refer to almost any people of crude and unlearned ways who were from little-known countries to the north.[24] Ezekiel pictures them as coming from the north[25] and as being so numerous as to be like ". . . a storm, thou shalt be like a cloud to cover the land, thou, and all thy bands, and many people with thee."[26] Their purpose shall be to spoil and ravage the land of Israel.[27]

And yet strangely enough, it is out of this great catastrophe that the Jews will finally come to know their Master, Jesus of

---

[23]Ezekiel 38:1-7.
[24]F. N. Peloubet, *Peloubet's Bible Dictionary*, (Holt, Rinehart & Winston: New York, 1947), pp. 380, 598. See entries for "Magog" and "Scythians."
[25]Ezekiel 38:15.
[26]*Ibid.*, 38:9.
[27]*Ibid.*, 38:13.

Nazareth. Many of the latter-day prophets have spoken of this great event, and their predictions add more details to what is known concerning the last of the tribulations of the house of David—the battle known as Armageddon.

Elder Charles W. Penrose predicted that the nations of the Gentiles would come up against Jerusalem in order to take spoil of their wealth so that they could alleviate their own bankrupt positions. He then described the resulting war and final deliverance of the Jews.

> The bankrupt nations, envying the wealth of the sons of Judah, will seek a pretext to make war upon them, and will invade the "holy land" to "take a prey and a spoil." . . .
>
> His [Christ's] next appearance will be among the distressed and nearly vanquished sons of Judah. *At the crisis of their fate, when the hostile troops of several nations are ravaging the city and all the horrors of war are overwhelming the people of Jerusalem, he will set his feet upon the Mount of Olives, which will cleave and part asunder at his touch. Attended by a host from heaven, he will overthrow and destroy the combined armies of the Gentiles, and appear to the worshipping Jews as the mighty Deliverer and Conquerer so long expected by their race; and while love, gratitude, awe, and admiration swell their bosoms, the Deliverer will show them the tokens of his crucifixion and disclose himself as Jesus of Nazareth, whom they had reviled and whom their fathers put to death. Then will unbelief depart from their souls, and "the blindness in part which has happened unto Israel"* be removed.[28]

Orson Pratt explained that Satan would play a part in the gathering of this mighty army through the showing forth of miracles.

> He will gather up millions upon millions of people into the valleys around about Jerusalem in order to destroy the Jews after they have gathered. How will the devil do this? He will perform miracles to do it. The Bible says the kings of the earth and the great ones will be deceived by the false miracles. It says there shall be three unclean spirits that shall go forth working and they are spirits of the devils. Where do they go? To the kings of the earth; and what will they do? Gather them up to battle unto the

---

[28]Charles W. Penrose, "The Second Advent," *Millennial Star*, Vol. 21, pp. 582-583, September 10, 1859. (Italics added)

great day of God Almighty. Where? Into the valley of Armageddon. And where is that? On the east side of Jerusalem.

> . . . *There the Lord shall fight for his people, and smite the
> horse and his rider, and send plagues on these armies, and their
> flesh shall be consumed from their bones, and their eyes from their
> sockets. They will actually fulfil these prophecies,* with all their
> pretension to Bible and prophetic learning.[29]

The promises referred to by both Elder Penrose and Elder
Pratt refer to ancient prophecies given by Isaiah, Ezekiel,
Joel, Zechariah, and other Old Testament prophets. The
promises of deliverance for Jerusalem and the return of the
Savior are found most specifically in Zechariah where he
foretells of the Jews looking upon the wounds of Jesus and
the mourning that will result from their startling discovery;[30]
of the fountain springing forth;[31] of the great earthquake and
the resulting avenue of escape opened in the Mount of Olives;[32]
of the destruction of the army;[33] and of the resulting millennial era that will be ushered in.[34]

President Joseph Fielding Smith also wrote of this terrible
war and described in more detail the great earthquake that
would split the Mount of Olives and the earthquake which
would save the Jewish nation.

> All of them [the prophets] speak of it; and when that time
> comes, the Lord is going to come out of His hiding place. You can
> see what a terrible condition it is going to be; and the Jews besieged,
> not only in Jerusalem, but, of course, all through Palestine are in
> the siege; and *when they are about to go under, then the Lord
> comes. There will be the great earthquake. The earthquake will
> not be only in Palestine. There will not be merely the separation
> of the Mount of Olives, to form a valley that the Jews may escape,
> but the whole earth is going to be shaken. There will be some
> dreadful things take place, and some great changes are going to*

---

[29]Orson Pratt, *Journal of Discourses,* Vol. 7, p. 189, July 10, 1859. (Italics
added)
[30]Zechariah 12:10-14; 13:6.
[31]*Ibid.,* 13:1; 14:8. (This is evidently the water which Joseph Smith said would
come from the temple and heal the Dead Sea. See footnote No. 14 of this
chapter.)
[32]*Ibid.,* 14:1-7.
[33]*Ibid.,* 14:12-15.
[34]*Ibid.,* 14:16-21.

take place, and that you will find written in the book of Ezekiel (38:17-23), which I did not read to you.[35]

He went on to speak about the Jews recognizing their Savior and then President Smith said:

> Then they will fall down at His feet and worship Him. After these days will come their redemption and the building of Jerusalem. They will be given their own land again, and every man will live under his own vine and his own fig tree and they will learn to love the Lord and keep His commandments and walk in the light, and He will be their God and they will be His people, *and that is right at our doors.*[36]

In the Book of Revelation, John also spoke of this last struggle and told of the Gentiles treading down the holy city for a period of forty-two months, or three and a half years.[37] During this period, there will be two witnesses who will be given power to prophesy and to work with the people of Judah. John spoke of the tremendous power which they would have, which probably explains the success of the Jews in holding off such a powerful army for three and one-half years.[38] Joseph Smith explained that the two witnesses are prophets raised up to the Jewish nation prior to the end.

> Q.   What is to be understood by the two witnesses, in the eleventh chapter of Revelations?
>
> A.   They are two prophets that are to be raised up to the Jewish nation in the last days, at the time of the restoration, and to prophesy to the Jews after they are gathered and have built the city of Jerusalem in the land of their fathers.[39]

John went on to say that after the witnesses had finished their testimony, they would be caught and killed by the troops besieging Jerusalem. This would cause much rejoicing and merrymaking among the armies of Gog. Rather than the

---

[35]Joseph Fielding Smith, *Signs of the Times,* (Deseret Book Co.: Salt Lake City, 1964), p. 170. (Italics added)
[36]*Ibid.,* pp. 171-172. (Italics added)
[37]Revelation 11:2.
[38]*Ibid.,* 11:3-6.
[39]*Doctrine and Covenants* 77:15.

bodies being buried, John predicted that they would be left lying in the streets, evidently as a sign of Gog's triumph.[40]

In his pamphlet, *A Voice of Warning,* Parley P. Pratt explained how the Gentiles would race through the city plundering the Jews.

> John in his 11th chapter of Revelation, gives us many more particulars concerning this same event. He informs us that, after the city and temple are rebuilt by the Jews, the Gentiles will tread it under foot forty and two months, during which time there will be two Prophets continually prophesying and working mighty miracles. And it seems that the Gentile army shall be hindered from utterly destroying and overthrowing the city, while these two Prophets continue. But, after a struggle of three years and a half, they at length succeed in destroying these two Prophets, and then overrunning much of the city, they send gifts to each other because of the death of the two Prophets, and in the meantime will not allow their dead bodies to be put in graves, but suffer them to lie in the streets of Jerusalem three days and a half, during which the armies of the Gentiles, consisting of many kindreds, tongues and nations, passing through the city, plundering the Jews, see their dead bodies lying in the street. But after three days and a half, on a sudden, the spirit of life from God enters them, and they will rise and stand upon their feet, and great fear will fall upon them that see them. And then they shall hear a voice from heaven saying, "Come up hither," and they will ascend up to heaven in a cloud, and their enemies beholding them.[41]

According to John, it is then that the great earthquake strikes, felling one-tenth of the city and killing seven thousand people outright.[42]

Close to the End

For those closely watching the signs of the times, this event just spoken of shall signal the last of the world's existence. The prophets indicate that it is shortly thereafter that the great coming of the Lord in glory takes place, and the Millennium is ushered in. John, for example, after speaking

---

[40]Revelation 11:7-12.
[41]Parley P. Pratt, *A Voice of Warning,* Published by The Church of Jesus Christ of Latter-day Saints (first published in 1837), pp. 41-42.
[42]Revelation 11:13.

of the two witnesses being caught up to heaven, and the great earthquake says:

> The second woe is past; and, behold, the third woe *cometh quickly.*
>
> And the seventh angel sounded; and there were great voices in heaven, saying, *The kingdoms of this world are become the kingdoms of our Lord and of his Christ; and he shall reign for ever and ever.*[43]

Parley P. Pratt briefly summed up the entire closing scene.

> Suffice it to say, the Jews gather home, and rebuild Jerusalem. The nations gather against them in battle. Their armies encompass the city, and have more or less power over it for three years and a half. A couple of Jewish Prophets, by their mighty miracles, keep them from utterly overcoming the Jews; until at length they are slain, and the city is left in a great measure to the mercy of their enemies for three days and a half, the two Prophets rise from the dead and ascend into heaven. *The Messiah comes, convulses the earth, overthrows the army of the Gentiles, delivers the Jews, cleanses Jerusalem, cuts off all wickedness from the earth, raises the Saints from the dead, brings them with Him and commences His reign of a thousand years. . . .*[44]

President Joseph Fielding Smith indicated also that this would be one of the last events to be fulfilled before Christ came.

> One thing we are given by these prophets definitely to understand is that *the great last conflict before Christ shall come will end at the siege of Jerusalem. . . .*
>
> So we are given to understand that *when the armies gather in Palestine will be the time when the Lord shall come in judgment* and to make the eventful decision which will confound the enemies of his people and establish them in their ancient land forever.[45]

This miraculous deliverance of the Jews by their Redeemer will be something that the nations of the earth shall

---

[43]*Ibid.,* 11:14-15. (Italics added)

[44]Parley P. Pratt, *op. cit.,* p. 42.

[45]Joseph Fielding Smith, *Doctrines of Salvation* (Bruce R. McConkie, comp.), Vol. 3, (Bookcraft: Salt Lake City, 1956), pp. 46-47. (Italics in original)

speak of for many years. The destruction of the army is of such a magnitude that Ezekiel tells of the Jews burning the spoils of war for seven years without need of going to the fields or forests for fuel.[46] The number of the slain shall be so great that the entire house of Israel shall spend seven months burying the dead in an attempt to cleanse the land.[47] Thereafter, they will have to hire permanent burial teams to seek out the bodies which are as yet unburied to remove the stench of death from off the face of the land.[48]

It is not hard to understand why in a Proclamation of the Twelve Apostles the kings and rulers of the earth were warned that they could not remain neutral in the coming crises.

> You cannot, therefore, stand as idle and disinterested spectators of the scenes and events which are calculated, in their very nature, to reduce all nations and creeds to *one* political and religious *standard,* and thus put an end to Babel forms and names, and to strife and war. You will, therefore, either be led by the good Spirit to cast in your lot, and to take a lively interest with the Saints of the Most High, and the covenant people of the Lord; or, on the other hand, you will become their inveterate enemy, and oppose them by every means in your power.[49]

And so the tribe which produced the royal house of David, so long trodden down by their enemies, so long searching for their Messiah, so long without a homeland, shall come to know that the God of Abraham, Isaac and Jacob still lives and still remembers the covenants made with their fathers so long ago.

---

[46]Ezekiel 39:8-10.
[47]*Ibid.,* 38:11-13.
[48]*Ibid.,* 38:14-16.
[49]Proclamation of the Twelve Apostles, *Millennial Star,* Vol. 6, pp. 6-7, (end of volume) October 22, 1845. (Italics in original)

The End – And the Beginning

In the introduction to this work, reference was made to a frightened pilgrim who stood at the gates of the future and asked the keeper for a light to guide him through the darkness. And the keeper of the gate replied, "Go out into the darkness, and put your hand in the hand of God. That shall be to you better than a light, and safer than the known way." Throughout this work an attempt has been made to show that prophecy is the hand of a kind and loving Father extended to his groping and frightened children. Guiding his children through foreboding days of violence, war, corruption, and decay seems to be one of the major tasks of the Lord, and as has been amply demonstrated, he has abundantly marked the future course of the world and of his Church.

We know that the great turmoil and chaos that will reign in the earth prior to the return of the Master is necessary to prepare a world for his reign. We know that Satan shall rage in the hearts of men but shall not triumph. We know that God shall closely watch over the worthy, protecting them in times of crises and blessing them as they draw near unto him. We know that The Church of Jesus Christ of Latter-day Saints was restored specifically to prepare the world for the great millennial day. We know that the face of the future is known to God and he is anxious to prepare his children so that its dreadful visage may be smoothed into one of smiling promise. We know that the day shall come that the earth shall burn as an oven, and the wicked as stubble, but we also know that the signs of the times have been given so that the wicked may take heed and turn from their paths of self-destruction. We

know that the Lord Jesus Christ is coming to claim his kingdom, and this magnificent King shall set the affairs of the
world in order that peace shall dwell in the hearts of men.

> Now, we look for the coming of our Lord Jesus Christ, and
> we expect it just as much as when the sun goes down we expect
> it to rise above the hill tops in the morning. And when He comes
> we expect it will be Himself—Jesus of Nazareth, our Elder Brother,
> the first-born of God in the spirit world, the Only Begotten of God
> in the flesh. *We expect that He will come and reign over the earth*
> *as King of kings and Lord of lords. . . .*[1]

It is to this joyous culmination of the world's history that
we now turn our attention.

Those Who Will Not See

It seems a difficult thing to understand how any person
could live through the great events which lead to the return of
the Son of God and still refuse to change his heart in preparation for that coming. Yet, there will be vast multitudes of
people who shall be caught as were those in the days of
Noah[2]—living their lives of spiritual apathy; laughing at or
ignoring the mounting evidence that the day of reckoning
approaches. Parley P. Pratt spoke of the great number of
signs that would be shown to warn the world of the second
advent but still predicted that this singular event would catch
the world unaware.

> Whoever will look to the word of the Prophets, and to the
> sayings of Jesus Christ, on this subject, the same will be convinced
> that all the signs of which I have spoken are clearly pointed out
> as the signs of His coming. *But, notwithstanding all these things*
> *are written, His coming will overtake the world unawares, as the*
> *flood did the people in the days of Noah.* The reason is, they will
> not understand the Prophets. They will not endure sound doctrine;
> their ears are turned away from the truth and turned to fables
> because of false teachers, and the precepts of men. . . .[3]

[1]Charles W. Penrose, *Journal of Discourses*, Vol. 25, p. 222, July 26, 1884.
(Italics added)
[2]Matthew 24:37-41.
[3]Parley P. Pratt, *A Voice of Warning*, Published by The Church of Jesus
Christ of Latter-day Saints (first published in 1837), p. 46. (Italics added)

Elder LeGrand Richards explained how men would seek to rationalize away the most evident signs, even as they presently ignore the great signs which have already been given.

> While I was president of the Southern States Mission, one of our missionaries wrote in from Florida and said, "President Richards, I have been reading about the signs of the coming of the Lord." He said, "when the sun darkens and the moon ceases to give of its light and the stars fall from heaven, everybody will know that he is coming."
>
> And I wrote back and said, "Probably they will know. The newspapers might announce some great phenomenon in the heavens, misplacement of planets, that have caused consternation, and scientists will have their explanation to make of it, and unless they have faith in the living God, unless as Jesus said, they can read the signs of the times, they may not know anything about what is going on in the world."
>
> "Why," I said, "if the inhabitants of this earth had the ability and the power to read the signs of the times, they would know that already the Lord has given far more than the darkening of the sun or obscuring the light of the moon or causing the stars to fall from the heaven, for what he has accomplished in the establishment of his kingdom on the earth in these latter days, and the unseen power operating in the world for the accomplishment of His purposes, are greater signs than any of these phenomena that we read about—the signs of his coming."[4]

And so, ironically, the vast majority of the world will ignore the great abundance of evidence and the innumerable warnings given by the Lord and will be caught unawares. President Joseph Fielding Smith warned members of the Church that this may be true of some of them as well, if they are not watchful.

> In our own day messengers have come from the presence of the Lord declaring that it is even now at our doors, (D&C 110: 13-16) and yet many, *even among the Latter-day Saints, go about their affairs as though this coming of the Lord Jesus Christ and the ushering in of this reign of peace had been indefinitely postponed for many generations. I say this to you that it is at our doors.* I say this with all confidence because the Lord has said it. His

---

[4]LeGrand Richards, *Conference Report*, April, 1951, pp. 40-41.

messengers have said it as they have come from his presence bearing witness of him.[5]

Thus, as the last of the great signs are fully fulfilled, the
world will be tragically unprepared for the greatest event of
its entire history. As the last moments of the earth's telestial
history draw to a close, it is hard for the mind to imagine the
feelings that will strike the hearts of those who have been
eagerly watching and waiting for the coming of their king.
The Lord has described that last winding-up scene most
vividly:

> And there shall be silence in heaven for the space of half an
> hour; and immediately after shall the curtain of heaven be un-
> folded, as a scroll is unfolded after it is rolled up, and the face of
> the Lord shall be unveiled;
>
> And the saints that are upon the earth, who are alive, shall
> be quickened and be caught up to meet him.
>
> And they who have slept in their graves shall come forth, for
> their graves shall be opened; and they also shall be caught up to
> meet him in the midst of the pillar of heaven.[6]

Elder Orson Pratt spoke of this great silence and the
appearance of the Lord that would follow immediately thereafter:

> Immediately after the sounding of this trump there will be
> "silence in heaven for the space of half an hour." Whether the
> half hour here spoken of is according to our reckoning—thirty
> minutes, or whether it be according to the reckoning of the Lord
> we do not know. We know that the word hour is used in some
> portions of the Scriptures to represent quite a lengthy period of
> time. For instance, we, the Latter-day Saints, are living in the
> eleventh hour, that is in the eleventh period of time; and for aught
> we know the half hour during which silence is to prevail in heaven
> may be quite an extensive period of time. During the period of
> silence all things are perfectly still; no angels flying during that
> half hour; no trumpets sounding; no noise in the heavens above;
> but immediately after this great silence the curtain of heaven shall

---

[5]Joseph Fielding Smith, *Doctrines of Salvation*, (Bruce R. McConkie, comp.),
Vol. 3, (Bookcraft: Salt Lake City, 1956), p. 55. (Italics added)
[6]*Doctrine and Covenants* 88:95-98.

be unfolded as a scroll is unfolded. School children, who are in the habit of seeing maps hung up on the wall, know that they have rollers upon which they are rolled up, and that to expose the face of the maps they are let down. *So will the curtain of heaven be unrolled so that the people may gaze upon those celestial beings who will make their appearance in the clouds.* The face of the Lord will be unveiled, and those who are alive will be quickened, and they will be caught up; and the Saints who are in their graves will come forth and be caught up, together with those who are quickened, and they will be taken into the heavens into the midst of those celestial beings who will make their appearance at that time. These are the ones who are the first fruits, that is, the first fruits at the time of his coming.[7]

Two Zions Unite

It is evidently about this time that another great and significant event takes place. As the righteous from all ages— both living and dead—are caught up to meet the coming Lord, a group of people who long ago distinguished themselves for their righteousness will also descend and join the millennial band who are to take up abode with the saints on the earth. This group of saints were so righteous in an age of wickedness that the Lord took up the entire city to himself.[8] That, of course, was the City of Enoch. The latter-day prophets have made it clear that the return of this city shall be part of the great latter-day restoration of all things.

For example, the Lord implied that return in the song sung by millennial saints: "The Lord hath brought down Zion from above. The Lord hath brought up Zion from beneath."[9] Orson Pratt referred to that scripture in 1854:

. . . We expect that the Zion which was built up by Enoch, that had no poor in it, will come down again at the commencement of the Millennium to meet the Zion here, according to the song in the Book of Covenants . . . and they shall gaze upon each other's countenances, and see eye to eye.[10]

---

[7]Orson Pratt, *Journal of Discourses,* Vol. 16, p. 328, December 28, 1873. (Italics added)
[8]Moses 7:67-69. See also *Doctrine and Covenants* 38:4.
[9]*Doctrine and Covenants* 84:100.
[10]Orson Pratt, *Journal of Discourses,* Vol. 2, p. 103, September 10, 1854.

He Comes!

Many of the prophets, both ancient and modern, have spoken of this crowning experience of man's history, but perhaps none have done it more eloquently than President Charles W. Penrose, in his article, "The Second Advent."

> The tongue of man falters, and the pen drops from the hand of the writer, as the mind is rapt in contemplation of the sublime and awful majesty of his coming to take vengeance on the ungodly and to reign as King of the whole earth.
>
> He comes! The earth shakes, and the tall mountains tremble, the mighty deep rolls back to the north in fear, and the rent skies glow like molten brass. He comes! The dead saints burst forth from their tombs, and "those who are alive and remain" are "caught up" with them to meet him. The ungodly rush to hide themselves from his presence and call upon the quivering rocks to cover them. He comes! with all the hosts of the righteous glorified. The breath of his lips strikes death to the wicked. His glory is as a consuming fire. The proud and rebellious are as stubble; they are burned and "left neither root nor branch." He sweeps the earth "as with the besom of destruction." He deluges the earth with the fiery floods of his wrath, and the filthiness and abominations of the world are consumed. Satan and his dark hosts are taken and bound—and the prince of the power of the air has lost his dominion, for he whose right it is to reign has come, and the "kingdoms of this world have become the kingdoms of our Lord and of his Christ."[11]

The Great and Dreadful Day

On April 3, 1836, the Prophet Joseph Smith and Oliver Cowdery went behind the curtains of the pulpit in the Kirtland Temple and bowed in solemn prayer. As they finished, a marvelous vision opened to them, and they received several important visitors, including the Savior, Moses, Elias, and Elijah. The coming of Elijah was in fulfillment of a prophecy uttered by Malachi about four hundred years before the birth of the Savior.[12] As Elijah spoke to Joseph and Oliver, he

---

[11]Charles W. Penrose, "The Second Advent," *Millennial Star*, Vol. 21, p. 583, September 10, 1859. Perhaps it should be noted here that many people picture, incorrectly, the Savior coming in apparel which is brilliantly white. The scriptures explicitly tell us that at his coming he will be clothed, not in white, but in *red* apparel. (*Doctrine and Covenants* 133:48, Isaiah 63:2.)

[12]Malachi 4:5-6.

referred to this prophecy of Malachi's and explained that he was now fulfilling it. By this, he went on to say, ". . . ye may know that the great and dreadful day of the Lord is near, even at the doors."[13]

At first it may seem contradictory to use the adjectives "great" and "dreadful" to describe the same event. But further reflection will substantiate the appropriateness of both words. To those who have been eagerly watching and waiting for the coming of the Lord, who have made the necessary preparations so as to be included in that group which Christ described as his "first fruits."[14] it shall indeed be a great day. To those who have ignored or rejected the innumerable warnings, who have felt sure that the Lord was delaying his coming, who are not worthy to endure the brilliant presence of the Son of God, what better word to describe their experience on that day than "dreadful"?

It is for this very reason that the Lord has gone to such great lengths to warn his children. It is for this very reason that in the Doctrine and Covenants alone there are nearly fifty separate references to the coming of the Savior and pleas for his children to prepare for that day.[15] It is for this reason that the Lord warns:

> But the day soon cometh that ye shall see me, and know that I am; for the veil of darkness shall soon be rent, *and he that is not purified shall not abide the day.*
>
> Wherefore, gird up your loins and be prepared. . . .[16]

It is for this reason that the Lord predicts:

> And then they shall look for me, and behold, I will come; and they shall see me in the clouds of heaven, clothed with power and great glory; with all the holy angels; *and he that watches not for me shall be cut off.*[17]

---

[13]*Doctrine and Covenants* 110:16.
[14]*Ibid.,* 88:98.
[15]For a listing of these references see footnote "e" to *Doctrine and Covenants* 1.
[16]*Doctrine and Covenants* 38:8-9. (Italics added)
[17]*Ibid.,* 45:44. (Italics added)

It is for this reason that he promises: "And again, be patient in tribulation until I come; and behold, I come quickly, and reward is with me, and *they who have sought me early shall find rest to their souls.*"[18]

A New World Like unto Eden

Thus, in an unbelievable blaze of glory, the world of war, bloodshed, anarchy, slavery, pain, violence, immorality, depravity and despair comes to an end. After six thousand years, the troubled, turbulent world will be no more. Even though the end of the world as we have known of it for these sixty centuries will be a catastrophe in some ways, members of The Church of Jesus Christ of Latter-day Saints believe that this climactic end marks the beginning of something vastly more important—the millennial era.

"We believe . . . that Christ will reign personally upon the earth; and, that the earth will be renewed and receive its paradisiacal glory."[19] In other words, we believe that once again the earth shall become a paradise, much as it was during the time when Adam and Eve lived in the Garden of Eden. It is appropriately called a paradise, for the conditions then will be so markedly different from what presently exists.

> And in that day the enmity of man, and the enmity of beasts, yea, *the enmity of all flesh, shall cease* from before my face.
>
> And in that day *whatsoever any man shall ask, it shall be given unto him.*
>
> And there shall be *no sorrow because there is no death.*
>
> In that day *an infant shall not die until he is old;* and his life shall be as the age of a tree;
>
> And when he dies he shall not sleep, that is to say in the earth, but shall be changed in the twinkling of an eye, and shall be caught up, and his rest shall be glorious.
>
> Yea, verily I say unto you, in that day when the Lord shall come, *he shall reveal all things—*

---

[18]*Ibid.,* 54:10. (Italics added)
[19]Tenth Article of Faith of The Church of Jesus Christ of Latter-day Saints, *Pearl of Great Price.*

Things which have passed, and hidden things which no man knew, things of the earth, by which it was made, and the purpose and the end thereof—

Things most precious, things that are above, and things that are beneath, things that are in the earth, and upon the earth, and in heaven.[20]

For, behold, I create *new heavens and a new earth:* and the former shall not be remembered, nor come into mind.

But be ye glad and rejoice for ever in that which I create: for, behold, I create Jerusalem a rejoicing, and her people a joy.

And I will rejoice in Jerusalem, and joy in my people: and *the voice of weeping shall be no more heard in her,* nor the voice of crying.

There shall be no more thence an infant of days, nor an old man that hath not filled his days: for the child shall die an hundred years old; but the sinner being an hundred years old shall be accursed.

And *they shall build houses, and inhabit; they shall not plant, and another eat:* for as the days of a tree are the days of my people, and mine elect shall long enjoy the work of their hands.

They shall not labour in vain, nor bring forth for trouble; for they are the seed of the blessed of the Lord, and their offspring with them.

And it shall come to pass, that *before they call, I will answer;* and *while they are yet speaking, I will hear.*

The wolf and the lamb shall feed together, and the lion shall eat straw like the bullock: and dust shall be the serpent's meat. *They shall not hurt nor destroy in all my holy mountain,* saith the Lord.[21]

To achieve such an era, those who are not capable of living in a world of peace and harmony must be swept off. The rebellious and the wicked who refuse to live according to the laws of God will be destroyed so that the paradise spoken of may be ushered in. This explains the great judgments of the Lord. They are to prepare the world for its paradisiacal glory. According to President Joseph Fielding Smith, this will include all those who have been living a telestial law.

---

[20]*Doctrine and Covenants* 101:26-34. (Italics added)
[21]Isaiah 65:17-25. (Italics added)

When the reign of Jesus Christ comes during the millennium, *only those who have lived the telestial law will be removed.* The earth will be cleansed of all its corruption and wickedness. Those who have lived virtuous lives, who have been honest in their dealings with their fellow man and have endeavored to do good to the best of their understanding, shall remain.[22]

President Brigham Young described the hearts of those who bring the Millennium into existence.

The Millennium consists in this—every heart in the Church and Kingdom of God being united in one; the Kingdom increasing to the overcoming of everything opposed to the economy of heaven, and Satan being bound, and having a seal set upon him. All things else will be as they are now, we shall eat, drink, and wear clothing. *Let the people be holy, and the earth under their feet will be holy. Let the people be holy, and filled with the Spirit of God, and every animal and creeping thing will be filled with peace; the soil of the earth will bring forth in its strength, and the fruits thereof will be meat for man. The more purity that exists, the less is the strife;* the more kind we are to our animals, the more will peace increase, and the savage nature of the brute creation vanish away. If the people will not serve the devil another moment whilst they live, if this congregation is possessed of that spirit and resolution, here in this house is the Millennium. Let the inhabitants of this city be possessed of that spirit, let the people of the territory be possessed of that spirit, and here is the Millennium. Let the whole people of the United States be possessed of that spirit, and here is the Millennium, and so will it spread over all the world.[23]

Down through the troubled millennia of history, man has dreamed of a time when society would perfect itself and achieve harmony and peace. Plato dreamed of the "Republic," Sir Thomas More visualized the mythical country of "Utopia," Aldous Huxley saw a "Brave New World"; many have longed for it, but very few have found it. When the Son of Man comes to make the kingdoms of the world subject to his righteous rule the reality of this dream will come to pass.

---

[22]Joseph Fielding Smith, *op. cit.,* p. 62. (Italics added)
[23]Brigham Young, *Journal of Discourses,* Vol. 1, p. 203, April 6, 1852. (Italics added)

Free Agency Still Preserved in the Millennium

Some have pictured that all people will be forced to accept the gospel of Jesus Christ if they are to live during the thousand-year era of righteousness, but this is not the way the Lord works with his children. As President Joseph Fielding Smith indicated, only those living a telestial order of things will be swept off in preparation for the Millennium. This will leave many people who live good lives but not the kind of lives that would take them to the celestial kingdom. In short, there will be people living the terrestrial law and the celestial law during the Millennium.

All people will acknowledge that Jesus is the Savior and the King to whom homage must be given, but this does not imply that all peoples will accept the gospel in its fulness. Brigham Young explained it in this manner.

> When all nations are so subdued to Jesus that every knee shall bow and every tongue shall confess, *there will still be millions on the earth who will not believe in him; but they will be obliged to acknowledge his kingly government.* You may call that government ecclesiastical, or by whatever term you please yet there is no true government on earth but the government of God, or the holy Priesthood.[24]

A few years later President Young said:

> In the millennium *men will have the privilege of being Presbyterians, Methodists, or Infidels, but they will not have the privilege of treating the name and character of Deity as they have done heretofore.* No, but every knee shall bow and every tongue confess to the glory of God the Father that Jesus is the Christ.[25]

This agrees essentially with what the Prophet Joseph said about eighteen months before his martyrdom.

> While in conversation with Judge Adams during the evening, I said, Christ and the resurrected Saints will reign over the earth during the thousand years. They will not probably dwell upon the

---

[24]*Ibid.,* Vol. 7, p. 142, May 22, 1859. (Italics added)
[25]*Ibid.,* Vol. 12, p. 274, August 16, 1868. (Italics added)

earth, but will visit it when they please, or when it is necessary to govern it. *There will be wicked men on the earth during the thousand years. The heathen nations who will not come up to worship will be visited with the judgments of God, and must eventually be destroyed from the earth.*[26]

The Great Work of the Millennium

Isaiah spoke of the time when the people would have the privilege of enjoying the full fruits of their labor, and when their efforts to produce goods would not be in vain.[27] This would seem to indicate that the people then will find it much easier to provide enough food and materials to take care of their temporal needs. This would free man from much of the presently required time needed to produce enough for his wants. In the telestial world in which we live, the effort a man puts into sustaining himself and his family is often robbed by storm, pestilence, disaster, or through high taxes, vandalism, or robbery. In the conditions predicted for the Millennium, it seems as though a person would have to spend much less of his time trying to maintain life than he does today. This raises a natural question: What will people do with all of the extra time? Here again the prophets have given us the answer.

Joseph Smith taught the early members of the Church that there was no work as important as was the work for the salvation of the dead. So important was it that the very salvation of living members of the Church depends on it.

> It is sufficient to know, in this case, that *the earth will be smitten with a curse unless there is a welding link of some kind or other between the fathers and the children,* upon some subject or other—and behold what is that subject? *It is the baptism for the dead. For we without them cannot be made perfect; neither can they without us be made perfect.*[28]

The billions of people who have lived upon the earth without knowing of the saving principles of the gospel of Jesus Christ must have their work performed for them before the

---

[26]Joseph Smith, *DHC*, Vol. 5, p. 212, December, 1842. (Italics added)
[27]See footnote 21.
[28]*Doctrine and Covenants* 128:18. (Italics added)

final day of judgment. This work can be done only in the temples. The great burden of this vast project rests upon the faithful members of this dispensation. Although the Church has been working diligently since the time of Joseph Smith to build temples and carry out the work for the salvation of the dead, only a small proportion of the total work has been accomplished. *The completion of that great work will be the primary task of the faithful members of Christ's kingdom during the Millennium.*

President Brigham Young testified concerning the work of the Millennium on several occasions. In 1859 he said:

> When his kingdom is established upon the earth, and Zion built up, the Lord will send his servants as saviours upon Mount Zion. *The servants of God who have lived on the earth in ages past will reveal where different persons have lived who have died without the Gospel, give their names, and say, "Now go forth, ye servants of God, and exercise your rights and privileges; go and perform the ordinances of the house of God for those who have passed their probation without the law,* and for all who will receive any kind of salvation: bring them up to inherit the celestial, terrestrial, and telestial kingdoms.[29]

Three years later he explained in more detail how those in the Millennium will receive the information necessary to do the temple work for these people.

> The Gospel is now preached to the spirits in prison, and when the time comes for the servants of God to officiate for them, *the names of those who have received the Gospel in the spirit world will be revealed by the angels of God and the spirits of just men made perfect; also the places of their birth, the age in which they lived, and everything regarding them that is necessary to be recorded on earth,* and they will then be saved so as to find admittance into the presence of God, *with their relatives who have officiated for them.*[30]

President John Taylor predicted that the time would come when there would be thousands of temples built to accomplish this work.

---

[29]Brigham Young, *Journal of Discourses,* Vol. 6, p. 347, July 31, 1859. (Italics added)

[30]*Ibid.,* Vol. 9, p. 317, July 13, 1862. (Italics added)

This is a great work. Well might it be said to Joseph Smith, "You are laying the foundation of a great work"—so vast that very few can begin to comprehend it. We read sometimes about the millennium. But what do we know about it? It is a time when this work will be going on, and Temples, *thousands of them,* will be reared for the accomplishment of the objects designed, in which *communications from the heavens will be received in regard to our labors, how we may perform them, and for whom.*[31]

Elder George Q. Cannon said that redemption for the dead would be the "occupation" of the people.

. . . During that period, as God has revealed, *the occupation of his people will be to lay a foundation for the redemption of the dead,* the unnumbered millions who lived and died on the earth without hearing and obeying the plan of salvation.[32]

President Wilford Woodruff also referred to the great number of temples that will be built to accommodate the vast scope of this work.

When the Savior comes, a thousand years will be devoted to this work of redemption; and *Temples will appear all over this land of Joseph,—North and South America—and also in Europe and elsewhere;* and all the descendants of Shem, Ham, and Japheth who received not the Gospel in the flesh, must be officiated for in the Temples of God, before the Savior can present the kingdom to the Father, saying, "It is finished."[33]

Knowledge concerning these countless numbers who have died may come not only through angels and spirits but perhaps also through the Urim and Thummim, according to a suggestion of President Joseph F. Smith's.

The great work of the Millennium shall be the work in the temples for the redemption of the dead; and then we hope to enjoy the benefits of revelation through the Urim and Thummim, or by such means as the Lord may reveal, concerning those for whom

---

[31]John Taylor, *Journal of Discourses,* Vol. 25, p. 185, May 18, 1884. (Italics added)
[32]George Q. Cannon, *Journal of Discourses,* Vol. 14, p. 322, December 3, 1871. (Italics added)
[33]Wilford Woodruff, *Journal of Discourses,* Vol. 19, p. 230, September 16, 1877. (Italics added)

the work shall be done, so that we may not work by chance, or by faith alone, without knowledge, but with the actual knowledge revealed unto us.[34]

President Joseph Fielding Smith indicated that this communication with those who have passed on will be on a *daily* basis.

It is our duty to go to the temple and take our records and work for the dead of our own lineage as far back as we can go, but what about these others? I will tell you. *The great work of the millennium, of 1,000 years, will be for the salvation of these souls. . . .*

Those who will be living here then will be in *daily* communication with those who have passed through the resurrection, and they will come with this information, this knowledge that we do not have, and will give it to those who are in mortality. . . . And in that way every soul who is entitled to a place in the celestial kingdom of God will be ferreted out, and not one soul shall be overlooked.[35]

What an exciting thought! To live and work in such a way that daily communication with resurrected beings can be expected! Add to that the feelings that come when one realizes that he may raise his children in a land of peace, plenty, and love, when disease and death shall no longer run rampant through the masses of humanity, and what heart cannot help but long for the privilege to see the millennial reign of Christ ushered in!

The Final Scenes

For nearly a thousand years, the earth shall know a period of paradisiacal glory which shall be a great blessing to all the inhabitants thereof. But this state is not to continue forever. When Christ promised that Satan would be bound during the millennium he also told us that he would once again be loosed for "a little season."

---

[34]Joseph F. Smith, *The Improvement Era,* December, 1901, pp. 146-147.
[35]Joseph Fielding Smith, *op. cit.,* Vol. 2, pp. 166-167. (All italics in original)

> . . . And Satan shall be bound, that old serpent, who is called the devil, and shall not be loosed for the space of a thousand years.
>
> And then he shall be loosed for a little season, that he may gather together his armies.[36]

At the close of the Millennium, Satan shall once again begin to gain power over the hearts of the children of men, so much so, that he shall begin to stir them up once more to make war against the saints of the Most High God. George Q. Cannon taught that this power would result as mankind once again began to drift away from the principles of righteousness, including the Law of Consecration.

> I also believe that when Satan is loosed again for a little while, when the thousand years shall be ended, it will be through mankind departing from the practice of those principles which God has revealed, and this Order of Enoch (the Law of Consecration) probably among the rest. He can in no better way obtain power over the hearts of the children of men than be appealing to their cupidity, avarice, and low, selfish desires. This is a fruitful cause of difficulty.[37]

This rebellion will evidently lead to a last great conflict between the forces of Satan and the servants of Jesus Christ. The Lord described this great battle in the Doctrine and Covenants:

> And Michael, the seventh angel, even the archangel, shall gather together his armies, even the hosts of heaven.
>
> And the devil shall gather together his armies; even the hosts of hell, and shall come up to battle against Michael and his armies.
>
> And then cometh the battle of the Great God; and the devil and his armies shall be cast away into their own place, that they shall not have power over the saints any more at all.[38]

As the Lord describes the hosts of heaven arrayed in battle against the hosts of hell, it brings to mind the original war in heaven. It would seem that the original conflict was

---

[36]*Doctrine and Covenants* 88:110-111.
[37]George Q. Cannon, *Journal of Discourses,* Vol. 16, p. 120, June 29, 1873.
[38]*Doctrine and Covenants* 88:112-114.

not decisively settled as far as Satan is concerned and he still feels he can triumph over the work of the Almighty. This tremendous battle is also referred to as the battle of Gog and Magog. Joseph Smith said:

> The battle of Gog and Magog will be after the millennium. The remnant of all the nations that fight against Jerusalem were commanded to go up to Jerusalem to worship in the millennium.[39]

This may at first be somewhat confusing, since the vast armies of the Gentiles which are to gather against Jerusalem just before the second coming are also referred to as the armies of Gog and Magog.[40] Evidently, Gog is a name symbolical of all that is evil, militarily speaking, and thus is used to describe both great conflicts. According to President Joseph Fielding Smith, however, the first of these battles is more appropriately titled the battle of Armageddon, and the second at the end of the Millennium as the battle of Gog and Magog. *"Before the coming of Christ, the great war, sometimes called Armageddon, will take place* as spoken of by Ezekiel, chapters 38 and 39. *Another war of Gog and Magog will be after the millennium."*[41]

Elder Pratt described this great final war at some length in an address to the saints in 1877.

> He [Satan] with his army will come against the Saints, and the beloved city, and encompass them round about. His army will be so great that it will be able to come upon the Saints on all sides; he is to encompass their camp. Because of the favorable position he is to hold, in that great last battle, and because of the vast number of his army, he doubtless believes that he will get the mastery and subdue the earth and possess it. I do not think he fully understands all about the designs of God: for John tells us when this great army shall be gathered in position, around the camp of the Saints, that "fire came down from God out of heaven, and devoured them." Devoured whom? Not those who are fallen angels, for they have no bodies to be devoured; but this fire from heaven will devour the wicked apostate race who will have listened to them and who will have joined Satan's army; they will be consumed,

---

[39]Joseph Smith, *DHC,* Vol. 5, p. 298, March, 1843.
[40]Ezekiel 38:1-3.
[41]Joseph Fielding Smith, *op. cit.,* Vol. 3, p. 45. (Italics in original)

consequently the kingdom of Christ will not be overcome by Satan or taken away from the Saints.[42]

That final contest between the enemies of righteousness and the saints of God will end just as did the first one, fought so many years before this earth was inhabited. And just as the battle of Armageddon will signal the end of the telestial world and the coming of the terrestrial, so will the battle of Gog and Magog at the close of the Millennium signal the end of the terrestrial order and the coming of the celestial.

The Celestial Kingdom—The Final Destiny

It is at this time that the earth passes through its final stages of temporal existence and becomes the celestial kingdom.[43] It is then that those found worthy to dwell with God shall be given their home. It is then that the earth will become a gigantic Urim and Thummim as described by the Prophet Joseph:

> This earth, in its sanctified and immortal state, will be made like unto crystal and will be a Urim and Thummim to the inhabitants who dwell thereon, whereby all things pertaining to an inferior kingdom, or all kingdoms of a lower order, will be manifest to those who dwell on it; and this earth will be Christ's.[44]

This is the final glorious destiny of the earth, and gives added meaning to the Beatitude which says: "Blessed are the meek: for they shall inherit the earth."[45] Then shall the earth cease its temporal existence and become the residence of those beings who have kept the celestial law.[46]

Elder Orson Pratt spoke of this celestial law and how it qualifies those who keep it to dwell on this sanctified earth, and he also spoke of what would happen to those who did not keep the law.

---

[42]Orson Pratt, *Journal of Discourses,* Vol. 18, p. 346, February 25, 1877.
[43]*Doctrine and Covenants* 88:18-20.
[44]*Ibid.,* 130:9. See also 77:1.
[45]Matthew 5:5. See also *Doctrine and Covenants* 88:17.
[46]*Doctrine and Covenants* 88:22.

If we are not thus prepared, where shall we go? God is the author of many creations besides those that are celestial. He will prepare a creation just adapted to the condition of such people—those who are not sanctified by the Gospel in all its fullness, and who do not endure faithful to the end, will find themselves located upon one of the lower creations, where the glory of God will not be made manifest to the same extent. There they will be governed by laws adapted to their inferior capacity and to the condition which they will have plunged themselves in. They will not only suffer after this life, but will fail to receive glory and power and exaltation in the presence of God the Eternal Father; they will fail to receive an everlasting inheritance upon this earth in its glorified and immortal state.[47]

Thus it could be said that there shall be two times that the world comes to an end. *And both times shall be a new beginning.*

---

[47]Orson Pratt, *Journal of Discourses,* Vol. 18, p. 323, December 3, 1876.

Anxiety?... or Anticipation?

Shortly before his death, President Jedediah M. Grant, counselor to Brigham Young, asked a most intriguing question:

> Why is it that the Latter-day Saints are perfectly calm and serene among all the convulsions of the earth—the turmoils, strife, war, pestilence, famine and distress of nations?[1]

Why indeed? When that question was put to a group of college students, after a lengthy discussion, one replied: "What kind of a question is that? Who is calm and serene? If you ask me, a better question would be: 'How can one become calm and serene after hearing all of the horrible things that God has promised to send upon the world before the second coming?' "

His voice was sincere; his question was in earnest; his point was well taken. How indeed can one remain calm and serene in the face of promises of hailstorms so widespread that the crops of the earth are destroyed;[2] of earthquakes so powerful that even the heavens tremble;[3] of plagues so terrible that men's flesh will fall from their bones, and their eyes from their sockets;[4] of thunders so loud that they reach to the very ends of the earth;[5] of "blood, and fire, and vapors of smoke";[6] of times so frightening that men's hearts shall fail them;[7] of a

---

[1]Jedediah M. Grant, *The Improvement Era*, February, 1915, p. 286.
[2]*Doctrine and Covenants* 29:16.
[3]*Ibid.*, 84:118.
[4]*Ibid.*, 29:18-19.
[5]*Ibid.*, 43:21.
[6]*Ibid.*, 45:41.
[7]*Ibid.*, 88:91.

presence so brilliant that the sun hides its face in shame,[8] the elements melt "with fervent heat,"[9] the waters boil and the mountains flow down in the face of that presence?[10] The coming of the Lord and the events that precede it will be catastrophic. How can anyone find peace and serenity, be he Latter-day Saint or anything else?

Actually, the question posed by President Grant and the one posed by the student are not as different as they may at first appear. In fact, when one can answer the latter, he can easily see the answer to the former.

Be Not Troubled

In an outstanding address given in October conference in 1966, Elder Marion G. Romney quoted the Lord's words to Joseph Smith in 1831. The Lord was recounting to the Prophet the things that he had told his disciples before his death concerning the destruction of Jerusalem, the scattering of the Jews, and the other great calamities of the last days. "And now, when I the Lord had spoken these words unto my disciples, *they* were troubled."[11] —a most natural reaction; much the same reaction as that given by the student previously mentioned. But the Lord immediately said unto them:

> *Be not troubled,* for, when all these things shall come to pass, ye may know that the promises which have been made unto you shall be fulfilled. . . .
>
> Even so it shall be in that day when they shall see all these things, then shall they know that the hour is nigh.
>
> *And it shall come to pass that he that feareth me shall be looking forth for the great day of the Lord to come, even for the signs of the coming of the Son of Man.*[12]

Elder Romney then commented:

[8]*Ibid.,* 133:49.
[9]*Ibid.,* 101:24-25.
[10]*Ibid.,* 133:41, 44.
[11]*Ibid.,* 45:34. (Italics added)
[12]*Ibid;* 45:35, 38-39. (Italics added)

The fact that the Lord recounted these predictions to the Prophet Joseph in 1831 surely emphasizes their importance to us. And since the disciples were troubled when they were but being told of these calamities to come far in the future, *it is no wonder that we are troubled as we witness their occurrence. . . .*

It was in the light of Christ's foreknowledge. . . . that he said to his disciples, "be not troubled. . . ."

I hope we are all familiar with these words of the Lord and with his predictions concerning other coming events, such as the building of the New Jerusalem and the redemption of the old, the return of Enoch's Zion, and Christ's millennial reign.

Not only do I hope that we are familiar with these coming events, I hope also that we keep the vision of them continually before our minds. *This I do because upon a knowledge of them, and an assurance of their reality and a witness that each of us may have part therein, rests the efficacy of Christ's admonition, "be not troubled. . . ."*[13]

When President Grant asked the question cited above, he immediately answered it. And his answer is the same as that given by Elder Romney, viz., the foreknowledge of things which are going to happen helps to prepare us for them.

Why is it that the Latter-day Saints are perfectly calm and serene among all the convulsions of the earth—the turmoils, strife, war, pestilence, famine and distress of nations? *It is because the spirit of prophecy has made known to us that such things would actually transpire upon the earth. We understand it, and view it in its true light.* We learned it by the visions of the Almighty. . . .[14]

The Lord instructed his disciples that when they saw all of these things which he had foretold come to pass then they would know that his coming was near and he would shortly fulfill his promises to them. It is faith in the fulfillment of these prophecies that allows one to "be not troubled," for the Lord has abundantly promised that through all of the strife and turmoil, he shall prevail and conquer at last. And with him in that conquest shall be those who have qualified as saints of the Most High God.

---

[13]Marion G. Romney, *Conference Report*, October, 1966, pp. 51-52. (Italics added)

[14]Jedediah M. Grant, *op. cit.* (Italics added)

President John Taylor summed up in this manner:

> In relation to events that will yet take place, and the kind of trials, troubles, and sufferings which we shall have to cope with, it is to me a matter of very little moment; these things are in the hands of God, he dictates the affairs of the human family, and directs and controls our affairs; and *the great thing that we, as a people, have to do is to seek after and cleave unto our God, to be in close affinity with him, and to seek for his guidance, and his blessing and Holy Spirit to lead and guide us in the right path. Then it matters not what it is nor who it is that we have to contend with, God will give us strength according to our day.*[15]

During the terrible struggles of World War II, Elder John A. Widtsoe put it this way:

> Above the roar of cannon and airplane, the maneuvers and plans of men, the Lord always determines the tide of battle. So far and no farther does He permit the evil one to go in his career to create human misery. The Lord is ever victorious; He is the Master to whose will Satan is subject. *Though all hell may rage, and men may follow evil, the purposes of the Lord will not fail.*[16]

This is why President Heber J. Grant stated that Latter-day Saints have no fears for the future.

> While the world is in a state of commotion and there is perplexity among the nations, *the Latter-day Saints have no fears for the future.* The signs of the times indicate the near approach of the coming of the Lord, and the work that we are engaged in is a preparatory one for that great event. . . .[17]

The Lord Protects His Own

Having no fears for the future when the future is dark and foreboding is sometimes difficult to achieve, but the prophets have comforted this generation with the promise that the Lord will watch over and protect those willing to follow his counsel.

---

[15]John Taylor, *Journal of Discourses*, Vol. 18, p. 281, November 5, 1876. (Italics added)
[16]John A. Widtsoe, *Conference Report*, April, 1942, p. 34. (Italics added)
[17]Heber J. Grant, *Conference Report*, October, 1930, p. 5. (Italics added)

Therefore, verily, thus saith the Lord, let Zion rejoice, for this is Zion—THE PURE IN HEART; therefore, *let Zion rejoice, while all the wicked shall mourn.*

Nevertheless, Zion shall escape if she observe to do all things whatsoever I have commanded her.[18]

In the same talk in which he declared that the angels of heaven had been loosed to reap down the earth, President Wilford Woodruff spoke of those who would be shielded from the dreadful judgments coming upon the earth.

Can you tell me where the people are who will be shielded and protected from these great calamities and judgments which are even now at our doors? I'll tell you. *The priesthood of God who honor their priesthood, and who are worthy of their blessings are the only ones who shall have this safety and protection.* They are the only mortal beings. No other people have a right to be shielded from these judgments. They are at our very doors; not even this people will escape them entirely. They will come down like the judgments of Sodom and Gomorrah. And *none but the priesthood will be safe from their fury.*[19]

About fifteen years earlier, President John Taylor spoke of being in tune with God and the peace that would bring during times of strife.

We are, as the French would say, *en rapport,* with God; that is, in communication with God. . . . And while nations shall crumble and thrones be cast down, and the God of heaven arise and shake terribly the earth, while the elements melt with fervent heat in fulfillment of ancient as well as modern prophecy; while *these things are going on he will whisper, peace to Zion.*[20]

In October conference, 1905, President Joseph F. Smith promised:

You do not need to worry in the least, the Lord will take care of you and bless you, he will also take care of his servants, and

---

[18]*Doctrine and Covenants* 97:21, 25. (Italics added)
[19]Wilford Woodruff, "The Temple Workers' Excursion," *The Young Woman's Journal,* August, 1894, p. 512. (Italics added)
[20]John Taylor, *Journal of Discourses,* Vol. 21, p. 100, April 13, 1879. (Italics added)

will bless them and help them to accomplish his purposes; and all the powers of darkness combined in earth and in hell cannot prevent it. They may take men's lives; they may slay and destroy, if they will; but they cannot destroy the purposes of God nor stop the progress of his work. He has stretched forth his hand to accomplish his purposes, and the arm of flesh cannot stay it. He will cut his work short in righteousness, and will hasten his purposes in his own time. *It is only necessary to try with our might to keep pace with the onward progress of the word of the Lord, then God will preserve and protect us, and will prepare the way before us,* that we shall live and multiply and replenish the earth, and always do his will; which may God grant.[21]

In the talk previously referred to, Elder Marion G. Romney also discussed how one could recognize and resist the power of evil and be delivered from the judgments of God.

Naturally, believing Christians, even those who have a mature faith in the gospel, are concerned and disturbed by the lowering clouds on the horizon. But they need not be surprised or frantic about their portent, for, as has already been said, at the very beginning of this last dispensation the Lord made it abundantly clear that through the tribulations and calamity that he foresaw and foretold and that we now see coming upon us, *there would be a people who, through acceptance and obedience to the gospel, would be able to recognize and resist the powers of evil, build up the promised Zion, and prepare to meet the Christ and be with him in the blessed millennium. And we know further that it is possible for every one of us, who will, to have a place among those people.* It is this assurance and this expectation that gives us understanding of the Lord's admonition, "be not troubled."[22]

The Lord's protective care for those worthy to be called saints, will consist of much more than simply shielding them from the judgments which sweep the world. That is much, and for such protection one would be understandably grateful. But, there is much more. Elder Romney touched on it when he said that it is possible for those who are worthy of the Lord's protective care not only to be shielded from his judg-

---

[21]Joseph F. Smith, *Conference Report,* October, 1905, pp. 5-6. (Italics added)
[22]Marion G. Romney, *op. cit.,* pp. 53-54. (Italics added)

ments but also to participate in the exciting events which will prepare the world for Christ's coming and his millennial reign.

The Last Days—A Choice Blessing

For those so qualified, the opportunity to live through the last days preceding the return of the Savior shall be a blessing the likes of which few generations have enjoyed. Members of The Church of Jesus Christ of Latter-day Saints look back on the early history of the Church and its pioneer heritage with great pride and respect. We think of the persecutions in Missouri, look on the terrible sufferings at Winter Quarters, read of the exploits and triumphs of men like Joseph Smith, Brigham Young, Parley P. Pratt, Heber C. Kimball, Wilford Woodruff, and many others, and are proud of what our forefathers have done.

But project the mind into the future. Perhaps a hundred years from now, future Church history classes will speak with equal reverence of the marvelous return to Jackson County, Missouri, or of the tremendous faith of those who built the New Jerusalem and the temple there—and they may be speaking of those who are now living. Today, members of the Church rejoice over the stories left to them by their grandparents and great-grandparents—stories of faith, sacrifice, and inspiration. But think for a moment of the stories that this generation will have to tell their grandchildren and great grandchildren. *The future destiny of the Church holds as many opportunities for greatness as does the history of the past!*

Imagine, if it is possible, the thrill and pride that would come to a person assigned to work with the construction crew of the temple in Zion. President Wilford Woodruff had a dream in 1877 wherein he saw the temple in Missouri under construction. He described the scene he saw of twelve men who represented the twelve gates of the New Jerusalem. Then he continued:

> I saw people coming from the river and from distant places to help build the Temple. *It seemed as though there were hosts*

of angels helping to bring material for the construction of that building. Some were in Temple robes, and the pillar-like cloud continued to hover over the spot.[23]

Can the reader picture himself in such a scene? What an exciting thing it would be to pass on such scenes to one's posterity in family home evenings of the future!

Nor is that all. President Lorenzo Snow spoke of when the Savior would visit Zion and offered a most sublime promise:

> Many of you will be living in Jackson County and there you will be assisting in building the temple; and if you will not have seen the Lord Jesus at that time you may expect Him very soon, *to see Him, to eat and drink with Him, to shake hands with Him, and to invite Him to your houses as He was invited when He was here before.* I am saying things to you now, which I know something of the truth of them.[24]

Such a blessing is nearly beyond one's ability to comprehend. Shaking hands with the Lord Jesus Christ in humble greeting; spending an evening at dinner with him—the mind is overwhelmed! Imagine a husband and father coming home to announce that a special guest shall be spending some time in the home! Picture going to a special temple session where it is known that the Savior shall be present! Blessings beyond a person's most optimistic hopes are in store for those privileged to participate in such times.

Or to turn to another scene. Visualize, if possible, that day in the city of New Jerusalem when a commotion is heard in the streets, and someone shouts over the tumult, "Here they come! Here they come!" People pour into the streets and look northward across the plains to see a vast cloud of dust signaling the arrival of the ten tribes! What an experience to watch prophet grasp prophet in firm handshake, to watch as the people of Ephraim who journeyed over the plains from the west delightedly introduce them-

---

[23]Matthias F. Cowley, *Wilford Woodruff, History of His Life and Labors,* (Bookcraft: Salt Lake City, 1964), p. 505. (Italics added)

[24]Lorenzo Snow, *Deseret News,* June 15, 1901, p. 1. (Italics added)

selves to the people of Dan, of Issachar, of Reuben, Manasseh, and the other tribes, who traveled over the plains from the north. After the children are put to bed, many long hours could be shared around the table with members of this long-lost group. Think of the history and experiences they will have to share with us.

As the mind runs over the whole range of events prophesied for the last days, many other examples of exciting and stimulating experiences are suggested. Picture the feelings of those fortunate enough to participate in the council at Adam-ondi-Ahman with Adam, Christ, and all of the prophets who have held keys throughout history. Think of the missionary experiences those 144,000 high priests will have as they spread the gospel to every nation, kindred, tongue and people. Imagine the feelings of the heart as the heavens are rolled back like a scroll and the face of the Lord is unveiled! The examples could be multiplied again and again.

Joseph Smith included an editorial from the *Times and Seasons* in his *History of the Church* which summed up the whole point most adequately. Speaking of the prophets, priests, and kings of every age, the editorial says:

> . . . They have looked forward with joyful anticipation to the *day in which we live;* and fired with heavenly and joyful anticipations they have sung and written and prophesied of this our day; but they died without the sight; *we are the favored people* that God has made choice of to bring about the Latter-day glory; it is left for us to see, participate in and help to roll forward the Latter-day glory. . . . *Our name will be handed down to future ages; our children will rise up and call us blessed; and generations yet unborn will dwell with particular delight upon the scenes that we have passed through, the privations that we have endured; the untiring zeal that we have manifested; the all but insurmountable difficulties* that we have overcome in laying the foundation of a work that brought about the glory and blessing which they will realize.[25]

Those Counted Worthy to Stand

These things will, of course, be true only of those who have endured faithfully in the covenants they have made

---

[25]Joseph Smith, *DHC,* Vol. 4, pp. 609-610, May 2, 1842. (Italics added)

with the Lord. The judgments for the wicked in these last days will be as terrible as the blessings are glorious for the righteous.

It is as though each person stands at the entrance to two separate corridors. The one is dark and threatening, filled with frightening shapes and shadows and menacing threats to personal safety. The other is bright and lighted, filled with beauty and pleasant fragrances and joyful experiences. The Lord stands at the entrance pleading with those who approach to avoid the one and choose the other. Some people read descriptions of the calamities coming upon the earth and speak as though God were trying to force them down the dark corridor to make them repent, when in actuality he has only described that corridor to us so that we could wisely choose to avoid it and pass through the more pleasant one. But some will not heed the counsel and they refuse to walk where God would have them walk.

The servants of God are working feverishly to help today's generations choose their path wisely and thus be preserved, for God does seek to preserve his people.[26] But, as President George Albert Smith asked:

> Are we going to be worthy of that preservation? *Because only those who are worthy will be preserved.* He has said that unless we keep His commandments we will forfeit our blessings and the calamities that already are abroad on the earth and are spreading day by day will find us.[27]

Melvin J. Ballard also pleaded with the saints to be awake to the importance of these days.

> These are the last days spoken of by the prophets of old. These are the signs. Oh, Latter-day Saints, let us, though we be in Zion, be not asleep, for this is the day when no man can be at peace, nor shall we remain at peace in sin or in transgression; for everything will be shaken that is not built upon righteousness, and *every man, whether in Zion or elsewhere, who does not keep the com-*

---

[26]*Doctrine and Covenants* 35:13-14.
[27]George Albert Smith, *Conference Report,* October, 1941, p. 100. (Italics added)

*mandments of God, shall be shaken and shall fall, and shall feel
the chastening hand of the Almighty.*[28]

What a tremendous choice it is that lies before each person
today, and yet how few find themselves even vaguely concerned over that choice and its consequences!

A natural question arises when one considers the importance of being prepared for the critical times coming upon
us. It can be asked in many ways but it is essentially the
same question asked by the young college student. "How
can I prepare myself so that I may remain calm and serene?
What can I do to make sure I will enjoy the tremendous
blessings of the future rather than suffer the terrible judgments? In short, what must I do that I might look forward
to the future not with anxiety, but with anticipation?"

The Five Who Are Wise

Just prior to his crucifixion, Christ spent some time
teaching his disciples about the last days and the signs of
the times. When he finished, he described the condition of
men at that time with a parable, the Parable of the Ten
Virgins. The symbolism of the parable is simple and to the
point and yet very profound. Ten virgins were waiting for
the coming of the bridegroom with their lamps burning in
welcome. The bridegroom tarried and the virgins drowsed
off. Suddenly at midnight the cry was raised that the bridegroom was coming. Five of the virgins found that their
lamps had gone out during the long delay, and asked the
others for oil. They were refused by the wise virgins, for
they said that they would then have no oil for their own lamps.
While the foolish virgins rushed out to buy more oil, the
bridegroom came, the wedding party entered the wedding
chambers and the door was shut. Later the five foolish
virgins returned and pleaded with the Lord to let them in.
But they were refused because, the Lord said, "I know you
not." Then the parable was concluded with this warning

---

[28]Melvin J. Ballard, *Conference Report*, October, 1923, p. 32. (Italics added)

to all: "Watch therefore, for ye know neither the day nor the hour wherein the Son of man cometh."[29]

The key to the interpretation of the parable lies in the symbolic meaning of the oil, for the lack of oil was what made the five virgins foolish. On March 7, 1831, the Savior once again referred to that parable and applied it to our own time. In that passage he also explained what the "oil" represented.

> And at that day, when I shall come in my glory, shall the parable be fulfilled which I spake concerning the ten virgins.
>
> For they that are wise and *have received the truth, and have taken the Holy Spirit for their guide, and have not been deceived*— verily I say unto you, they shall not be hewn down and cast into the fire, but shall abide the day.[30]

That also sums up the answer to the question of what preparations are necessary if one is to replace anxiety with anticipation. Those who have patterned their lives after the guidance of the Holy Spirit shall not be deceived. Elder Harold B. Lee, speaking to the Church in general conference, warned members of the Church that the only thing that would permit them to survive the great days of evil and deception would be an unshakable testimony.

> *Unless every member of this Church gains for himself an unshakable testimony of the divinity of this Church, he will be among those who will be deceived in this day* when the "elect according to the covenant" are going to be tried and tested. Only those will survive who have gained for themselves this testimony.[31]

Several other latter-day prophets echoed this message. Brigham Young warned the saints not to be overly anxious for the second coming unless they were sure they were properly prepared.

> Are you prepared for the day of vengeance, to come, when the Lord will consume the wicked by the brightness of his coming?

---

[29]Matthew 25:1-13.
[30]*Doctrine and Covenants* 45:56-57. (Italics added)
[31]Harold B. Lee, *Conference Report,* October, 1950, p. 129. (Italics added)

No. Then do not be too anxious for the Lord to hasten his work. *Let our anxiety be centered upon this one thing, the sanctification of our hearts, the purifying of our own affections, the preparing of ourselves for the approach of the events that are hastening upon us.* This should be our daily prayer, and not to be in a hurry to see the overthrow of the wicked. . . . Seek not to hasten it, but be satisfied to let the Lord have his own time and way, and be patient. *Seek to have the Spirit of Christ, that we may wait patiently the time of the Lord, and prepare ourselves for the times that are coming. This is our duty.*[32]

In 1956, Elder Lee spoke of four steps that would prepare an individual for the Millennium and the coming of the Lord.

Now, I have asked myself, this being the time to prepare for the millennial reign, how shall we set about to prepare a people to receive the coming of the Lord? As I have thought seriously about that matter, I have reached two or three sure conclusions in my own thinking. This preparation demands *first that a people, to receive the coming of the Lord, must be taught the personality and the nature of God and his Son, Jesus Christ. . . .*

To my thinking, another requisite of that preparation to receive the Lord at the beginning of his millennial reign demands that the *people be taught to accept the divinity of the mission of Jesus as the Savior of the world. . . .*

[There is] still another requirement, as I see it, for a people to be prepared to receive the Savior's coming. *We must be cleansed and purified and sanctified to be made worthy to receive and abide that holy presence. . . .*

And now, finally, there is still one thing more that is necessary, to my thinking, before that preparation is made for the millennial reign. *We must accept the divine mission of the Prophet Joseph Smith as the instrumentality through which the restoration of the gospel and the organization of the Church of Jesus Christ was accomplished.*[33]

Every member of the Church should seriously examine his own testimony and personal life on the basis of these four steps, to see if his testimony is "unshakable." In October con-

---

[32]Brigham Young, *Deseret Evening News,* May 1, 18f1, p. 1. (Italics added)
[33]Harold B. Lee, *Conference Report,* October, 1956, pp. 61-62. (Italics added)

ference, 1970, now in the First Presidency, Elder Lee added one additional important step of preparation.

> Now the only safety we have as members of this Church is to do exactly what the Lord said to the Church in that day when the Church was organized. *We must learn to give heed to the words and commandments that the Lord shall give through his prophet, "as he receiveth them, walking in all holiness before me; . . . as if from mine own mouth, in all patience and faith."* (D&C 21:4-5) There will be some things that take patience and faith. You may not like what comes from the authority of the Church. It may contradict your political views. It may contradict your social views. It may interfere with some of your social life. *But if you listen to these things, as if from the mouth of the Lord himself, with patience and faith, the promise is that "the gates of hell shall not prevail against you; yea, and the Lord God will disperse the powers of darkness from before you, and cause the heavens to shake for your good, and his name's glory."* (D&C 21:6) [34]

If Ye Are Prepared, Ye Shall Not Fear

If the emotions one feels as he contemplates the foreboding days ahead are primarily fearful, then perhaps what is needed is a serious evaluation of one's personal relationship with Jesus Christ. It is he to whose coming we look, and if it is with frightened eyes, perhaps it is because we are not completely comfortable with our present relationship to him. In quotations already cited in this chapter, Jedediah M. Grant, and his son, Heber J. Grant, both spoke of Latter-day Saints being without fear in the face of the future. What they seem to mean is the *prepared* Latter-day Saint. At a conference of the Church in Fayette, New York, held before the Church was a year old, the Lord spoke through Joseph Smith and gave a most profound truth, and a promise, saying: ". . . if ye are prepared ye shall not fear." [35] Elder John A. Widtsoe spoke in conference during World War II, using that scripture as his theme. His words are as significant in our own day as they were when he uttered them.

---

[34] Harold B. Lee, "Uphold the Hands of the President of the Church," *The Improvement Era,* December, 1970, p. 126. (Italics added)
[35] *Doctrine and Covenants* 38:30.

Fear, which "shall come upon every man," is the natural consequence of a sense of weakness, also of sin. Fear is a chief weapon of Satan in making mankind unhappy. He who fears loses strength for the combat of life, for the fight against evil. Therefore, the power of evil ever seeks to engender fear in human hearts. In this day of sorrow, fear walks with humanity. It directs, measurably, the course of every battle. It remains as a gnawing poison in the hearts of the victors as of the vanquished.

As leaders in Israel, we must seek to dispel fear from among our people. A timid, fearing people cannot do their work well. The Latter-day Saints have a divinely assigned world-mission so great that they cannot afford to dissipate their strength in fear. The Lord has repeatedly warned His people against fear. *Many a blessing is withheld because of our fears.* He has expressly declared that man cannot stop his work on earth, therefore, they who are engaged in the Lord's latter-day cause and who fear, really trust man more than God, and thereby are robbed of their power to serve.

The key to the conquest of fear has been given through the Prophet Joseph Smith. "If ye are prepared ye shall not fear." (D&C 38:30) That divine message needs repeating today in every stake and ward. Are we prepared in surrender to God's commandments? In victory over our appetites? In obedience to righteous law? If we can honestly answer yes, we can bid fear depart. *And the degree of fear in our hearts may well be measured by our preparation by righteous living, such as should characterize Latter-day Saints. . . .*

In this world upheaval, in this day of wanton destruction, we, as a people, must look upward. There must be trust and faith in our hearts. Hope must walk by our side. We must remember charity also. We must treasure the warm words of the Father to His Church, "Be of good cheer, and *do not fear, for I the Lord God am with you, and will stand by you.*" (D&C 68:6)[36]

Oh! that each heart could honestly repeat the words spoken by President Joseph F. Smith during World War I.

No matter what may come to me, if I am only in the line of my duty, if I am in fellowship with God, if I am worthy of the fellowship of my brethren, if I can stand spotless before the world, without blemish, without transgression of the laws of God, what does it matter to me what may happen to me? I am always ready,

---

[36]John A. Widtsoe, *op. cit.*, pp. 33-34. (Italics added)

if I am in this frame of understanding, mind, and conduct. It does not matter at all. Therefore, I borrow no trouble nor feel the pangs of fear.[37]

Much has been said concerning the coming of the Lord. Much more could be said. The world rushes headlong toward disaster and many live in fear of that "dreadful day." But many others look forward with poignant longing for the "great day" of the Lord.

The advice of Elder Orson Pratt should be in the forefront of the mind of every Latter-day Saint in these troubled and ominous times.

> *With a work of such magnitude before them, the Latter-day Saints should be wide awake, and should not have their minds engaged in those fooleries in which many indulge at the present time. We should put these things away, and our inquiry should be, —"Lord how can we prepare the way before thy coming? How can we prepare ourselves to perform the great work which must be performed in this greatest of dispensations, the dispensation of the fulness of times? How can we be prepared to behold the Saints who lived on the earth in former dispensations, and take them by the hand and fall upon their necks and they fall upon ours, and we embrace each other? How can we be prepared for this?" How can all things that are in Christ Jesus, both which are in heaven and on the earth, be assembled in one grand assembly, without we are wide awake?[38]*

When we can make such questions the code for patterning our daily living, we too can truly be prepared for the coming of the Lord.

---

[37]Joseph F. Smith, *The Improvement Era,* July, 1917, p. 827. (Italics added)
[38]Orson Pratt, *Journal of Discourses,* Vol. 16, p. 326, November 22, 1873. (Italics added)

Index